Dear [ ],

It's been lovely to meet over Zoom. I'm looking forward to our collaboration. Thank you for the opportunity. I hope you find this book useful & you enjoy it.

Best Wishes,
Vivek

# INSIGHT EDGE

## Praise for the book

'In his typically interdisciplinary way, Vivek Banerji unpicks the art and science of "insight". This excellent book is long overdue. The phenomenon of insights – distinct from ideas or information – remains largely unexamined. This book is a meta-analysis, offering insights into "insight" itself: a blend of high concept thinking and practical examples. In exploring topics such as "interactional expertise", "methods of abstracting", and "pragmatic polymathy", Banerji brings a rich and much-needed language to the field.'

– **Ed Fidoe, founder and CEO,
London Interdisciplinary School**

'The book showcases Vivek's rare gift to see what's hidden in the light of what truly matters.'

– **Vibha Paul Rishi, former Global Head
of Marketing (Flavours), PepsiCo International**

# INSIGHT EDGE

## Crafting Breakthroughs in a World of Information Overload

Vivek Banerji

JOHN MURRAY

First published in India in hardcover in 2025 by Hachette India
(Registered name: Hachette Book Publishing India Pvt. Ltd)
An Hachette UK company
www.hachetteindia.com

1

Text Copyright © 2025 Vivek Banerji
Cover design and illustrations by Anna Thomas
Author photograph by Dr Kathleen Puech

*The Bull*, stages second, fourth, eighth and eleventh © Succession Picasso 2025

'Graphs in Statistical Analysis' by F.J. Anscombe © American Statistical Association, reprinted by permission of Taylor & Francis Ltd

Vivek Banerji asserts the moral right to be identified as the author of this work.

All rights reserved. No part of the publication may be copied, reproduced, downloaded, stored in a retrieval system, or transmitted in any form or by any means without the prior written permission of the publisher, nor be otherwise circulated in any form of binding or cover or digital format other than that in which it is published and without a similar condition being imposed on the subsequent purchaser.

Subsequent edition/reprint specifications may be subject to change, including but not limited to cover or inside finishes, paper, text colour and/or colour sections.

The views and opinions expressed in this book are the author's own and the facts are as reported by him and have been verified to the extent possible. The publishers are not in any way liable for the same.

Hardback edition 978-93-5731-744-3
Ebook edition 978-93-5731-358-2

Hachette Book Publishing India Pvt. Ltd
4th & 5th Floors, Corporate Centre,
Plot No. 94, Sector 44, Gurugram 122003, India

Typeset in ITC Galliard Std 11.2/16
by InoSoft Systems, Noida

Printed and bound in India
by Thomson Press India Ltd.

*For my parents, Debashis and Mridula Banerji,
whose love of learning and life shaped my own*

# Contents

*Foreword* ix

Introduction 1

1. The Gift That Keeps Giving and Is Ignored 11
2. Insight Is a Way of Attending 33
3. Are You Solving the Right Problem? 75
4. Crafting Methods to Reveal Truth 107
5. Systematic Ways of Thinking Differently 161
6. Approaching the Five Archetypes of Unknowns 201
7. Getting the 'Insight Wheel' in Motion: Embedding Insights 253
8. The Practice of Pragmatic Polymathy 284
9. A Checklist for Building Your Aha! Insight Quotient 308

*Notes* 314
*Index* 329
*Acknowledgements* 346

# Foreword

SOMETIMES INSIGHTS ARRIVE LIKE THUNDERBOLTS, BUT OFTEN they emerge more quietly – taking shape not as discoveries, but as recognitions. Once seen, they seem inevitable, as if they were always present, waiting to be named. Their power lies in this strange familiarity. A good insight doesn't surprise us – it settles something.

And yet, insight is not a passive occurrence. It demands something of us. It needs ambition – the willingness to step back far enough to see the whole, even when our questions seem rooted in the part. It requires patience, even comfort with waste. Not every enquiry will yield ore. The fear of not arriving at a 'so what' often keeps us from staying with uncertainty long enough for meaning to surface.

In *Insight Edge*, Vivek Banerji takes this work seriously. This is not a book of declarations; it is a careful and deliberate attempt to understand what it takes to make insight possible – within organizations, teams, and ourselves. Drawing on years of practice across sectors, and informed by disciplines ranging from neuroscience to martial arts, Vivek constructs a thoughtful scaffolding for insight: modes of attention, archetypes of the unknown, ways of noticing and connecting.

What I appreciated most about this book is its honesty. It doesn't pretend that insight is easy or linear. It recognizes the dissonance, drift, and failure that accompany any real act of seeing. It acknowledges that not everything will add up – and that's fine. In fact, some of the most useful ideas come from wandering off-track.

Vivek also makes a compelling case for breadth. In a world obsessed with expertise, he argues for something more vital: permeability. Insight, he suggests, thrives on inputs that don't come from the syllabus. From jazz to genetics, from public health to calligraphy – nothing is too foreign, or too trivial. The ability to make lateral connections, to import metaphors from other worlds, is not a flourish – it is the method. And it's that refusal to stay in one lane that gives the book its quiet depth.

As someone who works with cultural meaning, I have long believed that insight isn't about piercing the obscure – it's about making the obvious visible again. The most enduring insights feel like truths we already knew but hadn't yet articulated. They don't demand belief. They simply make sense – in retrospect.

This book stays with that sensibility. It does not offer shortcuts or templates. Instead, it invites a more reflective way of working – one that makes space for intuition without abandoning rigour, and values questions that don't immediately resolve.

*Insight Edge* is a book that is genuinely useful, not in the narrow sense of having ideas that are instantly implementable, but in the deeper sense of examining all dimensions of the process of arriving at an insight after accounting for all the variables that are at play. Vivek is able to mesh many parallel frames into a coherent whole, all the while taking the reader along. In its care, in its methodical generosity, in its ambition to take insight seriously without stripping it of its soul – it offers readers not just tools, but a temperament. One that seems increasingly rare, and increasingly needed.

**Santosh Desai, CEO of Future Brands
and author of *Mother Pious Lady***

# Introduction

GREAT CUSTOMER INSIGHTS TRANSFORM BUSINESSES. FLAWED assumptions about the market fail businesses. However, insight development is an art. It requires using different modes of thinking and feeling, and cross-fertilization of ideas, methods, and knowledge.

I stumbled into the world of insights quite by accident, joining Indian Market Research Bureau (IMRB) straight out of my MBA. Much of my early years were spent designing and analyzing quantitative market research for a range of clients. Amidst the long hours and meticulous data crunching, there were these rare, exhilarating moments when one of us would uncover a hidden pattern – not immediately evident in the data – or stumble upon a counter-intuitive finding that opened up entirely new possibilities for our clients. These moments brought a surge of euphoria, spurring us to dig deeper and validate the insight. In our presentations, we put great effort into building a compelling narrative around these breakthrough discoveries. It was always deeply satisfying when we succeeded in conveying the true power of insights to our clients.

As my career evolved, these moments became more frequent, the insights more nuanced, the impact greater, and my personal satisfaction deeper. There were pivotal transition points along the way, each offering valuable lessons.

At PepsiCo India, I began to see the real headroom for impact beyond just the marketing function – at the C-suite level, for instance, where insights could drive growth, and also at the grassroots level, where working alongside frontline salespeople could improve execution. Pepsi taught me how to collaborate effectively with creative teams, since much of the marketing focus was on developing innovative campaigns and programmes.

At McKinsey & Company in New York and London, I saw how insights could help solve complex problems faced by the C-suite and drive transformational outcomes for organizations. It also underscored for me the critical importance of clearly defining the problem before beginning the search for insights. I realized it was essential to work closely with various stakeholders within companies to ensure that those insights were translated into actions and effectively implemented.

Starting Insight Dojo has been the most rewarding part of my journey. I have been running the company for over a decade and have established a track record of substantial business impact for my clients. At the heart of it is a polymathic approach to develop insights. Not only does the approach reflect a synthesis of all my professional learnings, but it draws upon my deep involvement with my hobbies – music, karate, yoga, literature, and extensive reading related to a variety of subjects. These interests have shaped how I think, filling my mind with many metaphors and helping me be more present, imaginative, and intuitive when developing insights.

I have had the chance to explore the world of insights from multiple vantage points. For instance, I have helped shape the commercial strategy of a US-based biotech – an insight-backed approach that led to its acquisition by one of the world's largest pharmaceutical companies. I supported a Korean chaebol beat a formidable Japanese rival to become a market leader in the consumer electronics category in the US. I guided a leading European genomics provider through a cloud migration while preserving customer satisfaction, and I helped an underperforming European women's health brand rise to market leadership.

My work as an insights professional has also supported the UK's National Health Service in reducing smoking rates, an Asia-based entrepreneur in launching a line of innovative climate control devices in the US, and South America's largest beer company in building a stronger brand strategy from its base in Colombia. I have presented to WHO members on obesity reduction strategies and contributed to the development and launch of breakthrough oncology treatments in both the US and Europe.

Beyond my experience, I have attempted to learn about insights outside the business world and looked at the perspectives of many thought leaders on related topics, notably Iain McGilchrist's work on the divided brain, Stephen Johnson's work on the birth of ideas, Robert and Michèle Root-Bernstein's thinking tools for creativity, Daniel Kahneman's work on heuristics and biases, Gary Klein's work on intuition and insight, and Richard Rumelt's work on strategy. A book that I found especially useful is *The Nature of Insight* by Janet E. Davidson and Robert J. Sternberg, which brings together diverse perspectives on insight. These are just a few examples.

To better inform the content of the work, I have conducted brief interviews with people who are intimately connected with the world of insights in different capacities.

- Ed Fidoe is the founder and CEO of the London Interdisciplinary School (LIS), which has been described as the 'most radical new university to open in decades' by the *Times*. Previously, he co-founded a 4 to 18 school in Stratford called School 21 and the UK's leading oracy education charity called Voice 21. He also consulted at McKinsey & Co., ran a theatre production company, and acted in the 80s hit TV show *Woof!*

- Hitendra Wadhwa is an educator and entrepreneur, currently serving as a professor at Columbia Business School. He is also the founder of the Mentora Institute, an organization that focuses on developing new models of leadership that are adaptable, authentic, and achievable. He teaches courses on personal leadership, strategic impact, and inner mastery, and has received numerous accolades for his teaching.

- Neerja Wable has been an insights and analytics leader, who has led and grown many market research companies in Asia, including the CEO of TNS in India and Sri Lanka; the Chief Client Officer for Millward Brown, Africa Asia Pacific; and a Senior Vice President and Executive Director at IMRB.

- Nivedita Banerji, my older sister, is the co-founder of Samaj Pragati Sahayog (SPS) in Madhya Pradesh, one of India's largest grassroots initiatives, and the founder of Kumbaya, which empowers women and disabled individuals by teaching them stitching. Made in recognition of their work, the film *The Kumbaya Story* won the 'Transforming Society Short Film Award' at the tve Global Sustainability Film Awards at BAFTA in London.

- John Copeland, a global insights and analytics leader who aptly describes himself as a 'customer obsessed and data polymath', is based in the US. He has been a leader in a wide variety of companies, including ServiceNow, eBay, Adobe, AvalonBay, Rosetta, Zyman Group, Prophet, Accenture, McKinsey, and Envision.

- John Forsyth is a customer insights thought leader based in the US who co-founded Forsyth Insights LLC. He was a leader of the Consumer Dynamics Institute and has worked in companies such as Nestlé and McKinsey. John was the partner who built and led McKinsey's Global Marketing Insights & Analytics Practice for over 20 years.

- Marco Renoldi is a global commercial leader in the life sciences business. Trained as a medical doctor, he leads a Swiss radiopharma start-up, Blue Wave Therapeutics. He previously held global commercial leadership roles in companies such as Novartis, Amgen, and Nordic Nanovector.

- Rita Banerji, my younger sister, is a wildlife filmmaker, a conservationist, and the founder of Green Hub and Dusty Foot Productions. She is an Ashoka Fellow, a winner of the prestigious Panda Award, also known as the Green Oscar, and the National Geographic – CMS Prithvi Ratna Award in 2017.

- Santosh Desai is the CEO of Futurebrands, the founder of Think 9 Consumer Technologies, and the author of the bestselling book *Mother Pious Lady*. His work has shaped the strategies of numerous successful brands. His weekly column, 'City City Bang Bang', published in the *Times of India*, looks at contemporary Indian society from an everyday vantage point.

- Takashi Takenoshita is an entrepreneur, a business builder, and a leader in the field of life sciences. He is the founder of the LivBio Venture, and has held CEO positions in various pharmaceutical companies. He was a senior counsel for University of Oxford's life science open innovations. He also co-founded McKinsey's Patient Behavior Change service line with me.

- Vibha Rishi is a seasoned marketing and business leader who has advanced brands such as Titan, PepsiCo, Max India, and Future Group. She has held marketing and innovation leadership roles across India, the US, and the UK, and was a founding member of Pepsi in India. She serves on various boards and supports Pratham, an NGO that works to provide education to underprivileged children in India.

## THE SCOPE OF THIS BOOK

### The target reader

This book is written for those keen to generate insights and make a positive difference to their organizations and businesses. It could be a CEO determined to identify the next game-changing idea and drive profitable growth. It could be an entrepreneurial market research manager who wants to create an insights-driven culture to improve the performance of the company. It could be the Head of R&D in a technology company who wants to better connect their scientists to customer needs and generate ideas; it could be the Head of HR who wants to create a culture where people are stimulated, insightful, and happy. It could also be an entrepreneur in a start-up who wants to know how to compete with limited resources against bigger companies or an NGO trying to figure out how to scale up the impact to a national level after having achieved results at a regional level. It could also be an analyst in an investment firm who provides insightful reports on market trends.

Insight alone will not help achieve goals, but it will increase the likelihood of success and, in the process, create well-being for those involved.

## Real-life case studies

I have illustrated all the principles with real-world case studies. There is a breadth of industries that I have chosen – consumer goods, technology, B2B, healthcare, and non-profit organizations. Even if you do not find your industry represented in the book, the principles described should apply across sectors. Clayton Christensen, the Harvard Business School professor and the creator of Disruptive Innovation Theory, wrote[1] about how Andy Grove, the CEO of Intel, reached out to him to understand the implications of Clay's theory for Intel. He wanted Clay to provide the explanation in 10 minutes. Clay resisted and explained the theory for 30 minutes in the context of other industries he had studied. Andy Grove then told him that he had figured out the implications for Intel and knew what to do. He had experienced the insight firsthand in his mind. My hope is that even if your precise context, e.g., industry, is not covered, you will, like Andy Grove, be able to draw helpful implications for your business.

## Focus on usefulness rather than provocativeness

You will find the concepts in the book helpful in stimulating novel ways of approaching insight development. However, there are certain tried and tested approaches that I have included because of their usefulness. For instance, in Chapter 3, I have also written about breaking down problems into smaller components using issue trees and hypothesis trees. The idea of such logic trees is not new and has been in use by management consultants for many decades. However, I believe that these tools are essential for effective problem solving.

## Breaking down concepts into separate components to enable training

There are many concepts that I have broken down into different categories – five types of unknowns or eight thinking modes. Many of these concepts, when experienced in the real world, are not mutually exclusive. For instance, when I speak of different types of unknowns, for certain hard problems, all five types of unknowns may be present in a specific situation. However, I have separated these concepts into different components and disentangled them for greater clarity. When you break down anything complex into individual components, it becomes easier to train oneself on each of them. This is very similar to how we learn music or sports – we isolate the different skills, practise them, and then put them all together.

## Emphasis on principles, not techniques

This book is about principles of insight development for organizational success. While the principles are inspired by practices in a variety of disciplines – art, science, and other fields – most of the detailed illustrative case examples relate to business. If you want to understand the intricacies of methods and tools such as ethnography, conjoint analysis, or neural networks, there are better and deeper books. A few of these are mentioned in the references. While methods constantly evolve, principles remain enduring. I have attempted to make the book accessible to everyone. Perhaps, Chapter 4 has the most technical content, but I am hoping the emphasis on principles will make even that chapter helpful, both for a generalist user of insights and for a deep expert.

## No shortcuts

It is tempting to write a book with a stepwise linear process, e.g., seven steps to develop insights. There are many books that take to that style, and to their credit, they do it well. But I believe that developing insights is an area of mastery, and there are no simple linear steps. That is what makes it so rewarding and stimulating. I expect the reader to draw their own interesting lessons based on the content. The focus on principles is my attempt to simplify the complex and fascinating world of insights.

# 1

# The Gift That Keeps Giving and Is Ignored

> 'If you don't want to be replaced by a machine, don't try to act like one!'[1]
>
> – **Arno Allan Penzias**

WHEN AJAY BANGA, THE CURRENT PRESIDENT OF THE WORLD Bank and former CEO of Mastercard, read the slogan[2] 'Mastercard, the heart of commerce' on his company staircase, it struck him that whilst commerce was mostly about cash, people in his company were talking about credit cards. Subsequent analysis revealed that 85 per cent[3] of all retail transactions in the world were in cash. Ajay Banga noted that for Mastercard to remain in its current market of digital transactions, alongside other credit card companies, kept the company in a much smaller box relative to its potential. Thereafter, competing with cash, and not Amex or Visa, became the core of Mastercard's strategy.

The company adopted new technologies, expanded into adjacent spaces such as cybersecurity and data analytics and worked on making its business model financially more inclusive. Banga's crucial insight here reframed the vision for Mastercard, and 'killing cash' became the basis for tripled revenues, increased net income and market capitalization from under $30 billion to more than $360 billion.[4] Moving beyond Mastercard, Ajay Banga became an advocate for the benefits of going cashless, given the significant benefits to society of adopting this mode of payment. He pointed out that vast populations are excluded from the digital economy and that the unnecessary handling of cash costs a nation as much as one per cent of GDP. A simple insight can transform, create conviction to take bold actions, build purpose, and lead to positive business outcomes.

Although one cannot peer into the mind of Ajay Banga, the process of arriving at his insight is possibly decipherable. As in the case of many consequential insights, or the arrival of an 'Aha!' moment, there was a trigger in the form of the slogan that highlighted facts known to many others. That most retail transactions were in cash or that Mastercard competed with credit cards was not news. Yet, he was able to make an original connection in his mind, thereby creating a novel framing of the situation. It was an experience that galvanized Banga to mobilize many others to achieve the vision of a cashless society. In fact, according to Banga,[5] any employee of Mastercard could articulate the mission of the company, which was to create a world beyond cash. The insight might have arrived unprompted on the surface, but it was the result of several developments underneath: Banga's vast experience and expertise as a business leader, his ambition to make Mastercard successful, his deep immersion in the context, and his ability to sense the emerging zeitgeist early – in the last decade, many countries, notably India, the Nordics, South Korea, and the Netherlands, had been making a shift towards a cashless economy[6] – put him ahead of the curve. The Banga story also illustrates the importance of translating insights into initiatives that can be implemented. Creating and executing transformational insights requires a diverse set of abilities for an individual, a conducive culture, and inventive processes. In this book, I highlight the elements that help leaders develop and turn insights into real action – building the right skills, fostering a supportive culture, and creating processes that drive meaningful change and business success.

We can trace many innovations in business to an insight that was often arrived at serendipitously. Consider these well-known examples of serendipitous insights:

- Steve Jobs attributed the beautiful typography used in the Mac as an outcome of a calligraphy class he had once attended.[7]
- The founders of Uber formed the company after they had struggled to hail a cab.[8]
- Reed Hastings got a late fee for a rented video, went to the gym immediately after, and was inspired to start

Netflix because of the subscription model he observed at the gym.[9]

Insights fuel innovation in every human endeavour, not just in business. The process underlying the arrival at the 'aha!' has many common features across different disciplines.

My curiosity has led me to explore questions such as:

- What led Miles Davis to conceptualize the legendary album, Kind of Blue?
- How did Jennifer Doudna and Emmanuelle Charpentier think of leveraging CRISPR for gene editing?
- What was the insight behind Indra Nooyi's vision, 'Profiting with Purpose'?
- What prompted Yvon Chouinard to commit to making Patagonia a leader in corporate environmental activism?
- What led Nandan Nilekani, the co-founder of Infosys, to conceptualize Aadhaar, India's revolutionary biometric ID system?
- What makes Maria Popova, the founder of Marginalian, prolific in providing insights by synthesizing lessons from diverse disciplines?
- What are, in fact, the characteristics of Philip Tetlock's 'superforecasters'?

- How does author and columnist Santosh Desai uncover subtle nuances of everyday life in India that we know are true, once revealed, but couldn't see before?

It is worth mentioning that though a few of the above-mentioned examples are discussed explicitly, many of the lessons from my research are woven more implicitly into the narrative. My hope is that looking at the subject across multiple domains might enrich our understanding of how to be more productive in generating breakthroughs.

## WHY INSIGHTS ARE MORE RELEVANT NOW

Insights have been transforming the world from time immemorial, yet right now their role is particularly significant due to the high levels of uncertainty that businesses currently face. The World Uncertainty Index (WUI) developed by the IMF is a single measure of uncertainty that quantifies global uncertainty by analysing the frequency of the words 'uncertain,' 'uncertainty,' and its variants within the Economist Intelligence Unit's country reports. A report published in April 2022 reports that the index has grown significantly since 2012.[10] In January 2020, Kristalina Georgieva, the former Managing Director of the IMF, had said, 'If I had to identify a theme at the outset of the new decade it would be increasing uncertainty'.[11] The statement couldn't have been more prescient. The COVID-19 pandemic had just begun and had wreaked havoc globally not long after Georgieva made her statement about uncertainty. After that, the wars in Ukraine and in the Middle East began and have not yet ended, there's been a recession, and during all this, generative AI has emerged as one of the most powerful and disruptive technologies. Making sense of what's going on has become difficult. Being insightful can help leaders gain clarity and cope with the uncertainty.

There are at least five factors that make developing insight vital to building resilience and flourishing in contemporary times.

## 1. Understanding the macro environment of business has become radically more important than in the past.

We are surrounded by hard problems that cannot be solved using our own mechanistic methods. Horst Rittel and Melvin Webber categorize problems as 'wicked' or 'benign'.[12] 'Wicked' problems are ambiguous, difficult to define, constantly changing, unique in nature, hard to solve, with unclear solutions, and require creative thinking, such as adapting one's business to new geopolitical trends, adopting fast-changing technologies like AI, and transforming one's company to get to net zero. 'Benign' problems are well defined, with a known set of solutions whose value can be objectively ascertained.

Formerly, strategy was mainly based on understanding one's own capabilities, the needs of customers, the strengths and weaknesses of a well-defined set of competitors, and the capabilities of suppliers. The macro-environment was a contextual factor, not a primary driver. Many strategic frameworks were built around such thinking.

Today, we are more likely to be wiped out by a new technology, a digital competitor, or a geopolitical development such as the Russia-Ukraine war. If you were running a business in Britain in 2016, you would have found it hard to predict that in the next seven years the business would be directly and profoundly affected by at least Brexit, COVID, the Russia-Ukraine War, a recession, and the emergence of generative AI. Depending on your context, there would be many other surprising disruptions. There is too much going on that is changing fast. Indra Nooyi, the ex-CEO of PepsiCo, captured the plight of leaders when she said,[13] *'The CEO today has to be a diplomat, a foreign policy expert, has to be a sociologist, (and) understand all the social trends... everything that we had 15 years ago has been turned on its head'*.

In this type of a complex environment, there can be no silver bullet. Insight will not be a panacea. Yet it can help companies adapt and improvise. Richard Rumelt,[14] an author, educator, and consultant on business strategy, has said that, if we can see 10 per cent better than others through the fog, it is a huge advantage. Insight allows one to do that.

## 2. AI is transforming the world.

While machine learning had been advancing rapidly, generative AI has leapfrogged the diffusion of AI to a new level. It is expected to affect every sphere of life, to be integrated in business processes, to increase automation, to boost productivity and efficiency, and to drive innovation and personalization. Specifically, within the market research and customer insights industry, tools and techniques will soon be automated and jobs related to these will be replaced. We can see these disruptions happening now – questionnaire and discussion guide design, qualitative or quantitative analysis, and even report writing are happening in an automated manner. Increasingly, we will have AI agents that conduct deep interviews. Yet, according to Yann LeCun,[15] the Chief AI Scientist at Meta, AI is far from achieving human-level intelligence because it can't plan or reason, it has no persistent memory, and it has no understanding of the physical world. In fact, these and other human gifts that are at the heart of creating insights will help us utilize technologies such as generative AI more effectively.

We can already see how outputs from ChatGPT can improve dramatically through insightful probing and by providing contextual understanding. To thrive in this world, enriched by technology, we must fully develop and utilize our multi-faceted capacities. That will help us guide the technology and make a positive difference to our lives and to the world. That is what will give us the edge. In 1978, Martin Gardner,[16] a recreational maths enthusiast and *Scientific American* columnist, wrote, '*The computer, making an exhaustive trial-and-error search, may solve a problem in a few seconds... Even the writing of such a programme often calls for aha! insight.*', and later, '*It would be a sad day if human beings, adjusting to the Computer Revolution, became so intellectually lazy that they lost all their power of creative thinking.*' These thoughts are even more relevant now.

While we might love AI – and there is a lot to love – the belief that we can relinquish our ability to generate insight to a machine as we sit back and enjoy the fruits, is a dystopian vision of the future. Besides, it would be tragic for us to not continually hone our capacity to develop insights. In fact, guiding AI imaginatively to discover patterns and make connections can be a great source of enjoyment, learning, and value.

**3. The field of human understanding has witnessed many disruptions in terms of available information, analysis methods, technologies, and disciplines.**

Traditional market research companies were mostly reliant on knowledge of statistics and a set of concepts from the social sciences. Now, the disciplines have expanded to include machine learning, generative AI, design thinking, behavioural economics, and cognitive neuroscience. Consider the following routinely applied methodologies:

- Behavioural economics to test and design marketing campaigns using heuristics and biases such as anchoring, loss aversion, social proof, and reciprocity

- Tools from cognitive neuroscience like **fMRI** (functional magnetic resonance imaging) or **EEG** (electroencephalography) to study brain activity when consumers view advertisements

- Design thinking techniques to conceptualize and design new products
- A wider set of supervised and unsupervised machine learning models that are applied to a range of business problems
- Generative AI-based campaign optimization, trend identification, and bot-assisted interviewing.

We are also living in a virtual world that requires a significant degree of constant adaptation. In such an environment, insight development must happen in a manner that takes advantage of these changes, with lifelong learning being a priority. We need to build a level of fluency and depth in these disciplines whilst not losing the ability for integrative thinking. There is a real danger of hyper-specialization. Most organizations need significant up-skilling without creating knowledge silos. Also, our adoption of new streams of knowledge must be grounded in enduring principles of truth finding. For instance, you might be excited by the potential to generate insights by analysing synthetic datasets, but if you do not have the tools to evaluate the accuracy of the work, you are likely to be misled.

## 4. There is a modern-day paradox where despite the abundance of information, eliciting truth has become challenging.

In the recently concluded US elections, it was impossible to make sense of what was actually going on. The ramifications of the outcome on businesses are huge. Consider how many electronics and automobile companies started fleeing from China to Vietnam, Thailand, and Malaysia in anticipation of a Trump victory because of the threat of tariffs on goods from China.[17] Yet, no one could predict such a resounding victory for Donald Trump.[18] One had to go to poll aggregators such as Fivethirtyeight Interactives or Real Clear Polling to get an idea of the vast number of opinion polls that were being conducted. The results varied by organization and the only conclusion that one could draw was that the election is close. The narratives we heard were different based on the ecosystem of media where we situated ourselves. The version of reality depended on whether we sourced information from CNN or Fox News, Twitter or TikTok, Joe Rogan or Marc Cuban, the *New York Times* or the *New York Post*. Additionally, AI algorithms serve content that caters to people's biases.[19]

While these days we always have to worry about fake news, that is not the only problem. Many legitimate institutions are under pressure to stand out by communicating provocative positions that often lack in-depth research and analysis. Immediately after the US elections, the same pundits who got their predictions wrong about the outcomes offered their quick diagnoses of the main reasons for Trump's victory. The certitude was astonishing, especially because there was no consensus amongst different pundits. Was it anti-incumbency in the context of inflation and immigration? Was it the demonization and victimization of Trump? Was it a disconnect between Democrats and the working class? Was it misogyny or racism? What role did Elon Musk play? The post-mortem varied significantly between the different political pundits. If you are a leader of the Democratic Party, insight into the causes of their failure is crucial to develop the strategy to enable success in the future.

Often, a significant part of our contribution as insights providers is to sift through vast amounts of information, clear the fog and enable senior leaders to act with clarity. As we explore later in the book, truth and insight are inextricably linked. Having the mindset and methods to arrive at truth is becoming even more important now.

**5. Over-reliance on technology, remote working, and a general mechanization of processes are creating mental health issues for many employees, especially young people.**

There are many reports that emphasize the lack of connection, rising academic pressures, the stress due to social media, and hopelessness amongst young people.

In the face of this, it is extraordinary to see the uplifting nature of insight development. Young people feel valued and inspired when they see their insights being accepted and implemented by senior clients.

For instance, one of the associates in my company, a graduate in psychology, made a presentation to the senior leadership team of an organization on the role of cognitive dissonance in creating attitude and behaviour change. This was then translated into a programme to drive engagement amongst their customers. Such an experience is a tremendous self-esteem builder. A motivating aspect of my work is that we create a feeling of well-being and self-efficacy amongst our clients and internal teams. I am always caught by surprise when I speak with past clients and discover how emotionally they talk about the enjoyable process, not just the outcome, of developing insights with us. It is a gratifying experience, indeed.

Nakamura and Csikszentmihalyi, writing about 'vital engagement,'[20] a concept in positive psychology, wrote, *'In vital engagement, the relationship to the world is characterized by completeness of involvement or participation and marked by intensity. There is a strong felt connection between self and object; a writer is "swept away" by a project, a scientist is "mesmerized by the stars".'* Insight development, when done well, creates vital engagement. Since most of the insight work is about understanding people, it puts humanity at the centre, as a guide for the use of all the advances in information, knowledge, and technology.

## BARRIERS TO HARNESSING INSIGHTS FOR IMPACT

Business leaders face many hard problems routinely that need insight and cannot wait for chance connections to occur. There is a timeline within which problems must be resolved, e.g., how to secure investment in the face of a looming recession, how to adapt one's business to technological innovations, or how to launch businesses successfully in new geographies. To help leaders, we need a systematic way of generating insights whilst acknowledging that serendipity plays a significant role. Currently, there are many obstacles to getting high-quality insights.

First, we grasp the value of insights at an intuitive level, but the intangible, inconspicuous, and unpredictable nature of insight poses difficulties for most companies. We like to deal with controllable and tangible processes and outcomes. Leaders often acknowledge the value of insights; Steve Jobs famously spoke about connecting the dots,[21] and Richard Branson's mantra is ABCD[22] (Always Be Connecting Dots). However, if one observes actual practice for most companies, it appears that insights are not perceived as an essential aspect of doing business.

Insights are mostly perceived as 'nice-to-haves' or 'top-ups' to the everyday grind of getting 'real' business done – an indulgence when times are good – a topic for a stimulating breakout group discussion at an off-site event.

This is not unusual for other 'soft' concepts. For instance, there are similar barriers to creativity as well, when attempts are made to include it as part of the routine workings of an organization. Yet, creativity finds prominent external manifestations such as a brilliant advertising campaign or a breakthrough new product. Its contributions are visible.

> But, insight, being the somewhat introverted sibling of creativity, works in the background, and even when it develops into transformative action, people might forget the insight at the source or the process that led to it.

For instance, I found vast amounts of literature on Banga's insight about going cashless and the subsequent impact, yet there was only one source for the fortuitous event when he was walking down the stairs when the insight struck him. At other times, because of its subtle nature, we lack the sensitivity to notice the significance of an insight. Even when insights are considered part of everyday working, the assumption is that the capacity for it seems to develop organically as a side effect of our work experience. We do not think of it as a separate skill that can be improved by training. We also have ideas about ourselves or other people being insightful or not insightful, as if it were a fixed trait.

The second barrier is that in our desire for control, we reduce insight to what we can measure and reproduce easily. We become mechanistic in our pursuit of objective facts and focus on tools and techniques that produce those at the expense of human judgment. This leads to confusion about what the term means and often conflates insight with data. The conflation is so common that even well-regarded consulting firms, during the recent cost of living crisis, have presented rather obvious survey findings – such as inflation being a top concern for people in Europe – as a 'consumer insight'. Inflation being a top concern of people is a measured fact, indeed, an expected one, but not an insight.

High-quality facts are crucial for insight development. However, even to get such facts, we often need to use many different sources and a high degree of quality control by human beings. Leaving insight development to methodologies robotically applied can take us even further from the truth, and from insight. One is reminded of Arnold Toynbee, the British historian and philosopher, who said,[23] *'No tool is omnicompetent. There is no such thing as a master-key that will unlock all doors.'*

> Furthermore, if we equate gaining insight to the mere production of facts, and strip insight of all its intangible and human qualities, such as subjective interpretation, empathetic understanding, keen observation, and imagination, we work with a devitalized and less effective version of insight that does not inspire people.

We also deny the reality that insights are experienced in the human mind and do not sit outside us. When we are inspired on hearing the story about Ajay Banga's insight, we seldom pause to think that we ought to strive to systematically generate and diffuse such breakthroughs in an entire organization.

The third barrier is that there are systemic challenges faced by the market research or customer insights departments – the home for insights in most organizations – in delivering business impact. I have met many talented and insightful people in the market research industry who are constrained by certain factors that limit their ability to generate transformational insights for businesses. These factors are given below:

- Customer insights teams are distant from the senior leadership of companies. Historically, this group has evolved to support the marketing function. Whilst the C-suite executives might be focused on how to evolve the company in the face of the uncertainty due to big changes in the environment, e.g., an economic slowdown or the rapid development of generative AI, the insight function is focused on testing advertising copy or tracking a brand's performance on consumer funnel metrics. It is not that the latter is unimportant. However, the skills and tools required to execute such projects do not translate to the ability to solve C-suite problems. This misalignment creates a vicious cycle. The customer insights team is not represented in the C-suite, and they cannot fully appreciate uncertainties that the leaders are dealing with. The C-suite, on the other hand, do not associate the customer insights team with solving hard problems. It is a dynamic that can be changed. This requires that leadership teams in companies give insights people a seat at the table and that the insights team function to adapt their capabilities to serve the C-suite. There are entrepreneurial insights leaders who achieve tremendous impact and transform the way their department is positioned within the company. Similarly, there are CEOs who understand the value of insight and ensure that the decisions of the C-suite are sufficiently grounded in insight. But such leaders are exceptions.

- Being in the marketing silo, customer insights teams do not connect enough with other functions. According to John Copeland.[24] the insights team often has the purview of the totality of the customer experience. Yet, they might report to a CMO, whose domain pertains mainly to advertising and signage with limited influence on other aspects, such as product innovation and pricing. This constrains the impact that a customer insights person can have.

- The customer insights practitioners within companies are often positioned as the custodians of methodologies and data rather than as insightful thinkers who need to be consulted for their opinions. This reflects our general preoccupation with fact production. Additionally, the repertoire of methods used tends to be limited. For instance, in many situations, studying an analogous business case is likely to provide more insight than conducting primary market research. Yet, customer insights teams rarely draw insights from analogous cases. Furthermore, there is a need to speak to a wide variety of stakeholders – distributors, retailers, regulators, and experts in different fields – not just customers. This, again, is not routine practice amongst insight teams.

The fourth barrier is that insights often do not transmit through different layers of an organization and to the minds of employees. This is necessary for large-scale effect. One can assume Mastercard went through a transformation because Ajay Banga, as the CEO, was fully empowered to act on his insight. However, even if the source of the insight is a regular employee, we need to be able to make others experience it. People respond to stories, not to a collection of facts. Daniel Kahneman famously said,[25] *'No one ever makes a decision because of a number. They need a story.'* We are fundamentally social beings, and conversations are a medium through which effective communication happens. Narratives need to be created. Conversations, often informal ones, need to happen. However, a large part of business communication takes place with thick PowerPoint decks, which are designed to share facts rather than to trigger insights.

With these barriers, the language around insight and practices related to its development is vague or reductive. The role of intuition, emotion, and creativity, the euphoric Aha! experience, or a conducive culture – which are essential and inspiring aspects of the insight development process – are downplayed. There is no attempt to systematically train people on these elements.

## PETITES IDEES THAT TRANSFORM

The eclectic intellectual, economist, and social scientist, Albert O. Hirschman, was known for being interested in *petites idees*, or little ideas, that he would jot down in notebooks throughout his life. He knew that some of these little ideas could become powerful insights and big ideas. He was against grand theories and ideologies, which he contrasted with his approach described by his biographer, Jeremy Adelman,[26] as *'the attempt to come to an understanding of reality in portions admitting the angle might be subjective'*. He wanted to figure out what was going on around him by observation rather than through abstract theoretical thinking. Adelman noted[27] that *'piccole idees, small ideas... lesser thoughts that yield great insights, close-up shots that give way to a new panorama, these were touchstones of Hirschman's intellectual style'*. This may have aptly described Ajay Banga's observation triggered by Mastercard's slogan that commerce is mostly done in cash, leading to the big insight that there is huge headroom to 'kill cash'.

> Many breakthrough and game-changing insights in business arise from such little observations and ideas, not by constructing grand theories. However, for the little idea to convert into a big insight and be acted upon, a prepared and receptive individual and organization are needed.

My attempt in this book is to share certain principles that make this possible in a more systematic manner and at scale. I will demonstrate through case studies how insights can generate substantial business value, for instance, doubling a market opportunity, achieving market leadership within a year of launch, turning around plateauing sales or achieving substantial sales growth in a short duration. Correspondingly, I have drawn attention to how the lack of insight can cause products, businesses, and leaders to tragically fail. Whether it's Blockbuster or in the context of BREXIT, when David Cameron was not able to see the future, the failures were catastrophic because of a lack of insight.

## THREE CENTRAL IDEAS

There are three central ideas that underpin the content in this book that are worth highlighting:

1. To be game-changing, insights must be focused on solving hard problems that business leaders face. These problems are characterized by a high degree of uncertainty with huge potential impact on the outcomes. Being able to see the impact of a changing geopolitical event, such as BREXIT, on your business; finding a way to serve the needs of your customer when your industry is at the intersection of different technologies and scientific fields that are rapidly changing; creating a market for a product that doesn't exist – these are some of the hard problems that need the benefit of insight. We need to make a significant shift towards allocating insights budgets for solving

such problems rather than for confirming what is already more or less known.

2. Developing effective real-world insights is ultimately a very human affair and needs great craftsmanship. The transformational power of insight comes from its non-linear relationship with information. If the relationship had been linear, more information would have led to greater insight, and vice versa. This is not the case. Often a single observation or piece of data can trigger complex workings in our minds to create groundbreaking insights. The non-linearity is a result of multi-faceted human skills that come into play to generate and deploy insights; for instance, making imaginative leaps, hearing what is unsaid, acquiring knowledge and transferring it across domains, communicating and working with other people. It also requires strong values, e.g., openness and curiosity, humility, genuine truth-seeking, and being purposeful.

3. Insight generation is a skill that individuals and organizations can develop through systematic training – like any form of mastery, it improves with practice. We need to adopt a growth mindset and not a fixed one with respect to insight. We must believe that individuals and organizations can get better at developing and implementing insight with practice. It also requires that organizations create a conducive environment for insight. To be truly effective, insights should be embedded across organizational levels and functions.

# 2

# Insight Is a Way of Attending

'Do not mistake the menu for the food. Stop eating the menu.'[1]

– Zen saying

## INSIGHT AS A LIVED EXPERIENCE IN A WORLD OF ABSTRACT DATA

THIS BOOK IS ABOUT THE DISCOVERY AND APPLICATION of insight in a pragmatic context. To enrich our understanding, it is worth delving deeper into the nature of insight. In this chapter, I will dwell on one of the central ideas of the book – that insight is an embodied experience, i.e., it is realized in our minds and bodies.

The pivotal role of the mind-body connection, which refers to the intricate link between physical and mental states, must be emphasized. It is central to how insights appear. For instance, noticing something unusual requires us to be in a deeply attentive state. Exercising, sleeping, or mindfulness practices can help us get into such a state. Feeling stressed will have the opposite effect. Similarly, the appearance of an insight is often accompanied by emotions that we feel in our body – we may feel a sudden tranquillity descend upon us after having cracked a problem or a rush of excitement at a new discovery.

The contemporary world is abundant with information and sophisticated tools and technologies. Therefore, it has become far too common to disregard the human experience related to insights. We mistakenly refer to information that is distant from us, whether it is in a presentation, or sitting somewhere in a digital cloud, or on a dashboard of metrics that appear on a screen, as insights. The conflation of insight with information is so deeply entrenched that we often find apps, e.g., fitness tracking apps providing a summary of data with the title 'insights'.

## THE NON-LINEAR RELATIONSHIP BETWEEN INSIGHT AND INFORMATION

Even those who understand the distinction between insight and information often assume a strong link between insight and large amounts of data. This is evident in how the two are frequently paired in phrases like 'data and insights.' The relationship between information and insight is not straightforward. You can have vast quantities of information and no insight. As discussed in the last chapter, a glaring recent example is the failure to predict Trump's decisive victory in the 2024 US election despite the availability of vast quantities of information, including many opinion polls. Equally, a single observation or an experience, such as when Steve Jobs encountered sans serif in a calligraphy class, may trigger an epiphany and a subsequent innovation.

> The relationship between information and insight is non-linear, which we often don't acknowledge.

First, to satisfy our urge to be in control and to manipulate information, we like to deal with discrete units of data, preferably the kind that is suitable for quantitative analysis. For instance, understanding customer experience for a product or service has many facets: the way the product fits in the customer environment, the look and feel of the product, the performance on relevant features, the intuitiveness and ease of use, the difference it makes to the life of the consumers, the emotional benefits it offers… the list goes on. Immersive approaches such as ethnography allow us to observe and understand deeply how customers actually use the product in their own context. Yet, it is common for companies to default to only conducting surveys for measuring customer satisfaction on a subset of dimensions. Customer experience, often called CX, is reduced to the ratings on a few metrics or Key Performance Indicators (KPIs) that are then monitored periodically. Though it gives the companies a feeling of control, these 'CX KPIs' are abstract measures that do not capture real customer experience. They can make companies blind to innovation opportunities and vulnerable to customer attrition or to possible disruptions from competitors. The foundation for insights is often the continuous stream of sensory and unstructured data that we receive through our senses by living in the physical world and connecting with other human beings, e.g., Darwin's observations[2] of different beak sizes of finches in the Galapagos Islands, which helped him develop his theory of evolution based on natural selection, or how the melody of the song 'Yesterday' came to Paul McCartney[3] in a dream.

Second, the prevailing metaphor for developing insight is one of information processing – we receive data that is analysed by a model that will provide an output that is mistakenly called 'insight' rather than a 'result' or a 'finding'. The actual process of an insight emerging is far more haphazard, random, and serendipitous, with new information often colliding with retrieved memories and ideas stored in the subconscious. Sometimes the process is fast, almost instantaneous, and many times it first takes the form of an inkling or a slow hunch that develops over time. While both high-quality information and methods for elicitation of the information are crucial, if we do not train our minds to be receptive, insights will elude us.

We must not assume that the reductive approach I have described above is a criticism of just quantitative research. There are plenty of examples of qualitative research that are equally reductive, e.g., using random statements made by a few consumers to make big decisions on the design of products, brands or advertising. At the same time, the best users of quantitative research immerse themselves and try to find meaning by thinking in different ways. While talking about a quantitative consumer tracking study (CTS) used in PepsiCo, Vibha Rishi[4] said that 'if you are receptive, the CTS will talk to you'.

A large part of the preparation is learning how to attend to the world. The profound work of Iain McGilchrist,[5] the British psychiatrist, literary scholar, neuroscientist, and philosopher – a true polymath – emphasizes that our experience of life is dependent on how we direct our attention. Furthermore, while the two hemispheres of the brain are implicated in most processes, the manner in which they attend to the world is markedly different, with the right hemisphere more likely to play a significant role in the appearance of novel insights. Many people are concerned that with the explosion of AI innovation, professional insight developers will become redundant. On the contrary, the behaviour that will be replaced is that of human beings mechanistically using tools and techniques to provide data.

Later in this chapter, I describe the competencies that an insights professional must strive to acquire. Let us begin by looking at how a simple insight can positively transform the fate of a brand in trouble.

## USING INSIGHT TO REVERSE PLATEAUING SALES

A large global pharmaceutical company acquired a natural product that alleviated menopausal symptoms and marketed it in a European country. Within a year of the launch, the sales plateaued. The client could not understand why and brought us in to diagnose the issue and revive sales. We spoke to the leadership team to understand their view of the problem, which ranged from an inadequate number of sales visits to the gynaecologists to a lack of awareness amongst patients. After a few working sessions with the client team and reviewing their existing market research reports, a consensus began to emerge on the possible root cause of the problem. They believed that the communication to the gynaecologist about the product needed to be improved. They came to this conclusion by assuming that gynaecologists, being scientists, were fundamentally sceptical about natural products and therefore were hesitant to recommend the product. Their strategy was to use strong evidence to persuade the gynaecologists that the product was not like other natural products on the market. When subjected to rational scrutiny by the gynaecologists, the product would emerge as something closer to a pharmaceutical product, thus overcoming its 'naturalness' disadvantage. They wanted to develop communication material that told this story and test its validity in the research. The reasoning seemed entirely plausible.

We embarked on our research project. The standard market research practice is to invite the gynaecologists to a central venue for in-depth interviews or focus groups. It is an efficient process that allows one to conduct interactions with many gynaecologists in a single day with the additional advantage that the client team members can observe the research through a one-way mirror. We decided to break away from this practice.

Our belief was that by staying close to their natural environment where they met patients, we would get a glimpse of what really happens. For us, seeing their office could provide different cues and spark new lines of enquiry. For the gynaecologists, being in their natural habitat, without the pressure of being observed by employees from pharmaceutical companies, would help them feel more relaxed and open. What we discovered shifted our perspective.

The first gynaecologist I interviewed spoke about how beneficial natural products were for menopausal symptoms. Far from being sceptical, they produced material from training courses on natural products that they had attended, and excitedly talked about how they matched natural ingredients, such as black cohosh or red clover, to different symptoms of menopause, such as hot flushes or night sweats. They enthusiastically pointed to product samples of natural products in their office while speaking. I began to experience dissonance. I was expecting the doctors to be critical, but instead I was finding unabashed enthusiasm for natural products. It struck me as counter to my clients' beliefs – I thought this doctor might have been an exception. But then this pattern started recurring across most of the people in our qualitative sample, and we knew we were on the trail of discovering something new.

It became clear that there was a distinct group of physicians who believed in the value of natural treatments. We couldn't measure the prevalence of this behaviour in the market with a qualitative sample of just twenty people. However, we could identify certain variables that were associated with this group, such as that they tended to spend more time in private rather than public practice. Using such variables, we analysed our client's database of all the physicians and estimated that the 'natural believers' segment comprised more than half of the target population.

Our research revealed that the barrier to using the client's treatment was not that it was natural but that the gynaecologists did not understand how the ingredients of the product worked on typical menopause symptoms, such as mood swings or hot flashes.

Our client's medical team developed a simple explanation for how the treatment worked on the symptoms. This explanation was added to the communication material. Our client focused their marketing strategy on the 'natural believer' segment. The brand grew by 40 per cent in sales in the next six months. Following the same strategy, after seven years, today, it is the market leader and one of the strongest brands for the company. With a total budget of less than $100,000 on the project, the return on investment was dramatically high.

Many powerful insights are like this. Just a small shift in perception that creates a dramatic improvement in the outcome. It was like Hirschman's 'petit idee' – nothing very dramatic, just an observation of something we had not expected.

This case study also illustrates a few important aspects related to insight as applicable in business practice.

First, one must choose where to look. The problem definition was clear – that we had to reverse the plateauing sales. However, we could have pursued many different paths. Combining some fact-checking and working with our client's experience and intuition, we were able to narrow the focus of our effort towards improving the communication material for the gynaecologist, rather than randomly looking at some other area, e.g., expanding the sales force.

The second learning is that one must look at ground reality in a fresh manner, as opposed to buying into deeply entrenched notions that remain unexamined. We heard our client but still went into the project with an open mind, believing that there could be more to the story.

Third, subjective interpretation is important. A significant part of academic research on insight is based on studying how the subjects in a study solve brain teasers, riddles, and geometric and mathematical puzzles. These problems tend to be well defined, with a limited set of variables and a clear right answer.

> Real-world problems are different. They are often unclear and keep changing, with many moving parts. It's impossible to know if an insight or its solution is the right or best choice at the time it is developed.

In our study for the menopausal product, focusing on the 'natural believers' segment was one compelling solution to increase sales that was arrived at with research and collaboration with the client. Unlike in the case of a puzzle, there might have been other solutions that we didn't explore because of the time constraint. Also, in another context this solution may not have been valid. Consider the assumption that physicians are sceptical about natural products because of lack of scientific evidence. This is a valid assumption in general, including for the treatment of menopause. In the UK, the treatment protocol for menopause, which is largely managed by general practitioners (GPs), favours the use of hormone replacement therapy (HRT) and is influenced by the guidelines of the National Institute for Health and Care Excellence (NICE). It's less likely to find a large group of 'natural believers' in the UK.

However, where private gynaecologists play a greater role in managing menopause, as in our study, we found that the situation was more amenable to the recommendation of natural products because many women were reluctant to take hormonal treatments. The fear of taking hormones is often attributed to a Women's Health Initiative (WHI) study[6] in 2002 that challenged the safety of hormones. Over the years, the design and findings have been questioned, and a 20-year follow-up study found that the fears are overblown.[7] Recommending natural products has been the gynaecologists' way of helping these women.

Fourth, one must be willing to move away from traditional research designs if the situation demands the shift. We could have tried to elicit feedback from gynaecologists by using a traditional approach such as conducting a focus group or a depth interview in a central location. Or we might have done a quantitative survey. However, a conversation in the gynaecologist's office allowed for a more truthful and deeper interaction.

Fifth, inspiring stakeholders to implement actions is crucial for impact. In our study, both the CEO of Europe and the country head participated in every workshop or presentation. This is not common for customer insights projects. It speaks to the receptivity of the client's senior leadership team. Having arrived at our insights, we had to convince the client team about the validity of our recommendations and then work with them to implement the actions. The leadership team had to agree to the strategy, the medical team needed to be willing to create the story for how the product worked, the sales team had to identify and target the 'natural believers', and the marketing team had to create material to increase the salience of the brand.

Significant effort was required to bring the insights to life through film clips, pictures, and other material, and then we had to design concrete actions to make them executable by different clients. This is representative of most business situations where insights, without implementation, have little value.

At the end of the project, the European CEO said, '*You are telling us to do something that is exactly the opposite of what we were doing, and we are convinced. This is a work of art.*'

## DEFINING INSIGHT AND UNDERSTANDING ITS MECHANISMS

There is no consensus on a definition of insight. Consider the following examples:

Richard Meyer,[8] while emphasizing the role of insight in problem solving, defines insight as '*a process by which a problem solver moves from a state of not knowing how to solve a problem to a state of knowing how to solve it*'. The Webster's New World Dictionary[9] brings out the role of insight in uncovering a hidden truth, especially through an intuitive process – '*Insight is seeing and understanding the inner nature of things clearly, especially by intuition.*' Gestalt thinkers, who believe that insight arrives as part of a special mental process, talk about[10] '*insight resulting from a sudden restructuring of a problem that is accompanied by the sensations of flashes of experience or unconscious leaps of thinking*'. These varied definitions demonstrate the rich and multi-faceted nature of insight, and I feel comfortable with there being no single definition.

My own working definition builds on these ideas, yet it attempts to be more inclusive of a wider variety of situations and mechanisms.

> Insight is a transition from a state of not knowing to a state of knowing, which empowers one to make a positive change in a specific context.

For instance, let us revisit the menopause medicine case study. It is hard to contest that the discovery of the 'natural believer' segment was an example of a powerful insight. Was it a transition from a state of not knowing to knowing? Yes. We discovered that several gynaecologists were in fact open to natural solutions. Did it empower us to make a positive change in our context? The answer is a definitive yes. The sales of the company increased by 40 per cent within six months of implementing the new approach. Did it help us see a hidden truth? Yes. Contrary to what was largely believed, many medical practitioners were open to alternative solutions that best suited their patients' needs. Was it a sudden flash of illumination? No, the process was more akin to the development of a slow hunch. Did intuition play a role? Yes, to the extent that we picked up cues in the environment that reaffirmed what the gynaecologists were saying about their preference for natural products. Did it involve making unconscious leaps? It was most certainly an Aha! moment, but it wasn't an obvious unconscious leap. Had we adopted a different definition of insight than the one I selected, it might not have recognized our gradual understanding as an insight.

## The Aha! Moment

Having that visceral and sudden feeling of clarity when an insight appears is perhaps one of the most euphoric experiences of working to develop insights. When clients feel completely inspired after an insight development workshop, it's often the 'aha' moment that creates the positive feeling. There is research that supports this occurrence of sudden and affective feelings of illumination that accompany the arrival of novel insights, notably by Janet Metcalfe and David Wiebe.[11]

> This 'aha' moment, in addition to being a positive emotional experience, increases the likelihood of an insight living longer in the minds of people.

Creating an environment that stimulates the 'aha' moment makes people happier.

The Zen monk, Thich Nhat Hanh, distinguishes between an idea and an insight by clarifying that an idea only becomes an insight when people can experience it firsthand.[12] Until that happens, it is simply a cerebral concept. When they suddenly grasp the significance of the idea, it becomes the basis of transformation. Perhaps some of our best learning takes place when an idea that we know is theoretically true is experienced as an insight. I got such a lesson recently whilst playing in a jazz jam session. We were playing a Thelonious Monk tune called 'Straight, No Chaser' in a pub. The performance went well, and the audience applauded. Later that night, watching a recording of the performance, I noticed that whilst the bass player was in the midst of her solo, I interrupted her and prematurely started playing the tune. Nobody in the audience had noticed this because it all happened fast without any break in the music. Yet, from the video, it was obvious to me that I didn't let the solo finish because I was neither listening to her intently nor watching her body language. That musicians must listen to each other and pay attention to body language is an idea that everyone knows. But that experience of seeing the consequences of not listening came as an insight. It transformed how I approach playing music with others. I now approached it with a renewed emphasis on deeper listening and maintaining eye contact with others. The insight was so powerful that it improved my ability to listen to colleagues in business contexts. I often find myself asking, 'What is this person really trying to say?'

In businesses, transmitting the revelation, or the aha! moment, to different stakeholders is an essential aspect of communication and requires creativity. Making our prior beliefs or hypotheses in a situation explicit helps people notice the newness of the insight. In the case example on the menopause product, our client believed that physicians were deeply sceptical about natural products. When the research contradicted that assumption, the clients experienced a sharp shift in their perspective. We often design our presentations in a manner that enables our clients to experience the insight rather than hear about it from us as a point of information. The presentation is punctuated with breaks, when clients can immerse themselves in the material without commentary. This creates the space for the insight to strike them independently.

## Mechanisms for insight

Many people have investigated the mechanism of insight appearing in the brain. I have reviewed a few of these models and reflected on my experience. Whilst there is no clear consensus, there is a lot of common ground in the different theories. What is common to all frameworks is that insight is created by intricate workings in our minds. Some of the common routes are given below, though these may not be exhaustive. It is worth noting that these routes are not mutually exclusive and may work in combination. Also, what I have proposed below is not new but a reorganization of frameworks proposed by others.

a. **Connecting disparate elements – 'I see it now. This is how it all fits.'**

Consider the example mentioned in the previous chapter, when it struck Ajay Banga that the real opportunity for Mastercard was to 'kill cash' rather than outperform other credit card companies. Banga connected a set of seemingly unrelated facts to arrive at a new framing of the situation. In everyday parlance, this process is called 'connecting the dots' and is a common mechanism through which insights occur. In Davidson's theory of selection,[13] such a mechanism is described as a case of 'selective combination' when one suddenly puts together features of a problem in a way that was not obvious to one before; Gary Klein,[14] in his triple-path insight model, talks about the connection pathway facilitating such an insight.

b. **Experiencing dissonance – 'something seems odd'.**

Ruchir Sharma,[15] an author, fund manager, and columnist, who has been consistently making accurate predictions each year, has forecast that in 2025 there will be a reversal in the recent pattern of American dominance in the world. One of the main factors underlying Ruchir Sharma's prediction is America's fiscal deficit which at 8 per cent of the GDP over the past decade is substantially higher than that of most countries. Ruchir Sharma calls the large fiscal deficit America's 'fatal flaw' that will lead to a slowdown in America's economy. We do not know whether the prediction will come true until later this year. Yet, this exemplifies the arrival of an insight by noticing something odd or dissonant in a situation. Many thinkers have supported the idea of dissonance leading to insight in different ways – notably Thomas Kuhn,[16] who suggested that anomalies lead to paradigm changes in scientific thought, Gary Klein,[17] who considers contradictions as a distinct path to insight, and Stephen Johnson,[18] who talks about the role of errors in sparking ideas.

Consider how we arrived at our discovery of the 'natural believer' segment. The insight first emerged in the form of incongruence relative to our belief that physicians are dismissive of natural products. As the research progressed, instead of ignoring it, we developed this dissonance until we came to a realization that this indeed was the insight.

Television and film script writers often depict this route for insight in their stories. In the popular television series *Suits*,[19] Mike Ross, the young associate, routinely notices discrepancies in facts that lead to an insight which helps his firm win cases. In *Dangal*,[20] a movie about the Phogat sisters – world wrestling champions – a neighbour complains to the father, played by Aamir Khan, about his young daughters roughing up a boy who was bullying them. While everyone else is horrified by the violence inflicted by the girls on an older boy, the father is in a daze, experiencing disbelief. Until that moment, he thought his dream of winning a gold medal in wrestling for India was unattainable as he had no sons. Suddenly, it dawned on him that his daughters could be top-class wrestlers.

c. **Analogies – 'I have seen this pattern somewhere before'.**

This is my favourite route for insight. When the pandemic struck, the disruption was huge. We had never experienced anything like that. My karate teacher, a real master, began to take classes on Zoom. It became obvious that his mastery helped him design much better classes than many other teachers. He visualized spaces and created routines based on that. He could anticipate the mistakes students would make and gave instructions pre-emptively. Knowing that he could not demonstrate techniques on the small screen fully, he took pains to explain everything in detail. Very soon, his classes were oversubscribed, with people signing up from all over the world. Suddenly, I realized that mastery over one's subject is a particular advantage in the Zoom world, and that might be an opportunity for us. Until then, most of our business came from the UK and European countries. Physical proximity defined our market. However, during the pandemic, we were no longer disadvantaged by geography or size. I reached out to people in the US and Asia immediately, and our business thrived. A simple analogy made it happen.

Analogies have been sources of insight in many different fields. For instance, Darwin's insight[21] about natural selection was triggered by Thomas Malthus's observation that in resource-constrained societies, the poor and weak are more likely to starve, and so survival is not a random process. Davidson's selection theory[22] includes analogizing as part of 'selective comparison' when one discovers a non-obvious relationship between new information and information in the past. Gary Klein[23] includes it in the 'connection' path. However, given their importance, analogical insights deserve to be mentioned as a distinct and separate process.

d. **Seeing hidden variables or patterns – 'I am noticing something I have never seen before.'**

Often an insight comes in the form of seeing, hearing, or feeling something hidden, almost invisible, which results in the discovery of something new. Recently, we were helping a client launch a portfolio of innovative climate control devices in the US. Our client's focus for the innovations was on the residential market. This was consistent with their strategy for their existing products. As we were doing qualitative work, a few of the people we interviewed suggested that they would prefer to have these devices in their businesses, where there was a much bigger need. We decided to speak to more business decision makers and then conducted a quantitative study with 900 consumers and 300 business decision makers. It turned out that the size of the opportunity in the B2B market was significantly larger than that in the residential market. Based on our research, our client changed tack and began developing products for both the residential and B2B markets.

### e. Overcoming obstacles – 'I am stuck and I need to find a way out.'

In the 1996 World Cup for Cricket, both Coke and Pepsi bid for the official sponsorship.[24] Coke outbid Pepsi by a significantly large amount of money and became the sponsor. PepsiCo India responded with the 'Nothing Official About it' advertising campaign, which is perhaps one of the best case studies of impact through guerrilla marketing, an approach aimed at achieving maximum impact through surprise and novelty. I have described the case in detail in Chapter 6. The birth of the campaign is an illustration of an insight that overcame an obstacle.

Albert O. Hirschman[25] described creativity as the *hiding hand* that gets invoked only when entrepreneurs face obstacles. Gary Klein's triple path model[26] describes this mechanism as the *creative desperation* route. This is a route that many purpose-driven people deploy. They invariably face difficulties that need to be resolved. Insights appear to clear the path.

Often people use a combination of these routes. Green Hub is a youth- and community-based fellowship and digital archive for work related to wildlife, indigenous knowledge, and biodiversity in India. The founder, Rita Banerji, told me[27] that the idea had been developing for about fifteen years.

During filming, she first discovered that across India, numerous grassroots efforts – often operating invisibly – were addressing issues related to poverty, health, and education. She realized that even for the short films that she was making, she was generating a lot of video footage that could be useful to create training videos to support those NGOs. In parallel, there was a realization that conservation needed many people to be involved and that there was no platform for youth, especially from disadvantaged backgrounds, to work in conservation filmmaking. Meanwhile, the technology for filmmaking had become more accessible and cheaper. This led to the creation of Green Hub, launched in Northeast India – a region rich in biodiversity and in urgent need of conservation. She believes that Green Hub is creating changemakers. Filming is a medium that enables one to see the world differently, experience insight, and create change. In this story, the many routes for insight development are evident – spotting hidden patterns, connecting disparate elements, analogous transfer of ideas, i.e., from video as a training tool for NGOs to enabling youth to participate in conservation, and overcoming obstacles.

## THE ROLE OF THE TWO BRAIN HEMISPHERES

Iain McGilchrist's work[28] on the 'divided brain' has profound implications on the way we think about insight, and I felt compelled to draw attention to a few essential ideas. It is worth noting that I am not an expert in this field of cognitive neuroscience, and I hope I will be pardoned for any inaccurate representations of the original work.

Both the hemispheres are implicated in most mental processes in a complicated manner, so it is hard to make clear-cut statements about their respective roles. Yet, there is a substantial difference in how they attend to the world. The left hemisphere is engaged with manipulating the world and helping us get ahead, whilst the right hemisphere simply attends to what is happening without preconceptions. The left hemisphere enables focus, whilst the right hemisphere allows us to have broader sustained vigilance. The left hemisphere wants to reduce uncertainty and make concepts graspable. In the process, though, it is subject to illusions of certainty. The right hemisphere, on the other hand, allows for exploration of possibility. The left hemisphere values consistency and looks for simple mechanistic explanations for everything, often confirming what it already knows. The right hemisphere is involved with novel experiences, learning, and ideas. The left hemisphere dissects phenomena into parts, whilst the right hemisphere perceives in a gestalt way and is concerned with the relationship between things. The left hemisphere is involved in encoding tools and machines, and the right hemisphere is associated with living beings. Empathy is the domain of the right hemisphere. The left hemisphere abstracts and generalizes, whilst the right hemisphere notices the aspects of a specific instance. Language and making things explicit are aspects of the left hemisphere, whilst the right hemisphere is associated with metaphorical thinking.

These are a few essential differences that suggested the hypothesis that not only is developing and using both hemispheres critical for insight, but that our obsession with treating data and mechanised approaches may be dominated by a left hemisphere oriented thinking. Iain McGilchrist argues that as a society we have become increasingly more left hemisphere dominant due to many factors, including its emphasis on utility, its simplistic models of reality, and its ability to articulate its case through language, unlike the right hemisphere, which has no voice. Perhaps one of the particularly interesting differences is that the right hemisphere considers the workings of the left hemisphere and integrates it into its own working. The left hemisphere, however, works with an assumption of self-sufficiency.

Therefore, a lot of what I am writing about is a type of correction of the left-hemispheric bias, which may be slowing down our ability to experience breakthroughs. Iain McGilchrist sees insight as being more associated with the right hemisphere. This is made evident by his writing,[29] *'There is a relationship between the pleasurable 'aha!' phenomenon of insight and the right amygdala that mediates the interactions between emotions and higher frontal cognitive functions.'*

The purpose of this section is to emphasize the perils of being one-sided, especially in attending to the world in the manner of the left hemisphere. The next section provides a framework for the skills needed by insights practitioners.

# THE WHEEL OF INSIGHT TO TRANSCEND ONE-SIDEDNESS

Given the rich and intricate nature of an insight and its appearance in the mind, how do we systematically prepare ourselves?

Specifically, how can we train ourselves to:

- Systematically think in different ways to create insight?

- Learn and apply knowledge/methods artfully to elicit truth?

- Engage with other stakeholders in an organization in a manner that transmits insight and inspires effective action?

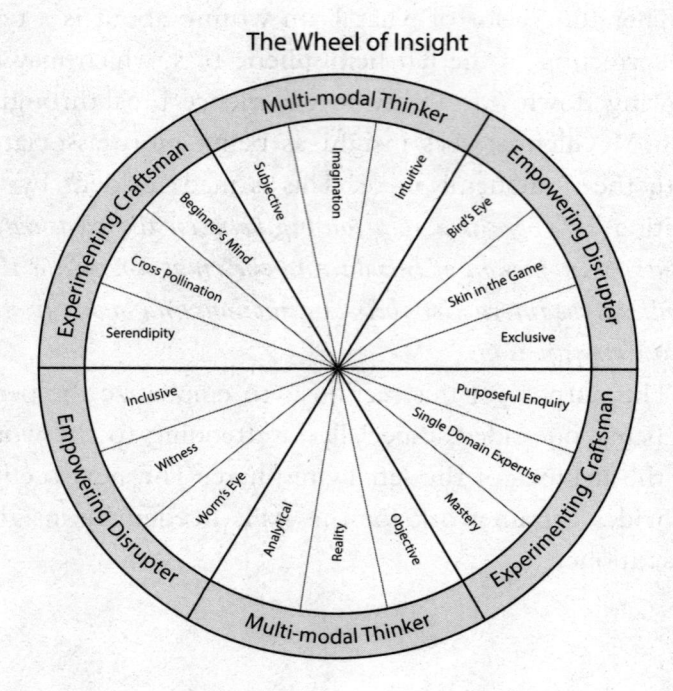

The Wheel of Insight

> One can imagine that an insights practitioner needs to wear three hats that reflect thinking styles, orientation to methods and knowledge, and how they work with organizations. I have called the three hats 'Multi-modal Thinker', 'Experimenting Craftsperson' and 'Empowering Disrupter'.

Each hat comprises certain competencies that represent seemingly opposing qualities that an insights professional must straddle to transcend one-sidedness. To be effective, we need to be always balanced on what one might call the 'yin and yang' of insight. It is very important not to confuse the end-points of each competency with the right or the left hemisphere. For instance, a popular notion might be that the left hemisphere deals with reality and the right with imagination. That may be incorrect because the right hemisphere's mode of being present in its attention to the world is what makes us see reality better.

## THE MULTI-MODAL THINKER

An insights practitioner must find latent opportunities for innovation, spot new markets and customer segments, and find novel ways to serve customers or discover a solution for a hard business problem. Creativity ought to be at the heart of an insights professional's work. However, the foundations of insights must be robust. This is akin to the requirements for scientists, who break new ground while adhering to fundamental principles of science; or composers of music, who ground their creations in the theory of harmony or, at times, break the rules, knowingly, to innovate; or architects, who design imaginative buildings while remaining true to the principles of structural engineering.

Often, we witness two cultures. There is the analytical, facts-driven, and evidence-based objective culture; in a generalized way, this culture is what the quantitative market research customer/insights world and management consultancies are associated with. In such cultures, the emphasis is on logic and quantitative evidence, and there is scepticism about anything that is qualitative and subjective, that is considered 'soft'. On the other hand, there is the intuitive, subjective, and free-thinking culture, more prevalent in innovation and qualitative research boutiques, which have the opposite proclivities and are often frustrated by the insistence of evidence, especially of a quantitative nature. This may be a broad generalization, but one can sample a fraction of posts on a professional network such as LinkedIn and witness the existence of these two cultures and the chasm between them.

An insights practitioner must be able to deploy multiple modes of thinking. Each of the competencies I have described below are closely related but warrant a separation because they are distinct from each other.

For instance, let's think of imagination. It can be conflated with being intuitive. Yet, we can be imaginative both analytically and intuitively. Einstein's thought experiment of travelling along at the speed of light,[30] which led to the theory of relativity, is an example of being imaginative and analytical. Thinking about more routine business situations, visualizing how the future for an innovation might unfold and instinctively knowing it might fail based on past experiences is an example of being imaginative and intuitive.

## 1. Subjectivity-Objectivity

Since our field is concerned essentially with understanding human behaviour, embracing subjectivity is intrinsic to what we do. People vary and interpret what goes on in their own unique way. The whole premise of customer segmentation is based on a view that there are multiple truths that make sense to different groups based on their situation. You cannot have empathy unless you appreciate the subjective nature of reality.

When it comes to our own thinking, subjectivity is often frowned upon. We believe that insights need to be built on objective facts to the extent possible. Yet, what is objective remains unchanged, irrespective of the experiencer. The obsession with objectivity often leads to absolutist views that can prevent insights from appearing. The notion of 'best practices' very much reflects this dogma, that there is one way or one framework for everything. For instance, people insist that there is a best way to segment customers, build a brand, or launch a product. We often find that all major players in an industry do market research, following a near-identical methodology, and share a common understanding of the market based on the collection of 'objective' facts. That does not translate into a differential insight or provide a competitive advantage.

> Subjectivity is the basis of differential advantage.

We need objective facts; that is what establishes the groundwork. Good insights people work with the same data yet come up with a more interesting story, less obvious to others. The widely known and hugely successful Dove 'Real Beauty' campaign[31] illustrates the difference between objective facts and insight. One of the facts underlying the campaign was that only a tiny fraction of women globally considered themselves beautiful, and most of them felt an enormous pressure to look good. A bigger, subjective, and contextual truth was that traditional stereotypes of beauty depicted in the media might be creating or reaffirming a self-esteem problem amongst girls and women. The insight was that challenging traditional stereotypes, by using real and relatable women in the campaigns, would help build self-esteem and bring the brand closer to women.

Interestingly, whilst subjectivity is often associated with qualitative thinking, it plays a significant role in our choice of quantitative models. Christoph Molnar[32] described different mindsets that underlie the choice of statistical and machine learning models and wrote, *'Models are like different lenses. All lenses show us a world, but with a different focus... in supervisory machine learning, for example, everything becomes a prediction problem, while in Bayesian inference the goal is to update beliefs about the world using probability theory.'*

## 2. Imagination – Reality

What's *really* going on here? According to Richard Rumelt,[33] the answer to this simple question is at the heart of strategy. For instance, why were the sales of the menopausal product plateauing? What was *really* happening? Such a question prompts us to dig deeper, past superficial answers, to get to the truth. We attempt to study people in their natural environments. We understand how they *really* make decisions using various heuristics. We analyse 'big data' to see what they *actually* buy. All this helps to understand what is going on.

However, we often create insights of a speculative nature. Steve Jobs' 'reality distortion field' (RDF) is a term that people within Apple[34] used to describe his ability to persuade himself, and others, to believe almost anything. This characteristic led him to imagine scenarios that did not exist, such as being able to reduce the booting time of the first Macintosh computer. The economist Milton Friedman,[35] echoing the possibility of theories being developed without realistic assumptions, had said, *'Truly important and significant hypotheses will be found to have 'assumptions' that are wildly inaccurate descriptive representations of reality, and, in general, the more significant the theory, the more unrealistic the assumptions.'*

Beyond speculative thinking, the interplay between reality and imagination goes on in everyday business situations. Even as we are observing 'reality', we are constantly imagining possibilities in our heads, matching it with our past experiences to make sense of what is going on.

## 3. Intuition-Analysis

I recall a problem we were set during an abstract algebra class when I was at university. Like most of my classmates, I set out to solve it analytically. Hitendra Wadhwa, now a prominent entrepreneur and educator, who was in my class, announced his solution almost instantaneously to the teacher. Then he turned to me with disbelief and said that he didn't know how the solution came to him! What was striking is that for his answer he used concepts from real analysis, a different field of mathematics. He himself was bewildered by how the solution came to him in a flash, unannounced, without his conscious awareness. This was my first encounter with the power of intuition that can help one grasp a situation by bypassing analytical reasoning and conscious thought. In a recent conversation with him, I reminded him of the incident. Whilst he did not remember the incident, he offered his reflection on what might have transpired based on his understanding of how intuition works. He said, 'One way to solve mathematical problems is to move away from the defined rigid structures (e.g., abstract algebra or real analysis) and go back to the few basics or axioms that form the basis of building a structure. In university, I remember wanting to get to the essence and understand what's going on. That type of understanding goes beyond logic and becomes a feeling – a feeling for the structure and system. That feeling sometimes enables flashes of intuition.'[36]

Over the years I have witnessed the intuitive appearance of an epiphany in a variety of fields, significantly related to my professional work. Intuition can be deconstructed into thinking tools such as analogizing, empathising, or abstracting, and people can be systematically trained on these tools as has been elegantly proposed by Robert and Michèle Root-Bernstein.[37] This is a topic that will be covered in Chapter 6. What is particularly inspiring about this approach is that it is different from common theories of training intuition, which suggest that the main method of training should be repetition of experiences in a specific context. While practising any skill is a reliable way to build intuition, it raises questions about the quality of intuition in situations that are unfamiliar. Robert and Michèle Root-Bernstein's approach focuses on building global cognitive skills that may serve us better in situations we haven't encountered before. The example of Hitendra Wadhwa is a case in point. It was not his experience in abstract algebra that helped him solve the problem. It was his ability to see an analogy between real analysis and abstract algebra. Training ourselves to be better at analogizing, one of the main thinking tools, would improve our intuition in many more situations, including unfamiliar ones.

While intuition must be celebrated, analysis lays the solid groundwork for insight. Most business problems need to be broken down into their component elements. Even a simple, well-defined problem, such as how to reverse plateau sales of a product, has many potential answers. Pursuing every avenue would be an inefficient and expensive way to get an answer. We need analytical thinking to structure and dissect the problem into its many components and then choose what we need to investigate. Even if an insight is generated intuitively, analysis helps guard against blind spots. Furthermore, the transparency and robustness of analysis inspires confidence amongst leaders in making the correct decisions.

In the information-abundant and uncertain world that we inhabit, a combination of the two is particularly important. We need sophisticated analytical tools to identify patterns based on the data that simply cannot be inferred intuitively; yet we need to sense-check what we uncover with intuition.

## THE EXPERIMENTING CRAFTSMAN

Getting immersed in new knowledge disciplines and learning new methods are essential to developing insight. Should we use ethnography, cognitive neuroscience-based methods, or conjoint analysis? Should we use principles of behavioural economics? How deeply must we understand the technologies related to an industry? The challenge in the real world is that problems are multi-faceted and messy; different disciplines intersect, and the boundaries are less clear. We need to be agile learners who go deep into a variety of knowledge areas and draw on a broad range of methods to develop insights that solve the business problem we are facing. We must be experimenting craftsmen and work on improving these three competencies.

## 1. Beginner's mind – master perspective

The notion of the importance of the beginner's mind is a concept that has been popularised by Zen practitioners, especially by Shunryu Suzuki, captured best in his statement,[38] 'In the beginner's mind there are many possibilities, in the expert's there are few.'

> The feeling of not knowing is vital to developing great insight. This is especially important because in many environments where expertise and knowledge are weaponized to support ambition, admitting to not having answers can be perceived as a weakness. Most breakthrough insights are preceded by a state of not knowing.

Research suggests that a big obstacle to insight is the formation of mental blocks or fixation. The Gestalt thinkers wrote about '*einstellung*',[39] or an installation in your mind, a kind of fixedness that prevents the appearance of an insight, and they suggest removal of a mental block as one of the primary ways to allow insight to appear.

Daniel Kahneman and Amos Tversky, in their groundbreaking work on decision-making, have demonstrated that we are all susceptible to systematic biases that distort our views of reality.[40] For instance, availability bias, the tendency for us to be swayed by easy-to-recall information, was at play when our clients assumed that the gynaecologists were likely to be sceptical about natural products based on past encounters they had had with doctors. Confirmation bias, the desire to find out what one already knows, prevents one from observing relevant new information. If we had simply accepted our client's assumption, it is more than likely that we would have confirmed their hypothesis. These are just a subset of biases that are at play. Anyone embarking on an insights project must learn how to be present and be like a beginner.

Yet, given the complexity of the world that we live in, having deep subject matter knowledge is useful because then our definition of problems and the questions we address are more nuanced. Mastery in a field allows one to see what may be invisible to a layperson. For instance, whilst working on making a new product successful, an expert will have a large repository of case histories of past innovations to draw upon. Ideas are 'chunked' together. They can use readily available frameworks without reinventing the wheel. In highly scientific areas such as genomic medicines, oncology, or machine learning, one cannot even begin to have a proper conversation with customers without a threshold level of knowledge.

So how do we marry the simultaneous need to be a beginner and an expert?

In my company, one of the practices we adopt is receptive mastery, described in detail in Chapter 7. The idea of a beginner's mind refers to being in a state of receptivity irrespective of one's knowledge. To explain this, I like to use the metaphor of a master musician, who is not only knowledgeable about music but can hear the subtleties of music better than most people because their ear is more trained. In that case, the beginner's mind refers to the capacity of the master to listen deeply and assimilate more than a layperson. At the same time, the master must have the humility to be receptive to new ideas, irrespective of the source.

## 2. Single-domain expertise – cross-pollination across disciplines

Traditionally we were reliant on classic social science disciplines and statistics. Now fields such as machine learning and generative AI, design thinking, cognitive neuroscience, and behavioural economics significantly influence how we develop insights in industry.

Many of these disciplines are rapidly evolving. To be on top of these fields and push the boundaries, one needs to develop mastery. For instance, you may want to use machine learning algorithms to develop a predictive model. There are many models available, logistic regressions, support vector machines, random forest, neural networks, etc. Going deep into the pros and cons of different models helps us find the best option to improve the quality of the insight.

However, most real-world problems have many angles, and often interdisciplinary hybrid methods are more suitable. Let us consider new product development, where insights play a big role. You may need to use design methods to test prototypes, conduct conjoint analysis to optimize features, conduct multi-variate analysis to identify early adopter segments, and create synthetic data based on your data for prior innovations to simulate the adoption trajectory of the product. We will illustrate this example in greater detail in Chapter 4.

Furthermore, cross-pollination across fields can be a source of breakthrough insights through analogies and metaphors.

> An insights team must have access to deep masters in the relevant knowledge areas, yet the leaders must be polymathic, with a threshold level of competence in many disciplines and the ability to cross-pollinate.

### 3. Serendipity-purposeful enquiry

Solving business problems requires purposeful, systematic, and focused work.

However, serendipity plays a big role in how insights and ideas appear. We ran a competition of machine learning algorithms for a client to understand which characteristics of a patient's lifestyle most impacted their experience of a particular medical condition. The idea came from an informal conversation with a client where we talked about machine learning. I sketched some shapes representing hypothetical relationships between two variables and mentioned how fascinated I was with the ability to model different non-linear patterns of data (e.g., circles or U-shaped curves instead of straight lines). That sparked my client's interest, and we collaborated on applying machine learning algorithms to the data from past quantitative surveys we had undertaken to understand drivers of patient experience. That led to a publication in a medical journal.

Informal, free-flowing conversation, the relaxed physical space, and downtime are factors which create the atmosphere for insights to appear. Psychologist Kevin Dunbar, in his research on scientific discovery, rigorously observed how scientists work in a lab and shed light on different aspects of scientific thinking and creativity.[41] He drew attention to the importance of the physical location and the role of informal discussions amongst scientists to generate and develop novel ideas.

Stephen Johnson, writing about the source of great ideas,[42] has dedicated a chapter to the role of serendipity in innovation, citing examples of Kekulé's discovery of the structure of benzene by seeing the image of Ouroboros, a serpent chasing its tail, in his dreams, or Henri Poincaré's discovery of Fuchsian functions. Stephen Johnson's writing urges us to take walks, read, and break walls between disciplines to invite serendipity. The novelist Murakami runs for 10 km every morning. This often unearths new ideas.

One of the perspectives that is particularly useful in this context is the prepared-mind approach, which is made up of four stages:

1. *mental preparation*, which comprises confronting the problem, dealing with its core components, followed by many attempts to solve it without success;

2. *incubation*, in which one takes a break and undertakes other activities;

3. *illumination*, when a flash of insight appears to solve the problem, and

4. *validation*, when one works out the details to implement the insight successfully. Originally conceived in *The Art of Thought*[43] by Graham Wallace in 1926, this approach has had its critics but has endured and been validated by many researchers.

My variation is to imagine that there are multiple cycles of the process with the stages juxtaposed, i.e., a non-linear and iterative version of this framework. An implication is that it is essential to punctuate a project with pockets of incubation – informal fun events, breaks from work, stimulating visits to museums or concerts, meditation breaks – all these activities help create space for insights to emerge.

## THE EMPOWERING DISRUPTER

When insights are truly breakthrough, they challenge the status quo and disrupt the normal way of working. To effect transformation, insights must reach, convince, and inspire people across functions and levels. This is not easy. There is a real tension. I have often seen harmonious and empowering insights leaders who can mobilize and inspire organizations but lack the ability to challenge the C-suite executives and convince them to change their minds. I have seen the opposite type, who function as brilliant visionaries but ruffle a lot of feathers and cause tension because of their disruptive style. It is rare to see both qualities present in one person. Striving to be both empowering and disruptive, when necessary, should be our aspiration.

## 1. Bird's eye – worm's eye

The metaphor of a bird's eye view represents having a global and holistic perspective, and that of a worm's eye view having a focused and detailed view. The bird's eye view allows us to have a strategic view, looking into the horizon, whilst the worm's eye makes us see the executional potential of actions in granular details. The bird's eye view allows us to communicate with CEOs and investors who are primarily interested in the big picture. The worm's eye makes us work with the frontline to ensure that the insights are implemented. Being able to move seamlessly between the two perspectives makes us more credible and effective. A good CEO, whilst focusing on the big picture, also understands the value of flawless execution. Such a CEO feels reassured by people who provide strategic insight while being cognizant of executional realities on the ground.

It also means you need strong and varied communication skills. For the C-suite, one needs to communicate well-synthesized executive summaries, for the marketing and advertising team an ability to bring insights to life to inspire creativity or explain analytical models to guide marketing spend or pricing, and for the front line, you must distil the insights into clear actions they can undertake.

## 2. Having skin in the game – Witnessing like an outsider

When you have skin in the game, typically the insights are sharper. You suffer if the insights are poor and benefit if the insights are breakthroughs. You identify with the goals of the company and passionately want to achieve them. You go the extra mile to overcome hurdles and find opportunities. To feel a compulsion to find a solution, you need to have stakes. Yet, feeling a strong sense of ownership can also blind one to what is happening. The role of an insights practitioner is also to provide an outside-in view. They need to understand the entire ecosystem, including customers, competitors, regulators, distributers, and influencers, and communicate that to the internal stakeholders. They need to examine a variety of trends and have a perspective on how the future is evolving. They need to challenge strategies and play the role of a sceptic. Having seen many insights leaders, the great ones feel fully committed and yet have the capacity to step back, see the big picture, and constructively challenge and improve a company's strategy. Strong CEOs value being constructively challenged.

## 3. Exclusivity-inclusiveness

For many functional groups, creating an exclusive team of skilled people is most effective. Creative and high-performance teams aim to build these centres of excellence based on high degrees of talent and capacities. In most fields where quality is important, elite and highly skilled groups are valued. There is a certain shared pride in being top class. Leaders of such groups tend to be perfectionists. There is a lot of merit in having such a world-class group. However, it is impossible to scale impact unless insights are disseminated to the entire organization. This requires collaboration across functions and geographies. The insights group must learn from other functions and geographies and be prepared to teach and bring insights to life. One must work with the relevant regions and functions – commercial, marketing, sales, engineering, design, and medical (if in pharma).

If one has the mandate of making a company customer-centric, exclusivity and inclusivity must go hand in hand. The regional point is particularly worth highlighting. Far too often, the 'headquarter mentality' creeps in when the insights leader at the head office views their role as serving only the leaders in their office and adopts a hierarchical view of how insights must be collected and applied. The business priorities of local offices are not taken into consideration. Even if the scope of the work is global, it is done in a manner using a standardized sterile format of collecting KPIs. The best leaders, rather than working in a top-down manner, agree on a common framework and tailor the work to local conditions. They empower internal stakeholders in the various markets, use knowledgeable experts on the local conditions, and conduct substantial qualitative work to test their assumptions before doing any quantitative work. They integrate the work from different countries by thoughtful problem solving rather than mechanically using the same method. They engage leaders from various markets whilst presenting the findings and cross-pollinating ideas from different markets. They act as facilitators of a collaborative process rather than hierarchical leaders.

The rest of this book describes how individuals and organizations can develop capabilities on these nine dimensions, though it is not organised linearly since many of these dimensions are related and can be developed simultaneously. At the end of the book, I have introduced the practice of pragmatic polymathy, which helps in acquiring these competencies in a natural manner.

# 3

# Are You Solving the Right Problem?

## THE FIVE TYPES OF UNKNOWNS

'It isn't that they can't see the solution. It is that they can't see the problem.'[1]

– G.K. Chesterton

MANY YEARS AGO, WHEN I INTERVIEWED WITH MCKINSEY & Company, John Forsyth, the Global Head of Customer Insights practice, gave me a case study to test my problem-solving and technical skills. He described a situation where a client from the auto industry was launching a new car and wanted to optimize the design. My task was to suggest a methodology to arrive at the optimal configuration based on what customers valued. John, adding to the complexity, emphasized that there were many features that had to be assessed, for instance, the power of the engine, fuel efficiency, the body type (sedan, coupé, etc.), and the exterior styling – as one can imagine, the list was very long!

I stepped back and asked a few questions about the context, including the client's market share in the industry, their current positioning, their goal of launching the new car, and the customer segment they wanted to pursue. After a brief discussion, I told John my conclusion was that the client was solving the wrong problem. That they needed to be clear on their strategy before diving into the nitty-gritties of product design. John asked, 'The client has asked you for a solution, and you will say that they are solving the wrong problem?' My nervousness faded away when I realized he was testing my resolve. He explained that most candidates plunged into the depths of creating a technical solution, e.g., designing a complicated conjoint-based approach, rather than stepping back and identifying the real question that needed answering.

While a case study in an interview is a miniaturised version of reality, the lesson imparted was a significant one. The lesson was one that I have discovered requires reaffirming. Over the years, whilst encountering many situations where I have had to tell a client to reassess the fundamental question to be addressed, my first interaction with John comes to mind.

A recent conversation with a commercial leader of a biotech company reinforced this lesson. This was a company that was headquartered in the US. They were developing a promising therapy for a rare neurodegenerative disease.

The drug was not going to be launched in Europe for another two years at least, as it had not been approved by the European Medical Agency (EMA).

The client's European organization was in the process of being set up, with several unknowns that could shape its future. They needed insights to address the uncertainties that the senior leaders were grappling with. For instance, the perception of the benefits and risks of the new drug by the physicians, the likely implications of different clinical trial outcomes, the likely patient groups for which the drug was particularly suitable, and the possibility of any new competitive drugs changing the paradigm of treatment. Yet, the bulk of the market research budget was allocated to a quantitative segmentation of physicians. Most of the study focused on the EU, where it was clear that the drug would not be launched for at least another two years.

A quantitative segmentation of physicians, which involves creating distinct groups of physicians based on common preferences, is useful for a drug that is *about to be launched*. It enables pharmaceutical companies to focus on priority segments, with tailored marketing. It is less useful for an early-stage drug in a market that is changing rapidly. Developing an expensive segmentation was not only misaligned with the business priorities, but it was also likely to be outdated by the time the drug was launched.

The EU commercial leader expressed their frustration to me as they had already expressed their reservations, yet believed it was not their battle to fight as the owner of the decision was the customer insights lead in the US.

Ultimately, the drug failed to meet its objectives in the trial and was not launched. The huge expenditure on market research was a waste.

This exemplifies a typical disconnect between the goals of the customer insights teams and business priorities. There are structural reasons underlying this common phenomenon. Historically, the market research function has evolved as a part of the marketing function and has served to improve decisions related to the Four Ps – product, placement, price, and promotion; this has created a certain distance from the C-suite, the top management.

According to a survey by McKinsey,[2] there is a significant misalignment even between the marketing function and the C-suite. More than 40 per cent of executive teams do not have a single growth- or customer-related role among their CEO's executive committee. On average, CEOs reported that marketing metrics relate to business impact less than 60 per cent of the time. In such circumstances, one can imagine that the classic customer insights department, which reports into the marketing function, is even more distant from the C-suite. They are not part of the C-suite conversations, and that limits their potential to understand and influence significant top management decisions.

In a recent conversation,[3] John Forsyth emphasized the importance and scarcity of 'translators', i.e., those who take research and convert it into actionable business recommendations. In that conversation, he also highlighted that while many new AI applications promise fast results, speed has never been the bottleneck for creating high-quality insights. He said, '*I don't think it's not having the time that stops people from creating insightful recommendations, it is not having the right skill set to help businesses*'.

> One of the fundamental purposes of developing insight ought to be to solve hard problems that leaders of an organization face and open the door to an advantage. The first step is identifying the right problem.

## THE BUSINESS QUESTION

Any insight project must be undertaken with a clear overarching business objective related to an outcome, such as market share, sales, profitability, customer satisfaction or any other goal that is being pursued. For instance, 'developing an actionable segmentation' must not be the objective. Segmentation is a means to achieving a business objective. Given below are three examples of business questions that guided projects that we undertook.

- How could the plateauing sales growth for a natural menopause product be reversed in Italy?

- How could our client launch three new, eco-friendly temperature control products for US households and grow this emerging category two to three times over?

- How could a genomics data services provider migrate customers from an on-premises platform to an AWS-based cloud service in a way that is profitable and keeps their customers happy?

Even without much context, it is easy to imagine that resolving these questions held substantial value for the entire organization.

Interestingly, customer segmentation was a crucial part of each project, but the way it was developed varied entirely based on the business goal. In the first case, we did not even consider doing segmentation when we began the project. We wanted to reverse the plateauing sales. During the research, as noted in Chapter 2, we discovered a segment that would potentially be receptive to our client's natural product. Targeting this segment unlocked the sales opportunity. The segmentation was the solution to the business problem. We had to simply classify the population into two categories: those who believed in natural products vs those who were sceptical.

In the second case, the product category of eco-friendly climate control devices was nascent. Only a third of the people in the US were aware of the category, and penetration was about 10 per cent of the total population.[4] To support the strong growth objectives of our clients, we had to find early adopter segments that had a significant unmet need for the new products, were willing to pay a premium, and had the potential to influence others.

We had to collect detailed information on their lifestyle, behaviour, and attitudes that could determine their needs – what were the weather conditions in their city? Did they live in an apartment in a city or a big house in the suburbs? Did they spend a lot of time outdoors, e.g., gardening or doing barbecues? Did they entertain people a lot? How important were style and design to them? Were there spaces and activities where they felt dissatisfied with the temperature control, i.e., it wasn't cool or warm enough? How much were they willing to pay?

There was a multiplicity of factors that determined the need for the products. In this case, we did a comprehensive segmentation based on many such variables and focused on identifying three early adopter segments that would be targeted for buying the innovative products.

In the third example, the primary issue was to understand what the users were trying to accomplish with the service and how satisfied they would be with the on-premises system vs the cloud. That led us to segment customers based on their level of fluency with respect to IT systems and bioinformatics. We could then prioritise the segments for cloud migration and recommend the features that the cloud-based service would need to make the customers happy.

In each case, the end goal determined the manner in which we segmented the customers. The importance of the business question is obvious in projects of a strategic nature. But, even for tactical work, e.g., developing an advertising campaign, framing the overarching business explicitly will change the nature of the work and increase the likelihood of success.

It's worth mentioning that the above discussion pertains to specific projects. Often, the question is more long term and implied. This is especially true if we have a clear purpose. For instance, for entrepreneurs or leaders of most organizations, subconsciously, there are always questions lurking in their minds on how to make their companies innovative or successful. Insights appear in response to such implicit questions.

## THE FIVE TYPES OF UNKNOWNS

My definition of insight, a 'transition from a state of not knowing to a state of knowing', underscores the significance of unravelling hidden truths. Problems that have a high degree of uncertainty with the greatest potential for business impact are the ones where insight is most powerful. Also, if you are a person who loves generating insights, nothing is more frustrating than hearing that what you've unearthed is obvious or that you've confirmed what the audience already knew. The findings might still be deemed to be accurate and useful but will not be considered insightful.

I have identified five recurrent uncertainty archetypes that can benefit from insight. Typically, a hard business problem has multiple types of unknowns present simultaneously, but for the purpose of clarity, it helps to think of these as distinct. Recognizing and appreciating these five archetypes can effectively shape our thinking and guide our approach for developing insights. This topic has been covered in greater detail in Chapter 6. I am providing a brief introduction here because it is an essential component of problem definition.

1. *Revealing what is hidden in a relevant context:* This is perhaps the type of unknown where insight has the potential to make a substantial positive difference to business outcomes on a regular basis.

The value of revealing what is hidden is obvious when the context is new and unfamiliar, what anthropologists call 'making the strange familiar'.

For instance, if an American company is launching a new consumer product in Japan, it would expect to learn many new and fascinating aspects about Japanese culture and consumer behaviour that can inform the product's launch strategy.

> It is the 'making the familiar strange' opportunity that is overlooked. Spotting something that is hidden in plain sight, in an environment that we believe we know well, can be a powerful source of differential advantage.

Such opportunities are missed because most of us use heuristics that make us systematically oblivious to what's going on around us. We carry many lazy assumptions and refuse to acknowledge that most real-world contexts are unique and can shape customer behaviour in a manner that may contradict many seemingly 'reasonable' assumptions. The case discussed in Chapter 2 about doctors liking natural treatments for menopause is an example of the significance of 'making the familiar strange' in improving business performance.

2. ***Making a creative idea relevant and practical:*** In business, innovations drive growth. A new product or service, a novel business model, or a creative marketing campaign can cause transformational

success. As insights practitioners, we are often tasked with assessing if a creative idea (product, service, campaign, etc.) will succeed in the market. By virtue of its novelty, the uncertainty related to the acceptance of such an idea is high. We never quite know how it will be received by people. Reducing this type of uncertainty with insight is applicable to a wide range of situations, other than new product or advertising launches, e.g., when an entrepreneur pitches to a venture capitalist for funding, or an author sends their book proposal to a publisher.

One might think that given the number of new products and advertising ideas that are tested, we would have mastered the approach to creative testing. Unfortunately, that is not the case. For instance, more than 90 per cent of new product launches fail.[5] Similarly, there are many examples of breakthrough innovations that were turned down initially – they didn't reach the product development stage. For instance, a team of engineers at Nokia had come up with the idea of a smartphone before the iPhone was launched;[6] it was rejected by the Nokia leadership team, paving the way for Apple to, yet again, create history. Such damning lack of foresight is not uncommon.

While breakthrough ideas are often particularly hard to assess because they challenge the limits of our imagination, even more mundane situations, such as testing a new variant of a product, a business model, a brand, or an advertisement, need to be done with care. Conventional thinking and methods that rely on asking customers about their future behaviour are often simplistic, potentially killing great ideas while letting mediocre ones go ahead. Most of the time, customers can't anticipate how they will actually behave with respect to an innovation.

3. ***Changing deeply entrenched attitudes and behaviours***: Certain problems are simply hard to solve because of deeply ingrained attitudes and behaviours. People have good hypotheses for the reasons for the problem, and yet they are unable to solve it. We were working at an academic private girls' school located in Surrey. Our task was to encourage more girls to take up physics as an A-level subject. In 2021, in England, only 23 per cent of the physics A-level entrants were girls, representing one of the widest gender gaps in STEM subjects, second only to computer science.[7] Alarmingly, this gender gap appears to persist over time, as demonstrated by a study conducted by the Institute of Physics (IOP).[8] Girls not taking up physics is an example of a deeply entrenched behavioural pattern. Whilst the school had a much higher uptake of physics than the national average, their aspiration was to be a leading school in science education, especially physics. Therefore, the primary objective of our work was to design a programme to increase the engagement with physics by gaining insights into the drivers and barriers that influence the selection of physics as an A-level at school. Our research confirmed that physics is considered one of the most difficult subjects. Maths

is perceived to be an easier subject that offers more career options in the future. For the girls, physics required high effort with limited opportunities, relative to maths.

> The role of insight is to find an opening that frees us from being stuck.

In this instance, one such insight was the disconnect between what the girls perceived about careers after completing a physics degree and the actual jobs that physics graduates took up. On average,[9] 90 per cent of the girls believed that people who pursued physics at university either ended up as academics or in careers that were deeply technical. Actual data shows a different picture: at least 40 per cent of physics graduates[10] do non-technical jobs. Making girls aware of this simple fact increased their level of interest.

Even if people are rationally convinced, the actual change in behaviour takes a long time. Conducting market research mechanistically throws up reasons that we already know. In such cases, the approach must be deeper, experimental, and informed by the behavioural sciences.

4. *Preparing for the future*: Recent world events have exposed our collective vulnerability due to a variety of disruptions, such as the 2008 financial crisis, the COVID-19 pandemic or, most recently, the emergence of generative AI. There is a greater

awareness of the distinction between risk, which is a form of uncertainty that can be statistically quantified with a known probability distribution, and radical uncertainty, which cannot be quantified. The original distinction was made by the economists Keynes and Knight, and more recently popularised by Mervyn King and John Kay in their book *Radical Uncertainty*.[11]

Similarly, we speak of black swan events,[12] an idea introduced by Nassim Nicholas Taleb, rare events with extreme impact that make sense to us only in hindsight. The recent discourse on black swan events and radical uncertainty have drawn special attention to our inability to see the future and to the limitations of quantitative models.

Yet, the record of misjudging future trends is both long and well established. In an article,[13] Paul J.H. Schoemaker lists some famous predictions that turned out to be false: 'Heavier-than-air flying machines are impossible' by Lord Kelvin, the British mathematician, or 'There is no reason for an individual to have a computer in their home' by Ken Olsen, the chairman of DEC. These were brilliant and capable people who could not see the future because it is inherently difficult to do so. Even with uncertainties related to the future looming large, leaders in business must make decisions. No one can predict situations that are extremely uncertain or are black swan events. In fact, the recommendation by leading thinkers in this field is to build greater resilience rather than attempt to predict accurate outcomes. Nevertheless, there is a wide range of events, from those that are easily predictable to those that are impossible to foresee, and this is where a good insights practitioner can contribute significantly.

History is replete with examples of both the success and failures of businesses based on an ability to see the future. The story of Blockbuster and Netflix is a classic example. Blockbuster, once a force to be reckoned with, failed to see the future and to adapt to changing market trends. Netflix, on the other hand, started as a DVD rental service and quickly pivoted to online streaming and succeeded. Blockbuster passed up the option of buying Netflix[14] and later filed for bankruptcy in 2010. John Antioco, CEO of Blockbuster, saw Netflix as a niche business and said,[15] 'The dot-com hysteria is completely overblown.'

Today Netflix has a market cap of around 400 billion dollars.

Moving to the political sphere, something as consequential as the outcome of the referendum for BREXIT for Britain, Europe, and the world, was not foreseen by Prime Minister David Cameron and his team. Since Cameron wanted Britain to remain in the European Union, it was in his best interest to have an accurate view of what was likely to happen. He was clear about the risks of Brexit. In a BBC interview a few weeks before the referendum, he said,[16] '...there are the experts: The Governor of the Bank of England, the IMF, the Institute of Fiscal Studies, all saying our economy would be smaller, and so therefore we'd have less money to spend on public services... there's a deep piece of common sense... In the single market we get free access to 500 million consumers. That's crucial for our economy.'

However, he miscalculated the extent of discontent with the EU[17] and concerns about immigration, which led people to vote to leave the EU. He placed more weight on rational factors, such as the impact of Brexit on the economy, rather than on emotional factors, such as the desire for sovereignty.

Like many other problems, seeing the future accurately is not just about using the right forecasting methodology. It is also about having the right mindset to make decisions. In behavioural economics, it has been well established that we often favour short-term benefits and discount future consequences in our decision-making. A common illustration is the tendency among smokers to downplay the risks of cancer associated with smoking.

Organizations suffer from this short-term bias too. There were many that questioned the wisdom of having a referendum on such a complex issue. Yet, David Cameron ignored these warnings – in part, to resolve an internal debate that was happening within the Tory Party with respect to EU membership. He took a decision to go ahead with the referendum despite being aware of the long-term risks of losing Europe as Britain's biggest trading partner. Not only was his method to assess the immediate future weak in not being able to forecast the referendum results, given that he believed that Brexit was a negative event for Britain, his decision-making appeared short-sighted. Unfortunately for Britain, it illustrates the negative consequences of lacking insight.

We respect companies that have a long-term view. But a good long-term view relies on an insightful understanding of how the future will evolve. We admire companies such as Apple, Nvidia, and Microsoft for having insight about the future and for their ability to adapt to it and shape it.

> According to the PWC 26th Annual Global Survey[18] on average, CEOs spent 47 per cent of their work time evolving their business and strategy to meet future demands and 53 per cent on driving current operating performance.

This is not surprising, given the world we live in. Leaders constantly need to assess the impact of macro trends, whether it is technology, the geopolitical situation, or the environment, and insight on these is invaluable.

More routine business problems are affected by uncertainty related to future events, as well. To forecast the sales of a new product, it is not enough to simply run predictive models or do concept tests without trying to understand how the environment might evolve. For instance, an innovation by a single competitor might completely alter the fate of a brand. P&G introduced Swiffer, which was a disposable cleaning system (mops and dusters) that was a game changer for its category in 1999. Its sales grew rapidly, achieving $100 million in the final four months of the year.[19] One can imagine how Swiffer's launch would have drastically altered the sales forecasts of its competitors.

5. *Simplifying complexity*: Samuel Arbesman,[20] a complexity scientist, defined complexity as not just having many parts in a system but the parts being connected and interacting in a manner that small changes in one part can cascade through the system. Such complexity surrounds us every day in life and in business. With the pace and the broader impact of scientific and technological progress accelerating, the environment we operate in is becoming increasingly more complex. Insight can help simplify complexity by finding patterns that underlie it. In fact, most theories and frameworks in different fields are illustrations of an insight of this nature.

Let us consider Clayton Christensen's theory of disruptive innovation.[21] He identified a pattern which found that incumbent companies that provide high profit margins in their quest to satisfy their existing customers are vulnerable to smaller players who target the 'low end' of the market, where customers are over-served by existing solutions, or those who create a 'new market' for people who previously lacked access to the product or service.

This insight helps many small companies disrupt traditional markets while helping established players guard against being disrupted. In fact, Netflix was a classic disrupter of the video rental market. Blockbuster, as an incumbent, dismissed the online business as small and unattractive. Christensen's insight simplifies complexities that businesses face and allows them to compete effectively.

Industries at the cutting-edge area of science are inherently complex because of the subject matter. In the project on genomics, referred to earlier, we interviewed top scientists with highly varied use cases; for instance, one identified mutational signatures for cancer, another ran Bayesian genetic association models for rare diseases, and another ran machine learning algorithms to identify patients at risk. Our task was to understand how these varied use cases translated to requirements for data, analytical tools, software, and other IT system-level features and then to communicate these to our clients. The challenge for us was to take in all the complexity of the field and simplify it without losing nuance when presenting our insights. This is representative of problems encountered by people who work in technical and scientific industries, where complexity is created by the interaction of subject matters from different disciplines. Complexity is not confined to these industries – technology's widespread influence brings it into non-technical fields as well. There are practitioners in the insights industry who ignore the complexity inherent in a specific industry. For instance, there is a widely prevalent belief that researchers can understand the user experience of customers without acquiring sufficient knowledge of the science and technology that sit under the products. This great asymmetry in the knowledge of customers who have deep expertise and these researchers who are novices often leads to superficial conversations. The researchers don't know how to ask nuanced questions or probe for details, and the customer oversimplifies their needs so that the researcher understands. This is a reductive approach that often blocks insight at the very outset. The complexity of business problems needs to be fully embraced first, before attempting to arrive at a simplification.

## CREATING A SUBSTANTIAL BUSINESS ADVANTAGE

While one might expect a business advantage to be the *raison d'être* for any effort to develop insights within an organization, as highlighted earlier in the chapter through the neurodegenerative rare disease case study, often that is not the case in practice. Having clarity about the potential positive impact on the performance of a business is essential. In certain instances, e.g., the reversal of plateauing sales, the business case is obvious and explicit in the question. The starting point for assessing the potential for impact is to assess the effect on business outcomes such as revenues, costs, or profitability.

Each of the three big business questions listed in the previous section had a clear statement of impact explicit in the question – reversal of plateauing sales, growing a category two to three times over, and migrating customers in a profitable manner.

However, beyond the likely impact on revenues and costs, it is helpful to look at three additional lenses:

## 1. What are the goals of the business, and what are the major obstacles?

At a recent meeting with a marketer of a pesticide-free food in India, we brainstormed about a variety of ideas, mostly about growth opportunities – new positionings, new markets, new segments, and new channels. The CEO then clarified that the priority was not really growth, but identifying a clear path to profitability, in the absence of which it was unlikely that the investors would sustain their current levels of funding and commitment. We discussed the hypotheses about what was preventing profitability. It became clear that given the power of retailers, both in the online and physical world, as a small player with an unclear positioning, the company would continue to bleed due to massive discounts and retailer margins. It was also evident that marketing and insight were just one part of the problem. The company had to take a hard look at the portfolio of its products in terms of financial performance and operational efficiency to identify opportunities for cost reduction.

The discussion shifted, and we had greater clarity about how to approach the question at hand. If we had not spent this upfront time on identifying the obstacles, we may have proceeded in a manner that was misaligned to the best interest of the business. Marketing and customer insights teams are often focused on top-line growth without thinking about profitability. This can lead to not only poor prioritisation but also a loss of credibility with the C-suite and investors.

## 2. What is the C-suite worried about?

Business leaders usually have an intuition about factors that are pivotal to the success or failure of a business. The intuition may arise from having privileged information about a specific technology or competitor, being aware of a conflict in opinion amongst the executive team, having doubts about the executional abilities of the team, a compulsion for a sudden shift in priorities, or experiencing pressure from the board. Identifying these thoughts and feelings enriches the understanding of the situation, and the potential for insight to have an impact increases.

We were serving a client that was developing a new therapy for two types of cancer. Our task was to provide insight to help design their clinical trials and to engage the community of oncologists. However, when we interviewed the Chief Medical Officer, they said that one of the big areas of conflict was whether the company should enter one of the cancer markets in the first place. The therapy was supposed to be given in conjunction with surgery. There were people in the company, led by a medical oncologist, who believed that the number of surgeries conducted for one of the cancer types was so low that the potential of the market was limited. Interestingly, as happens in many real-life situations, there are no clear sources of information that are easily available to resolve the issue. We decided to confront this question first. We estimated the size of the current and future market, which were substantially large to justify the client entering the market. This led to our client developing the product for this market with confidence, and it is currently executing clinical trials. This example is covered in greater detail in Chapter 6.

Often, to unearth more subtle issues, we conduct interviews amongst business leaders using projective techniques, such as role plays or creating collages. Whilst conducting a workshop to define the objectives for the launch of a product, we used Gary Klein's 'Pre-Mortem' technique, which involves imagining a future failure scenario and discussing what might have contributed to it. This is a technique to counter hindsight bias and develop intuition about the future. The head of strategy revealed that the salespeople would not feel confident about selling the product to retailers at the planned price. It was clear that before testing the concept externally, we had to work on establishing the value, and the basis, of the price premium internally within the organization. In general, there are certain topics, all listed below, that need consideration whilst interviewing business leaders. It is worth noting that some of these issues pertain to embedding insights, which is a topic discussed in the next section.

- **Background of the individual**: It can help you tailor the questions and test specific hypotheses.

- **Their view of the problem and hypothesis about the solution**: Most senior executives have hypotheses about how the problem can be solved or the opportunity can be realized.

- **Needs and concerns about the project**: Bringing out their aspirations and concerns at an individual, organizational, and team level can cast light on subtle nuances in the problem definition.

- **Preferred engagement mode:** Knowing how frequently and in what way the leaders would like to be involved is useful.

- **Internal political issues:** Understanding territorial issues, sensitivities, and other political issues is valuable, especially when working in large organizations.

## 3. Whose behaviour needs to change, and how?

Business success always involves change in behaviours, such as getting existing customers to pay a premium, customers of competitive brands to switch, retailers agreeing to stock the product without discounting, influencers willing to recommend, and regulators creating an environment conducive to the usage of the product and so on. There is an entire ecosystem that needs to be activated for the desired outcomes to transpire. Establishing the players, explaining their roles, and fleshing out the desired changes in behaviour makes the problem definition concrete.

This also allows us to design a project more expansively and speak to a wide variety of stakeholders and not just the customer. For instance, for the pestiscide-free company, it is essential to gain insight about not just the consumers but also about the different types of retailers and regulators. Only then can we attempt to effect the necessary changes in behaviour that are necessary to achieve the business goals.

## EMPOWERING THE ORGANIZATION TO IMPLEMENT

Insights must empower the organization to undertake actions that are easily implemented.

> Insights often fail because insufficient attention is paid to how the insight will translate into actions that the organization can implement.

Conversely, visualizing how recommendations can be implemented at the outset dramatically increases the usefulness of insights. Three simple questions can help make insights implementable.

### 1. Who are the main players, and what are their roles?

Understanding the contribution of people across functions, and engaging them, increases the chances of creating recommendations that can be executed easily. In our study to guide the strategy of the climate control devices, the commercial and strategy teams were based in one Asian country, the designers and engineers in another, and the sales team in the US. While the launch market was in the US, early engagement with the cross-functional teams in all locations ensured that we could create and test product prototypes rapidly with consumers. Ensuring cross-functional involvement early improves the quality of the problem-solving, the speed of execution, and the eventual 'buy-in' of recommendations. We get a clear sense of how the different parts of the organization are connected.

## 2. What kind of resources are available?

The scope of solutions is often determined based on available resources. For instance, if a company does not have a large salesforce or a big marketing budget, insights people need to be aware of that upfront. It is imperative to develop insights and solutions that help the company succeed within these constraints – be it a sharp focus on a specific segment, product innovation, brand differentiation, clever use of digital channels, or forming partnerships to grow faster.

## 3. What are the strengths and weaknesses of the organization?

Understanding the strengths and weaknesses of an organization in terms of their capacities can make the insights more relevant. For instance, for the manufacturer of the climate control devices, it became apparent that in the medium term the company needed to invest in building their design capabilities to compete with players such as Dyson.

## DISAGGREGATING PROBLEMS INTO COMPONENTS

Having framed the business question, one must disaggregate these into discrete, mutually exclusive sub-questions. The goal is to identify an efficient and effective structure that solves the problem in a minimal number of steps. A good way is to use logic trees to break down the original question into sub-components and then to prioritise those for further investigation. As an illustration, the figure below demonstrates how we broke the question about reversing the plateauing sales of the natural alternative to hormones.

The first subdivision in the tree represents a choice between focusing the effort on patients or on physicians. Subsequent subdivisions led to a list of branches that covered a complete list of possible actions for driving sales growth. We used existing information and conducted a workshop to understand which of the branches to tackle. The tree also helped us align the various stakeholders on what the most likely lever would be to turn sales around. A few points to note about creating logic trees:

- There are multiple ways to break a question, and the context will determine the best way to create the tree. For instance, in the example mentioned above, we

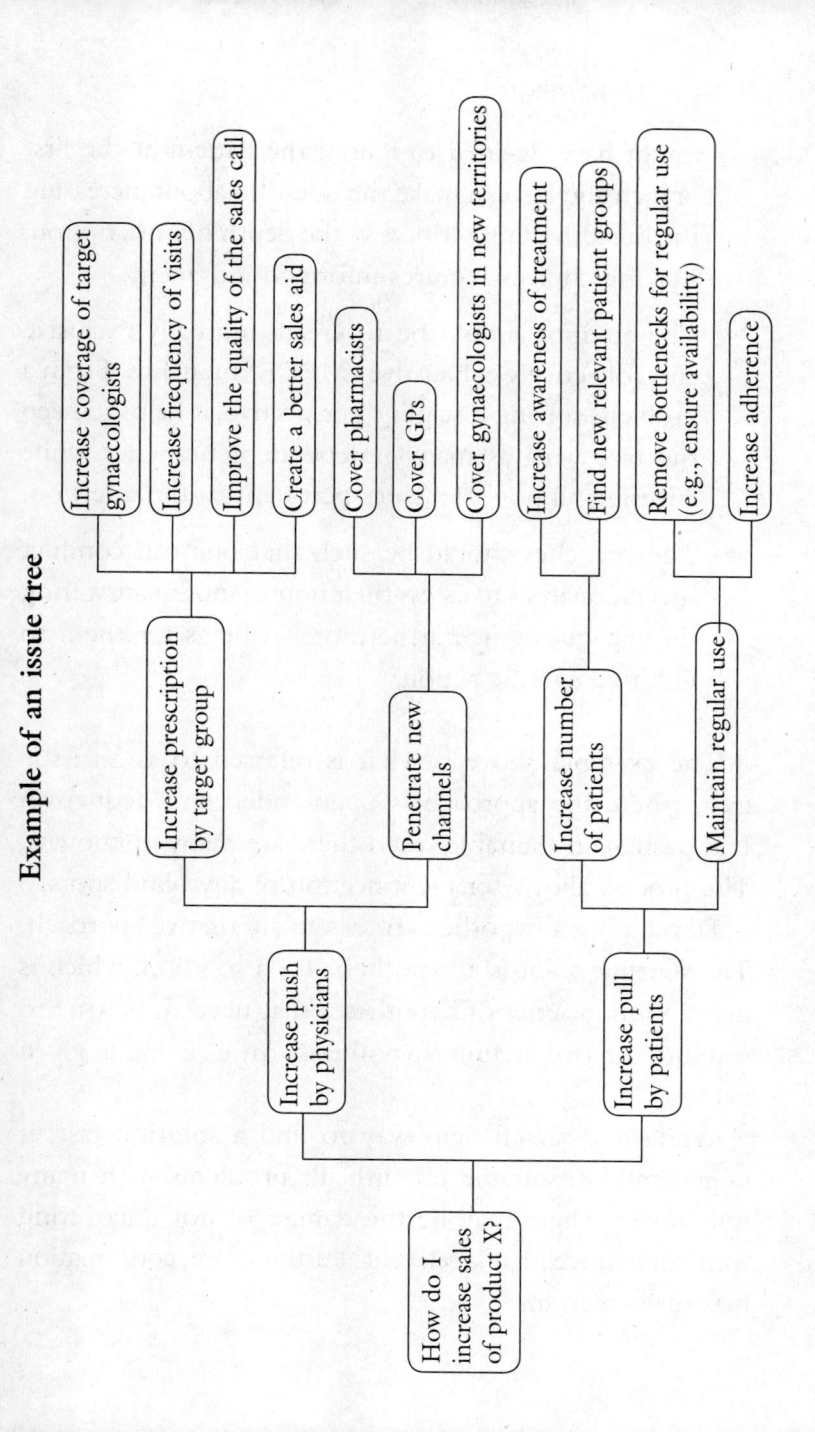

# Example of an issue tree

- **How do I increase sales of product X?**
  - **Increase push by physicians**
    - Increase prescription by target group
      - Increase coverage of target gynaecologists
      - Increase frequency of visits
      - Improve the quality of the sales call
      - Create a better sales aid
    - Penetrate new channels
      - Cover pharmacists
      - Cover GPs
      - Cover gynaecologists in new territories
  - **Increase pull by patients**
    - Increase number of patients
      - Increase awareness of treatment
      - Find new relevant patient groups
    - Maintain regular use
      - Remove bottlenecks for regular use (e.g., ensure availability)
      - Increase adherence

might have decided to ignore the patient at the first branch and instead make the question about increasing the breadth of prescribers vs the depth of prescription. Making choices requires informed judgment.

- The attempt should be to create mutually exclusive and collectively exhaustive (MECE) branches. From a problem-solving discipline perspective, it helps to keep the tree with as many independent branches while covering all possible issues pertinent to the question.
- The branches should be such that one can conduct specific analysis to assess their importance in answering the big question. Furthermore, it helps for them to link to a specific action.

The example above is what is referred to as an issue tree, where the approach is open-ended and deductive. It is particularly suitable when there are many unknowns. The process allows for identification of any blind spots.

Developing a hypothesis tree is an alternative approach. The starting point is a hypothesis for a solution, which is broken into a series of hypotheses that need to be true to support the overarching hypothesis. An example is given below.

While it is an efficient way to find a solution fast, it is generally unsuitable for difficult problems with many unknowns. There may be the danger of not uncovering something novel that is relevant. Furthermore, confirmation bias may creep in.

# Example of a hypothesis tree

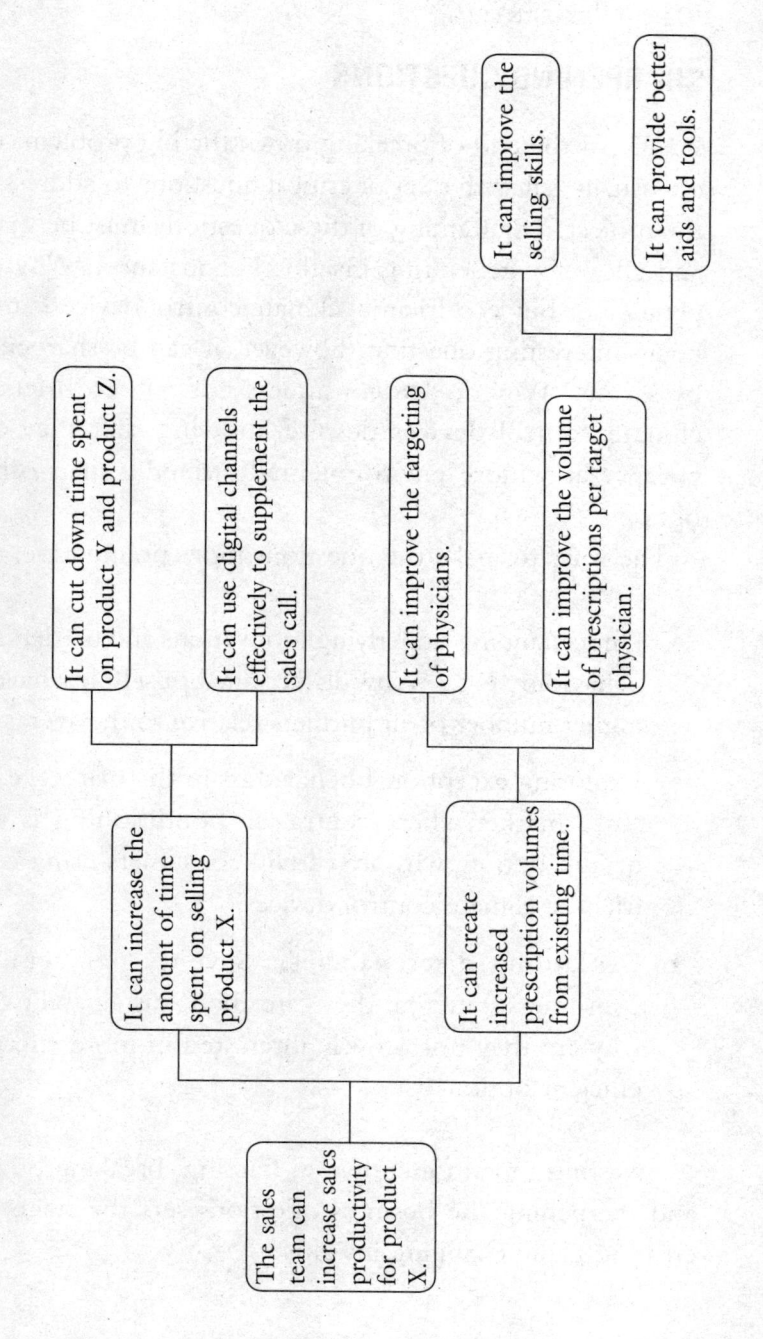

- The sales team can increase sales productivity for product X.
  - It can increase the amount of time spent on selling product X.
    - It can cut down time spent on product Y and product Z.
    - It can use digital channels effectively to supplement the sales call.
  - It can create increased prescription volumes from existing time.
    - It can improve the targeting of physicians.
    - It can improve the volume of prescriptions per target physician.
      - It can improve the selling skills.
      - It can provide better aids and tools.

## SHARPENING QUESTIONS

Finally, at the end of breaking down the big problem, we are usually left with a set of critical questions to address in the project. The framing of these questions must be sharp and allow for generating insight. For instance, 'Why do people not buy eco-friendly climate control devices?' may be an interesting question; however, it can be sharpened by asking, 'Why do US consumers not buy eco-friendly climate control devices despite knowing that they are cheaper and more environmentally friendly than other options?'

The ways to make the questions more pointed are:

- Understanding underlying motivations and barriers for behaviour, e.g., 'Why do certain households have a higher number of air purifiers relative to the average?'

- Exploring exceptional behaviours in the market, e.g., 'In a market where central air conditioning is the default option, why are certain consumers using eco-friendly climate control devices?'

- Explaining discrepancies, 'Seventy per cent of consumers state that they care about sustainability, so why are they not actively interested in more energy-efficient options?'

Investing time in identifying, framing, breaking down, and sharpening the business questions sets the stage for creating game-changing insights.

# TIPS TO IMPROVE THE PROBLEM DEFINITION AND STRUCTURING PROCESS

> It is essential to get the process of problem definition and structuring right. An easy way to lose credibility with the C-suite is by focusing on the wrong problem.

There are certain important issues worth highlighting about the process:

First, we must allocate a lot of time to defining and structuring the problem. It requires a few team meetings and many individual interactions.

Second, listening closely to the intuition of different stakeholders across functions is beneficial. People who have been running the business develop a lot of insight through real-world experience. For instance, salespeople being customer-facing can provide rich hypotheses about customer segments and sales messages that work. Of course, one must not take these at face value. We must continue to try to gather evidence. Ignoring the intuition and insights of experienced people in an organization is an unnecessary loss of learning. It is important to emphasize that gathering insight from stakeholders is not about just getting them to regurgitate their beliefs in response to questions. The interviewing must be done in a manner that makes them relive experiences so that they themselves are experiencing an insight.

Third, immersing ourselves in any technical areas that are relevant – industry details, technologies, scientific areas –

can have a bearing on the problem definition, issues, and hypotheses. Talk to experts, read articles, and familiarise yourself with all the research.

Fourth, it is a good practice to document all the existing knowledge and hypotheses and share it with the stakeholders. This helps focus the effort on real unknowns, prevents reinventing the wheel, and ultimately helps establish that the insights were genuinely new.

> Fifth, we must allow for the problem statement to change as the project progresses. This may be due to new learnings that are emerging in the project that require an adaptation in the definition of the problem, or it may be because the context of the business has changed.

For instance, if we are working on the brand architecture in a category, and the organization decides to acquire a new brand, this changed reality must be accommodated in the problem statement.

Defining the problem is the starting point. In the next chapter, we will explore how the problem influences the design of methodologies for insight.

# 4

# Crafting Methods to Reveal Truth

'Every good craftsman conducts a dialogue between concrete practices and thinking; this dialogue evolves into sustaining habits, and these habits establish a rhythm between problem solving and problem finding.'[1]
– **Richard Sennett**

IN 2024, A RECORD 642 MILLION PEOPLE VOTED IN THE INDIAN election; the scale of the event is unmatched anywhere in the world. Incumbent Prime Minister Narendra Modi achieved the remarkable feat of leading the country for the third consecutive term. Exit polls[2] had projected that his BJP-led National Democratic Alliance would win between 350 and 380 out of 543 seats, a bullish prediction which caused the Indian stock market indices, the Sensex and Nifty 50, to jump almost 4 per cent each to fresh record highs. The reality was different. NDA won 290 seats, and as a result, the indices dropped by almost 6 per cent, resulting in an immediate loss of over $3 trillion.[3]

Organizations that conduct exit polls must be commended for sticking their necks out and risking being wrong in public. Achieving accuracy is difficult in India because it is complex both in terms of its size and the sheer heterogeneity of any dimension that could influence voting patterns.

Interestingly, Yogendra Yadav, an activist, psephologist, political leader, and author, made accurate predictions[4] for each major party involved. He predicted that NDA would win 275 to 305 seats. While Yogendra Yadav is not infallible, the case illustrates certain important aspects regarding how we ought to think about insight, truth, and methods.

First, human judgment, with the help of data, outperformed the mechanistic application of a single method. In the future, one can imagine that with the broader diffusion of machine learning techniques, greater digitisation, and improvements in capturing election-related data, sophisticated predictive algorithms will play a greater role. Even then, humans would need to guide both the thoughtful integration of vast amounts of disparate data and the process of drawing insight.

Second, Yogendra Yadav, a Senior Fellow at the Centre for the Study of Developing Societies (CSDS), has worn different hats related to electoral politics. This enabled him to achieve a more nuanced interpretation of information, paving the way for better insight. He's been an academic researcher, fielded surveys on the Indian electorate, published papers, authored books, provided political commentary on television networks, and served as a founder and member of political parties.

Third, one of the main points of disconnects between Yogendra Yadav's forecast and those of others was that he could sense the dissatisfaction[5] amongst certain sections of the population. He was able to uncover this truth by travelling extensively and speaking to people.[6]

What is interesting is that Yogendra Yadav, being a psephologist, has expertise in quantitative survey methods. He knew he could not rely only on surveys and that having conversations would reveal what people were *really feeling*. This is typical. People who are experts in a method know its limitations and appreciate the role of other complementary approaches for pursuing truth. Yogendra Yadav, even while using qualitative information, is likely to have used his analysis and intuition to arrive at his precise predictions. Furthermore, he did not speak with just a few people but to many people across the terrains where his team travelled. While his approach was qualitative, he used the principles of sampling by ensuring sufficient spread and depth of information. It was a thoughtful and pragmatic approach.

Fourth, human values are critical for arriving at the truth. We must be curious about what's going on. That creates a humble mentality.

> When we are interested in the truth, we are likely to go deep, not be constrained by a single method, and cultivate a certain scepticism even about our own predictions.

This was evident in an interview[7] where Yogendra Yadav, in a self-deprecating tone, suggested that his precise prediction might just have been a stroke of luck, even as he was being praised.

This example highlights certain themes that need to be developed. I will discuss a way of approaching methodology more artfully to get us to the truth, which is ultimately necessary for insight.

## THE RELATIONSHIP BETWEEN TRUTH AND INSIGHT

Insight and truth are inextricably connected. Often, discovering the truth is the insight. Scientists routinely uncover a truth that is new to the world. For instance, Kekulé discovering the structure of benzene as a hexagonal ring by seeing a serpent chase its tail in a dream,[8] is an example of a truth that is also a breakthrough insight.

At other times, the insight comes in the form of seeing an implication of the truth. In the Mastercard example discussed earlier, that Mastercard competed with other credit cards and that commerce was conducted largely in cash were both true. However, Banga's grasping the significance and seeing the opportunity to compete with cash was the insight. In either case, insight and truth are deeply connected. The single biggest consideration for selecting or creating methodologies must be facilitating truth. A few caveats are worth mentioning. A truth can be bigger than a fact. It is a more holistic understanding of reality and may be subjective, as we discussed in Chapter 2.

Further, the output from any method, such as results of an exit poll, are estimates of facts. While facts are verified pieces of information, supported by evidence, estimates are approximations based on available assumptions, information, and models. This distinction between facts and estimates is important because without this realization, we conflate measurements with facts and are satisfied with whatever we can measure. We do not question the methods and assumptions underlying the creation of the information. We become less curious about what's going on. Later in this chapter, we will cover this topic in greater depth.

## THE ELUSIVE NATURE OF TRUTH

By now, we have referred to the failure of election forecasts in different contexts: Donald Trump's victory in 2024 and 2016, the Brexit referendum, the margin for the NDA in India's 2024 elections – the list is long. This is not to blame the forecasters but to highlight that even a seemingly simple task, such as the prediction of election results or a referendum, is difficult and prone to error. Therefore, it is not a surprise that we are not able to predict more complex events, what Nassim Nicholas Taleb calls Black Swan events[9], such as the occurrence of the COVID-19 epidemic, the duration of the Russia-Ukraine war or a financial crash. The difficulty in seeing the truth is not limited to the domain of election predictions.

Brian M. Hughes,[10] in his book *Psychology in Crisis*, talks about the problem of non-replicability of research findings in psychology. The Open Science Collaboration, with over 200 researchers, examined 100 experiments in psychology and attempted to re-conduct them. Over 60 per cent of the attempted replications failed. John Ioannidis,[11] an epidemiologist at Stanford University, tested 34 claims proven by randomised control trials, the gold standard of clinical trials, and yet 40 per cent of these could not be replicated.

Technology is not a solution either. Gerd Gigerenzer[12] points out how algorithms leveraging big data work in stable situations. He describes how initially Google Flu Trends developed based on the analysis of fifty million search terms and after trying 450 million models developed a predictive model with 45 search terms. After its initial success, there was an outbreak of swine flu that it completely missed.

## BARRIERS TO TRUTH

Trying to figure out what's going on is difficult for many reasons.

**The first barrier is that the world is genuinely getting more complex. As we observed in the first chapter,** there is too much going on that is changing too fast. By the time we have systematically studied the situation, reality has moved on.

**Second, whilst our minds are wonderfully brilliant at making sense of incomplete and ambiguous information, we are inherently susceptible to cognitive biases that get in the way of perceiving truth.** A variety of heuristics and biases identified in behavioural economics, which we referred to in Chapter 2, distort our vision of reality.

Steven Sloman and Phillip Fernbach have suggested[13] that our brains are not wired to be repositories of information. We have social brains, which require us to work with others, share our intentions, and divide cognitive labour. Yet, we imagine that we know a lot individually. We harbour an *illusion of explanatory depth* and overestimate our knowledge and ability to deal with complexity, even though we do not understand the mechanisms of simple everyday things we use, such as bicycles. This ignorance of our limitation causes us to seek less information, and yet, it does not prevent us from having an opinion on complex world issues.

While Judea Pearl and Dana Mackenzie[14] observe that the human brain is the most advanced technology to draw causal inferences, he states that we find it difficult to accept causeless correlation. We suffer from a bias called narrative fallacy,[15] which makes us create stories that connect disconnected events, making it hard for us to accept randomness or our inability to explain things. We are uncomfortable with data but can buy into a plausible story easily. We often have incentives to make our stories provocative at the expense of truth. In a competitive and polarised world, we find pushing our own agenda and demeaning our adversaries is at the heart of many campaigns of misinformation. We see that play out in a variety of arenas: politics, climate change, culture wars, etc. Insights professionals need to be particularly cognisant of this tendency. Often to sound interesting, one may say something which is simply wrong because it sounds counter intuitive! At other times, to please one's bosses, one may go along with their preferred hypothesis, despite having evidence that contradicts it. It takes phenomenal self-awareness and practice to loosen the grip of these flaws.

**The third difficulty in arriving at truth is that all methodologies have limitations that are often not taken into consideration.** No method is perfect. Qualitative approaches are powerful in uncovering motivations underlying people's behaviour or the latent needs that people might have related to a product category that they can't articulate or emotions they feel about a brand. But they do not provide quantitative estimates. Quantitative approaches, including machine learning, help us size opportunities, statistically identify patterns and study differences, and create robust predictive models; yet one must know what to measure, and that must be amenable to numerical analysis. So, without upfront qualitative work, especially in an unknown situation, one might end up measuring the wrong thing. But there are deeper challenges in the application of methods. A few of the common and recurring problems are described below:

- *Believing that measurements are facts*
  Most methods make assumptions about variables accurately reflecting what they intend to capture. Sometimes the underlying truth is an objective fact that can be easily estimated, e.g., awareness of a brand, captured in a survey; at other times, we are measuring

something more abstract, such as attitudes on a scale. In such cases, it is good to recognize that these measurements are approximations. Similarly, when we scan someone's brain through an fMRI test to measure their emotional responses to an advertisement, we are assessing the flow of blood across different parts of the brain, the roles of which are yet to be fully understood, and any inference about the truth is tentative and needs further validation. One can still make inferences, but that requires deep expertise in cognitive neuroscience.

- *The lost art of sampling and large volumes of unrepresentative data*
  Robust sampling, a basic requirement of obtaining high-quality information, is often ignored, especially with the abundance and the varied nature of the information available. Whilst the Internet has flooded us with data, we have lost the art of sampling. For instance, there are a variety of scraping tools on the internet that extract people's opinions from a myriad of sites but give no information about the population from which the data has been drawn; the challenge is that whilst it could be millions of users, it might represent the wrong audience. This is one of the reasons why it is so difficult to arrive at truth by looking at social media posts. Prior to the internet, when we conducted surveys, we drew starting addresses from electoral rolls in as random a manner as possible. Around each starting address, we would select a small number of households based on a specific rule

(e.g., the right-hand rule, which dictated that from the starting address, the interviewer would move right to cover other houses). To minimise bias, we would have strict protocols about the day of the week, time, and substitution of those absent. There would be a fieldwork supervisor making calls to ensure that data collection adhered to the high-quality standards. This approach to sampling has been replaced by large panels of people who have been amassed over the internet, who do surveys repeatedly. While we have realized time and cost efficiencies, we can never be quite sure of the quality of data. Fortunately, this is an issue that Market Research industry associations are attempting to address.

- **Unquestioning belief in quantitative information, and ignorance of risk and uncertainty**
  What we measure with our quantitative methods has a lot of uncertainty attached. Most people who have studied STEM subjects at an advanced level know this. The information is probabilistic and uncertain. Yet, in practice, quantitative analysts frequently ignore these aspects and present quantitative results with a high degree of certitude. Whilst Nassim Nicholas Taleb points to how black swan events[16] are so often missed because people routinely follow the normal distribution of probabilities in situations and perceive outliers as completely improbable, and therefore worth being disregarded. Being a critic of

the normal distribution, he suggests the existence of the Mandelbrot distribution, with a fat tail, which implies that extreme events are not as improbable as is suggested by the normal distribution. This is a criticism that is too advanced for many users of quantitative research who cannot engage in such a discussion because of their unfamiliarity with concepts such as probability distributions, risk, and uncertainty.

Quantitative metrics are also often lagging indicators and not sensitive enough to capture fast-changing reality. A client in a consumer electronics category had a low market share in the US. The market leader was a Japanese brand. We reviewed a consumer survey that showed our client lagging behind the leader on all metrics related to brand image. That would have led us to focus on a whole slew of activities related to branding and advertising. But we decided to observe what the consumers were doing in stores. This, being a more sensitive technique, revealed a different reality. Consumers were more open to being convinced at the store, disregarding their brand loyalty. A fundamental shift was taking place because of the increased pace of innovation, availability of information online, and the growing power of retailers. Our client shifted the battle to the retail front, enticing consumers with their displays and attractive offers, displacing the market leader in a few years. Had they focused only on the survey, they would not have sensed the change or realized the opportunity.

- **Weak pattern recognition by under-fitting or over-fitting**

  In quantitative modelling, it is important to find the right fit between a variable that is being predicted (say, sales of a product) and explanatory variables (distribution, price, marketing, etc.) from a dataset. There are two types of problems that we encounter – under-fitting and over-fitting. Under-fitting is when a model is simple (e.g., using a straight line for data that follows a curve) but does not fit the data properly, yet it can be generalized because it can accommodate many other datasets. On the other hand, an over-fitted model will perfectly describe a specific dataset, matching all the twists and turns. The challenge is that its highly tailored nature makes it not generalizable to other situations. While this situation is consciously addressed in quantitative work, the concepts of under-fitting and over-fitting affects most methods, even in qualitative research.

  Consider someone who is trying to understand how consumers use a specific technology at home. One might do qualitative research with a small sample by 'living with consumers' for a period. One might get deep insight about this sample, cover every nuance of their lives, and provide a 'thick description', yet generalizing the insights to the broader population becomes impossible. In contrast, the findings from a series of open-ended questions fielded online to a large number of consumers may help identify more generalizable findings, but the medium and format are likely to provide superficial answers. People are attempting to solve the problem with generative AI, but it still has a long way to go.

- **Many problems related to correlational data**
  That correlation is not causation is widely known. Causality explains why things happen; for example, pressing a light switch (the cause) makes a light turn on (the effect).

> Establishing causality with real-world data is difficult, and many leading statisticians and philosophers believe that true causality can never be established. In practice, though, having a strong hypothesis about the 'why' of an event of interest, e.g., what would increase the sales of my product, is immensely valuable in guiding us to make the right decisions.

For instance, if we know that an increase in television advertising will lead to a significant increase in sales and profit, then the decision to invest in TV advertising becomes easy. Conversely, making the wrong assumptions about causality can misdirect our efforts. Therefore, even if making causal inferences is difficult, one must take steps to improve our judgments on causality.

Conducting experiments where we set up test and control groups to understand the effect of an intervention, e.g., a sales promotion on and the outcome, e.g., sales of a product is an appropriate approach to arrive at causal inferences. That is the reason why randomized control trials revolutionised how various medicines are tested. However, implementing experiments is often difficult and expensive. We are largely reliant on observational studies such as surveys. We see variables that are associated, e.g., the daily temperature and the sales of soft drinks, and make common sensical inferences such as 'hot weather motivates us to consume soft drinks'. Specifically, snapshot surveys, which comprise a large part of quantitative market research, squarely fall in this category where you can only see associations, not causal relationships. Later in the chapter, we will discuss certain steps that we can take to improve our inferences.

This problem is particularly evident in large surveys that companies conduct amongst organizations on some aspect of business, e.g., what makes certain companies more innovative than others. The overarching question, one can imagine, is of high interest to CEOs. The idea is to compare the more innovative companies to the less innovative ones and draw conclusions based on the observed differences in what drives innovation. However, when the study is based on observational studies such as surveys without adequate controls and quality checks, one might arrive at misleading inferences, e.g., 'Large expenditure on consumer research drives innovation.' The observation is based on the survey results, which show that the more innovative companies tend to spend more on market research. The causality might work the other way. Innovative companies might generate greater profits and therefore have more money to spend on market research.

Another common pitfall in marketing is relying too heavily on correlations from past success – it tends to favour what has already worked, not what could work next. Take the example of launching a new smartphone. You might find that 'cutting-edge camera technology' is highly correlated with market success. That's likely because a dominant player like Apple or Samsung already excels in that area. While it's true that consumers value camera quality, trying to compete head-on in that space could backfire – especially if you're at a clear disadvantage on that front. A smarter approach would be to identify where the market leader is vulnerable and differentiate yourself there. But if you base your strategy solely on correlation with past winners, you're likely to land on a me-too approach that's neither distinctive nor competitive.

These problems are not trivial. Many market research companies, branding boutiques, and management consultants use correlations of brand attributes with loyalty as a measure of what's important. Even the language is misleading. Whilst running correlations of different attributes with a metric measuring loyalty, one often hears the term 'driver analysis', suggesting a causal relationship between loyalty and the high correlation attributes.

**Fourth, with the proliferation of methods for collecting data, there are many silos with hyper-specialized people who do not interact with other groups.** The disciplines, methods, and data insights that people use have exploded recently. Traditionally, the main disciplines for data collection were a combination of statistics and social sciences. Recently, a whole range of new disciplines have emerged and made powerful contributions to the industry. The most powerful and discontinuous disruption in the industry has been the digitisation of society and the consequent emergence of big data, which has propelled AI to becoming central to the operation of business.

AI has unleashed powerful innovations – machine learning models that work with large data sets and are vastly superior in pattern recognition to earlier statistical models, large language models that enable us to work with qualitative and quantitative data at scale, digital twins that help us create virtual representations of consumers, and many other such innovations.

In a world that already had many specialisms – commercial ethnography, design research, and conjoint specialists – AI has ushered in a new level of hyper-specialisms. For instance, in the past, the classic quantitative analyst had a background in social sciences or statistics, and the source of their knowledge was mainly statistics. The field of machine learning, however, draws knowledge from physics, maths, computer science, information theory, and statistics. There are other fundamental differences in the way statistical and machine learning models are applied. For instance, relative to statistical models, machine learning algorithms are far more concerned with accuracy of prediction rather than with being able to explain what's happening. Leo Breiman's classic paper[17] 'Statistical Modeling: Two Cultures' highlights the chasm between not just the methods but also between cultures and communities. Previously, quantitative researchers would typically work with software packages for statistical analysis such as SPSS, SAAS, or MATLAB, which had many 'ready-to-use' routines. The new generation of analysts are not only fluent in the knowledge about mathematics and statistics. They are also comfortable with programming languages such as Python and their vast libraries, big data technologies such as HADOOP, and visualization software. They know about version control systems like GIT, containerisation tools like Docker, Integrated Development Environments, and working with the cloud.

Consequently, there are many different groups of method-based hyper-specialized people. Such specialisation is essential to push the boundaries of a field. However, there are several challenges.

- People who are only focused on one class of methodologies may not appreciate the value of others and therefore get poorer insights. For instance, many big data analysts like to create behavioural segmentations without understanding the 'whys' underlying the behaviour, which makes it difficult to develop tailored and effective messages that would change behaviour. One of our clients used the time spent by their customers on programming as an indication of their technological sophistication. They had assumed that less sophisticated customers would use point-and-click menus and savvy users would prefer creating custom programmes. This data was available in their customer database, so such a categorisation by observing this variable was simple. But it was wrong. When we interviewed these 'sophisticated' users, we found it comprised a large group of researchers who didn't enjoy programming. They found it difficult, needed help, and spent a lot of time on it because they were new to it. They told us that they would have preferred ready-made programmes and point-and-click services that were tailored to the type of analysis they wanted to do. The right approach is to let the business problem lead the way, combine different lenses, and arrive at the right answer. Those who are narrowly focused on one set of methodologies often change the problem definition to suit the method.

- Second, methodology-based silos begin to form. In many organizations, there are separate departments for market research, data analytics, and design. This is despite the fact that there is a high degree of overlap in their skill sets and there are benefits to be gained from the complementarities of the disciplines. These groups do not talk to each other, and the integration happens at a high managerial level by someone who might not deeply understand specific methods. There is also an 'us vs them' mentality that is created. In conferences on qualitative research, practitioners are often overly critical of big data analysis, whilst big data analysts imagine they can substitute all the human skills that a qualitative practitioner deploys through an analysis of text. This divisive mentality exists even within close fields like design-based approaches and classic qualitative research, where each group thinks what they are doing is fundamentally different and superior, even though there is a high degree of overlap in techniques.

The factors mentioned above are barriers to the truth and are largely prevalent in actual business practice. My contention is that if we understand the strengths and limitations of different methods and interpret the emerging findings thoughtfully and with a certain level of pragmatism, we are more likely to facilitate the arrival of truth and development of insight.

## CRAFTSMANSHIP IN DESIGNING METHODS

The word craftsman typically conjures up images of artisans who are skilled people who work with their hands and apply techniques that have been refined through time to produce beautiful objects. Richard Sennett writes[18] about craftsmanship as 'an enduring, basic human impulse, the desire to do a job well for its own sake,' and that it serves varied human activities – computer programming, nursing, and even parenting – not just those that involve skilled manual labour. Just like craftsmen of physical products, techniques must be seen as an extension of our thinking. For instance, while constructing a conjoint analysis-based research methodology, we work through the concrete details of the design (e.g., attributes and levels, the number of tasks a respondent will be exposed to, the sample size), simultaneously imagine the output of the analysis and check if it is likely to answer the business question. Then, if necessary, we refine the method. Like craftsmen, we feel deeply engaged with the process of designing the research. Like craftsmen who understand that all materials have their unique qualities and purpose, we know that conjoint analysis can address only certain questions and will need to be supplemented by other methods. Like craftsmen, we appreciate that the quality of the research design matters and that elegant designs will produce creative and inspiring insights. Like craftsmen, we realize mastery in technique comes from mindful practice and experimentation.

So how do we go about displaying craftsmanship in designing methods?

Given below are certain essential principles related to crafting effective designs. It is worth noting that these eight principles are not meant to be a sequential process. Each principle must be in operation throughout the project.

## 1. Mindset first, truth always

We must actively cultivate a mindset of not knowing. We need to be aware of our biases and overcome those. That's how we create the space for insights to appear. Our attention cannot be fragmented across many activities. There are several things one can do to cultivate such a mindset:

- Create ownership by selecting a core team for the project. Insights work needs many people to contribute, but only a small team must lead the process from start to finish. They need to have stakes in the project.

- Set norms emphasizing the ground rules for interaction on the project. For instance, when we conduct qualitative fieldwork, we share guidelines for the participating team. We emphasize the importance of being relaxed. We suggest that people dress comfortably, listen to music or do other things that get them in the right mood. We request them to switch off their phones and pay close attention to what the respondent is saying and doing.

- Practise exercises to be mindful. Mindfulness helps us become engaged in the present moment and to pay attention to what's going on. There are many ways of getting into a mindful state. A walk in the park, a run, or a short meditation can do the trick. An example of a meditation exercise I created is given below:

    'Breathing in, I will listen intently to the respondent; breathing out, I will try to help them.'

    The exact words do not matter. Such a practice shifts one's focus to the customers. It enables people to feel fresh, empathetic, and energetic.

- Plan for serendipity by providing tools that capture insights that come out of the blue. We give journals to our clients so that if anything interesting strikes them, they can jot it down. Or seek inspiration by visiting interesting stores, art galleries, or concerts. The choice depends on the preferences of the team. For instance, the Insight Dojo team visited the 'In Real Life' exhibition at the Tate Modern[19] by Olafur Eliasson, whose work is a perfect fusion of mathematics, science, and art. His exhibition prompted many ideas. There was an expansive pin-wall, collaged with interesting text, data, and images, that showcased various aspects of climate change. This inspired us to create a similar 'wall of insights' in our own office for our current projects.

## 2. Problem determines method

If you state the problem and break it down into issues or hypotheses, the design choices become easy. You know the questions that need to be asked and the suitable research design for the answers.

> The mistake people make, though, is not acknowledging the nature of the unknowns. If the major uncertainty is about predicting the future related to a disruptive technology, e.g., how generative AI will affect an industry, the methodology must be tailored to that unknown.

Many organizations identify the right questions but then deploy the wrong method, e.g., they conduct a broad-based survey of people in the industry, elicit their views, and synthesize their responses to present a perspective about the future. This is misleading, because only a handful of people can accurately predict the future, especially of a technology that is evolving. Asking thousands of people will not solve the problem. A scenario planning approach is more suitable for long-term planning and allows for consideration of multiple versions of the future that could play out.

### 3. Think ecosystem of stakeholders, not just customers

Businesses rely on the behaviour of customers to achieve their goals. However, customers cannot fully understand or articulate how emerging trends may affect their behaviour. It becomes important to interview a whole range of people who can provide insight about how the environment might evolve and the implications of that. When we were helping a genomics data provider determine their strategy, we wanted to understand how the future would evolve for the field. The future comprised trends related to the amount of research funding for the field, concerns about privacy, the success of personalised medicine, etc. Customers were not cognisant of these broader trends. We interviewed knowledgeable experts who specialized in genomics but from different disciplines – scientific philosophers, regulatory experts, sociologists, leaders in pharma companies, heads of departments of genomics in medical schools, public health experts, and those specialising in AI for genomics. We complemented this by reading books, academic articles, and think tank reports on the subject. It allowed us to identify the main trends that would shape the future of the field and, consequently, the behaviour of the client's customers. Focusing only on customers would not have given us the insight. For instance, whilst there is excitement about the possibility of personalised medicine leading to cures for rare diseases and cancers, there are concerns about the inequality in access to these medicines, with affluent people benefitting more. Speaking to different stakeholders allows us to expose these tensions between alternative views and get a better understanding of the macro context.

## 4. Design as you go – be flexible, iterate, and combine

Rather than having a fixed methodology from start to finish of a project, the design should allow for adaptation and improvisation based on what one is learning.

> Whenever there is a complex problem, it is likely that a few of the initial assumptions underlying the project will not hold good, or new interesting leads will emerge. Sometimes the problem definition may shift. These are signs that a breakthrough might be on the horizon.

|  | Starting assumption/Learning from previous round | Business implication | Research design to explore/validate a hypothesis |
|---|---|---|---|
| Round 1 | Pain can originate from many medical conditions – cancer, rheumatoid arthritis, osteoarthritis, fibromyalgia, and many other chronic conditions. This meant that there were many different types of specialist physicians who could be involved in the initiation of the drug. | Our client thought that targeting a few specialist groups would be easier than targeting GPs. GPs comprised a significantly large population. The client would require a larger sales force to target them. | We conducted in-depth interviews and focus groups with various specialists and GPs, ethnographic interviews with patients, and observed mock consultations between physicians and patients. |
| Round 2 | Specialists, while being involved, did not have the time to manage the side effects of opioids in an ongoing manner. Even if they were interested. GPs and pain specialists were far more likely to be involved, yet they varied a lot in how they managed the side effects. | The focus shifted to finding segments of GPs and pain specialists which one could target. These segments were more likely to be receptive to a new therapy. | We conducted qualitative and quantitative segmentation research amongst GPs and pain specialists. We also conducted quantitative research to determine patient segments. The patients were those who were managing pain with strong opioids such as morphine or fentanyl. The underlying assumption was that managing the side effect was relevant only for strong opioids. |

| | | | |
|---|---|---|---|
| Adaptation to round 2 | When we interviewed GPs about the opioids that caused the side effect, a few of them mentioned codeine, a weak opioid, as a source of the problem. This was contrary to our client's belief that the problem was caused only by strong opioids. | If quantitative research could validate the hypothesis, the opportunity for the client would significantly increase by including patients on weak opioids. | We added questions on weak opioids to the physician questionnaire and additionally sampled 1000 patients on weak opioids. |
| Final insight | There were three segments of GPs and pain specialists who were particularly receptive to managing the side effect with a new treatment. The client decided to prioritise these segments for their sales effort, reducing the need for a large sales force.<br><br>The opportunity for the treatment doubled with the inclusion of patients of weak opioids. The quantitative research on patients and physicians helped estimate that the size of the potential market for the treatment amongst users of weak opioids was as big as that of users of strong opioids. | | |

However, these changes need to be explored, developed further or validated, and that requires a change in the methodology.

We were working for a client who developed a treatment for a side effect of opioids. They wanted us to help them develop their EU commercial strategy. The situation was complex – attitudes and regulations towards opioids vary by country, and both the physicians and the patients comprised a highly heterogeneous population. The following table describes a subset of the iterations that the design went through to illustrate the value of adaptation.

We discovered a new and large group of patients who were on weak opioids and were suffering from this side effect. This led to a doubling of the opportunity for the new treatment. Furthermore, identifying the three segments on whom the client should focus led to a strategy that was cost-effective. We could have easily missed the insights if we had not adapted our research design.

For instance, we might have accepted the finding that GPs and pain specialists managed the side effect and left it to the client to decide if they wanted to invest in a large sales force to engage GPs. Instead, we changed the research design to identify and validate physician segments that the client could target. Similarly, we could have treated GPs bringing up codeine, a weak opioid, as an aberration – after all, it was qualitative research. Instead, we expanded the quantitative work and modified the questions, which allowed us to realize and validate the hypothesis.

| | Business Decision | Technique | Purpose | Example of finding |
|---|---|---|---|---|
| 1 | Designing the product | Digital ethnography | Exploration of unmet needs with respect to climate control and hypotheses about potential segments Understanding of the product use environment both indoors and outdoors to guide the engineers to adapt the product. Ascertain responses to the client's three innovation concepts | There are 'dead' spaces in the house not covered by central air conditioning. There is an unmet need for effective climate control devices. There is a strong unmet need for better cooling for outdoor occasions such as barbecues. |
| | | Prototype testing with customers | Getting concrete feedback on usability, design, and performance. | The 'air throw' or the range of the coolers worked well indoors but not outdoors. The range was too low. |
| | | Concept test, Max Diff, Kano in quantitative research | Prioritising the product features | The quality of the rotating head and 'air throw' were the most important features for outdoor usage. |

| 2 | Determine the price level | Gabor granger in quantitative research | Estimating price elasticity | A $100 increase in the proposed price would lead to a 30% drop in the number of users. |
|---|---|---|---|---|
| | | Van Westendorp in quantitative research | Identifying price-value associations | The optimum price where people do not see it as too expensive or too cheap is $X. |
| | | Discrete choice-based conjoint in quantitative research | Measuring willingness to pay for additional features | People would be willing to pay an additional $Y for an optional heater. |
| 3 | Developing the brand strategy | Digital ethnography | Exploring emotional and rational needs | 'Environmental friendliness' is a latent driver of choice, i.e., it may not be salient in the minds of people currently but is likely to emerge as important in the future. |
| | | Brand funnel and image of competitive brands, attitudes, and concept reactions in quantitative research | Identifying compelling emotional and rational benefits that can be leveraged for differentiation | 'Allowing friends to enjoy outdoor celebrations' and 'having a stylish design that reflects my discerning taste' emerged as important benefits to be associated with one of the innovations. |
| | | Examine case studies of brands such as Intel and Shimano. | Assessing if the unique technology inside the innovations ought to be branded | The success factors underlying the Intel Inside story were having an established brand a large customer base, and high marketing spend. These factors were not true for our client's situation. |
| | | Discrete choice-based conjoint in quantitative research | Assessing brand premium of existing brands such as Dyson | Dyson commanded a premium of $Z because of its brand equity. |

| | | | | |
|---|---|---|---|---|
| 4. | Developing the go-to-market plan | Analysis of real sales data available of e-retailers | Assessing the structure of the current market | Most of the current products were being used for indoor use. |
| | | Simulation of shopping in digital ethnography | Understanding heuristics that shoppers use in their buying process | While reading reviews, the ones in the middle were ignored. Consumers either looked at the most recent reviews or at the top and bottom reviews. |
| | | Analysis of channels used and sources of influence in quantitative research | Understanding the relative value of different channels and sources of information in influencing purchase | The 'Chic and Connected' segment could be reached based on media based on their affinities – cooking, gardening, fashion, DIY, celebrity news, and beauty. |
| 5 | Developing and selecting priority segments | Digital ethnography | Developing hypotheses on segments | There is a segment called 'Chic and Connected' who entertain guests a lot with their houses designed for socialising. The products they used demonstrate their discerning taste. |
| | | Multivariate analysis (factor and cluster analysis) on attitudinal and behavioural data from quantitative research and profile on all variables | Developing robust and actionable segments<br>Identifying early adopter segments to guide go-to-market plans | The 'Chic and Connected' segment, comprising 12 per cent of all users, was more likely to buy the innovation and were willing to pay a premium for it. |

Another lesson from the above case study is that using multiple methods – in-depth interviews, ethnography, and quantitative research – allows us to get richer insight.

Most business situations involve multiple decisions that leaders need to make. For the client who wanted to launch three innovative and environmentally friendly climate control products in the US, we made recommendations for a whole range of decisions – brand strategy, product design, target segments, pricing, and channel mix. We used many techniques throughout the project, which are summarised in the table below. The study had five distinct components – digital ethnography with customers for three weeks who were directed to upload videos, answer open-ended questions, and react to concepts with 35 customers; physical prototype testing with 20 customers for feedback on usability, look and feel, and performance of the prototypes, both indoors and outdoors; quantitative research with 1200 customers; studying analogous case studies to help with branding decisions and analysing sales data for certain retailers to understand which were the dominant channels. The table below summarises how the research was used to inform the main business decisions.

Each technique was fit for a particular purpose. For instance, only ethnography could give us a rich understanding of the customer environment where the product would be used. Physical prototype testing allowed us to give granular recommendations on how to improve the features to the client designers and engineers.

I have deliberately listed all the methods to illustrate what a hybrid design looks like in practice. When we present the case study to most organizations, they are impressed by the insights and the varied underlying methods. They express surprise that we accomplished all the work in six months and in a cost-effective manner. However, there are two crucial success factors. First, there must be continuous problem solving with the client to know the relevant business decisions. Second, the team must be highly versatile in using various methods to design a hybrid approach. Expertise enables reducing each technique to its essential elements so that the research is not cumbersome for the customers.

## 5. Be analytically robust

In problems with a high degree of uncertainty, we cannot get quantitative evidence for every aspect. There will always be a certain level of speculation. However, for most business decisions, you need prioritization of insights for senior leaders and, therefore, quantification. For instance, it is not good enough to know that there is an unmet need for an innovation without having any idea about its market potential. This is necessary for developing a business case. It may be difficult to quantify accurately, but getting even a rough sense of the magnitude can be helpful in most instances. So, whether it is qualitative or quantitative work, striving for analytic robustness is necessary. There are certain critical elements that must be considered:

- *Robust sampling:* This, as argued before, is one of the most overlooked aspects in most insights work and needs to be addressed. In quantitative research, sample size is usually not an issue. These days it is easy to amass large data sets with a variety of online panels. The issue for quantitative research is having representative samples and managing the quality of the sample. The implication is that one must spend significant effort evaluating vendors to arrive at a robust sample design. This also implies being cautious of opinions gleaned from social media or large language models without understanding how the data is sourced. In qualitative research, usually, there is greater control over the quality of the sample. The bigger issue is that qualitative researchers are often satisfied with small samples. In my company, Insight Dojo, we do a lot of qualitative research, especially in areas where quantitative research is ineffective and impractical. For instance, if we are speaking to a highly specialized but varied group of individuals, quantitative research is a blunt and costly methodology. We need to have tailored qualitative interactions. Robustness is nevertheless necessary. We always find that there are distinct segments of customers in every category. We cannot pick these differences with research conducted with a small number of respondents. We solve the problem by doing substantially large qualitative research studies relative to other companies, usually in the 40–100 sample size range.

- ***Checking construct validity:*** The importance of measuring what you intend to measure cannot be emphasized enough. For instance, in surveys, framing questions to get accurate responses requires great craftsmanship. Yet, there are questions that simply cannot be answered by the customer, such as their likely behaviour at a future time. These questions take us further from the truth. In qualitative research, where we interact directly with human beings, one might expect that we won't face such issues. However, with the advent of digital qualitative research, we sometimes work with text only and do not have the benefit of observing body language and tone. We also may not understand what the consumer really means when they express a thought. We begin to face similar challenges of abstraction. It is important to be thoughtful in both the usage and interpretation of such measurements. Recognizing the level of abstraction in the measurements that we use encourages us to look for alternative methods. It also makes us less dogmatic about our findings.

- *Improving inferences about causality:* One of the biggest challenges in data analysis is distinguishing between correlation and causation. While statistical and machine learning techniques provide valuable insights, they rarely offer definitive answers to the question of 'why'. Making the right causal inference, however, is critical for decision-making in business, policy, and science.

A good way to build an intuition about making causal inferences is to think about a few questions to consider. Let's take a recent example. Elon Musk spent millions of dollars on the Trump campaign. What role did that expenditure play in causing Donald Trump's victory?

**Five questions to consider**

a. Is there a strong association or correlation between the two variables of interest? Yes, Elon Musk's investment and Trump's victory are associated.

b. Did the cause occur prior to the effect? Yes, all the expenditure happened before the actual election event.

c. Can one rule out other possible causes for the effect? No. There were many other factors. There were long-run factors such as the increasing alienation of the working class and the culture factors and short-term factors such as inflation and immigration. There were two wars going on. Additionally, one had to consider the strengths and weaknesses of the two candidates.

d. Would the effect still have occurred if the cause had not occurred? This is difficult to answer. If Elon Musk had not spent the money on the campaign, we don't know what the outcome might have been.

e. Do we have an explanation of the process through which causation takes place? Yes, we can construct a plausible story about how Elon Musk's campaign might have encouraged Trump supporters to vote

In balance, drawing a causal inference is particularly difficult because of (d) and (e). There are far too many potential causes. This is the reason why diagnosing the US election results has been so difficult. You can almost be sure that any immediate analysis of the results has a high likelihood of being wrong. Asking such questions is a useful exercise to help us think about making causal inferences before making decisions about methodologies.

**Methodological guidelines**

Several methodological approaches help strengthen causal inferences. Below are five key strategies:

1. **Stratifying the study with the right test and control groups**

   When analysing causality, it is essential to compare groups appropriately. In large surveys, for example, if we want to examine the impact of smoking on exercise frequency, we must stratify the sample into relevant subgroups – such as regular smokers, occasional smokers, and non-smokers.

   Additionally, we need to account for potential confounders – variables that may influence both smoking and exercise habits, such as age, gender, and existing health conditions. Proper stratification ensures that we are making more accurate comparisons and isolating the effect of smoking itself rather than other influencing factors.

2. **Using longitudinal data to understand the sequence of events**

   Longitudinal data – where observations are collected over an extended period – allows us to track cause-and-effect relationships rather than relying on cross-sectional snapshots.

   A relevant example comes from Pepsi's marketing strategy. Pepsi teams aimed to increase Top-of-Mind Awareness (TOM) – the percentage of consumers who name a brand first when asked to recall soft drink brands. Since TOM was highly correlated with loyalty and market share, it was an important metric. Many sales and marketing teams assumed that increasing advertising would improve TOM, which in turn would increase sales. The idea was based on the intuition that frequent advertising makes the brand more memorable and top-of-mind for consumers. However, longitudinal analysis revealed a different causal pathway: TOM actually lagged behind consumption. Consumers didn't remember Pepsi more often just from advertising; instead, it was their regular consumption of Pepsi that made it surface to the top of their minds. In markets where Pepsi's distribution was weaker relative to competition, additional advertising had little impact on TOM. Instead, the key driver was the distribution strength and promotional activities that encouraged consumption. Aiming for a high TOM in these markets was still a worthy goal because it preceded achieving brand loyalty, but the path to improving it was very different from what the teams had initially imagined.

3. **Running Experiments**

   Experiments are robust methods for drawing causal inferences. Unlike surveys, where we passively examine associations, experiments actively manipulate variables to test their impact.

   For example, businesses can:

   - Run A/B tests on marketing campaigns to determine which messaging drives higher engagement. For instance, a company might create two versions of a webpage, with just one element different between them, e.g., the choice of the image. They then show these versions to different visitors at random and observe the effectiveness of each version.

   - Adjust pricing strategies to observe how demand changes in response.

   - Test new product features on select customer segments before a full rollout.

   In digital environments, such as e-commerce and social media, experiments are relatively easy to conduct. Platforms like Amazon and Meta continuously run controlled experiments to optimize user engagement, pricing strategies, and content recommendations.

4. **Building Causal Maps and Using Counterfactuals**
Advanced causal inference methods[20], pioneered by Judea Pearl, emphasize using causal diagrams and counterfactual reasoning. This is a growing field. Studying Judea Pearl's work on causal inference is highly recommended. His work opened many doors in my mind. I have attempted to provide a simplified description of the steps.

- Visually map causal relationships between variables – the technical term is Directed Acrylic Graph (DAG). For example, a DAG could illustrate how talent, years of practice, and access to high-quality instruction may impact the likelihood of mastering a musical instrument. One can draw these causal maps by using one's intuition, leveraging existing knowledge, or by interviewing experts.

- Mathematical models help quantify the causal influence of one factor over another.

- Counterfactual questions – asking 'What if X had not happened?' – aid in testing alternative scenarios.

    For instance, we might meet an accomplished pianist and ask, 'What if this person had not received instruction from a maestro – would they have still achieved a similar level of mastery?' By simulating different scenarios, counterfactual reasoning strengthens our ability to infer causality.

5. **Analysis to Control for Confounders and Identify the Effects of Different Variables**

   Regardless of the method used, robust analysis helps establish the strength of the relationship between the hypothesised cause and effect. For that, analysis must account for confounders – variables that obscure the true causal effect. For example, when studying the relationship between smoking and exercise frequency, age may be a confounder. Younger people might both smoke more and exercise more, leading to misleading correlations. Applying multivariate analysis techniques, e.g., regression analysis, ANCOVA, and structural equation modelling, is very effective.

- ***'Triangulating' with many data points:*** It is a good practice to crosscheck one's inferences with data from multiple sources. This becomes particularly important whilst dealing with situations that are highly ambiguous, e.g., the future. Often there are conflicting pieces of information. Resolving the tension in such situations will lead to an insight through the 'dissonance' path.

## 6. Do not reinvent the wheel

There are many theories and frameworks that have been well researched and tested. The application of these will accelerate insight development. The theories and frameworks may pertain to innovation, marketing and branding, behaviour change, or other fields that we routinely access. Knowledge of these can prevent us from spending a lot of time developing everything from scratch and will enrich our understanding. There is no need to reinvent the wheel.

For example, Clayton Christensen's theory of innovation[21], discussed in Chapter 2, can help entrepreneurial companies spot opportunities for disrupting an incumbent systematically by finding new markets, or new dimensions, for competing.

## 7. Deliberately practise thinking differently

As we discussed in Chapter 2, insight requires us to be simultaneously imaginative whilst being grounded in reality' to use both our intuition and analytical skills, to be objective and to be subjective in our interpretation. This requires us to think in many ways – observing, abstracting, empathising, etc. Chapter 5 is dedicated to the different thinking modes necessary for insight. Deploying these throughout a project is essential. This also means that we need to create an environment in projects that is conducive to creativity and serendipity to occur. For instance, it is necessary to plan for relaxation or be exposed to novel ideas (e.g., by visiting an art gallery) so that insights can incubate.

## 8. Engage the C-suite and cross-functional teams

Ultimately, we want to translate insights into action that creates value. That involves mobilizing C-suite and cross-functional teams. The path to action from insight takes several steps. The first step is to inspire the stakeholders with the insight. They must believe it is truthful, useful, and something genuinely new. In the case study for the genomics provider, we pressure tested our finding with the design team, the bioinformaticians who routinely met customers, and some of the leaders in the executive team. Then we presented them to the entire organization and finally to the CEO. We brought our findings to life with videos.

The second step is to convince leaders that there is a real, sizeable business opportunity.

In most quantitative research studies, that is easy to show. In qualitative research work, once we identify the opportunities, we use desk research, e.g., analysing industry reports, journals, and government publications, to estimate the size of the opportunities. That is a critical input to enable senior leaders to make decisions.

The third step is to develop concrete actions that can be implemented easily. When we were working on increasing the sales of the natural menopausal product, the first was to help the sales team identify the 'natural believers'. We provided characteristics of the segment, which the salespeople could use to allocate the gynaecologists in their database to estimate the size of the segments. The second action was to create a compelling story about the mechanism of action of the product. We ran a brainstorming session with gynaecologists, who were knowledgeable about the product, and with the medical team of the client, to help describe how the treatment is likely to be working and affecting the symptoms. The advertising agency took this story and incorporated it in the sales aid.

Although I have described it above in a sequential manner, when the stakeholders are involved from the beginning, the translation from insight to action happens continuously. Stakeholders contribute to the insight creation process and start thinking about the relevant actions long before the end of the project.

It is necessary to use varied styles of communication. In certain cases, one might use a top-down structure with a clear executive summary. This is useful for senior executive communication, especially when there is limited time. In other situations, one might share the material from research in a raw form and give the stakeholders the opportunity to absorb the material and arrive at the insights themselves.

## CORE KNOWLEDGE AREAS AND METHODS

Given the vast number of disciplines and methods that intersect to enable us to see the truth, it is impossible to come up with a list that is complete. However, having a set of core disciplines and tools can help one create methods tailored to a wide range of problems.

## Methods

### *Mastering the basics*

First, we must master the basics of methodologies related to insight. This includes skills such as designing research, selecting qualitative and quantitative techniques, sampling theory, writing discussion guides and questionnaires, learning how to do fieldwork, preparation, analysis and synthesis of various types of data sets, synthesizing secondary research, conducting statistical significance testing, and presenting findings. The quality of outputs is dependent on the level of craftsmanship on these aspects. Below are some examples of mistakes that have occurred because people had not learned the basics:

- A team concluded that low prices were not an important driver of loyalty for discount stores. This sounded like an interesting and counter-intuitive finding, especially as in an earlier period there had been a strong correlation between a measure of loyalty and a measure of whether a store was perceived as low priced. When we looked closely at the data, we found that in the previous period loyalty and low-price perception were both measured on a 7-point scale. In the current period, the loyalty measure was conducted on a 3-point scale! The lower correlation was because of the difference in scales, not because of the decreased importance of price. It was a technical mistake.

- Asking people to rate the importance of an attribute on a scale, such as a 1–10 scale, is not very discriminating. You may have a question such as, 'On a scale from 1 to 10, where 1 means 'not important at all' and 10 means 'extremely important', how important is (attribute) to you when choosing (product/service)?'. A large number of attributes, incorrectly, often emerge as important because of the way the question is phrased. Experts in customer insights work around this problem by changing the phrasing of questions – an example of a rephrased question would be introducing trade-offs (e.g., allocation of 100 points based on what's important or using a conjoint-based research design) or using other indirect measures such as correlations of attributes with brand preference. (Please note that challenges with using correlational data discussed previously apply in this case as well.)

- Sequencing questions in a manner that creates a bias, making people answer in a particular way; for instance, inadvertently revealing the brand of interest. A client showed me research that showed that their brand was rated highly on satisfaction by the customers. I discovered from the questionnaire that the respondents would have guessed the name of the sponsor from the first few questions, as it was mentioned in the questions themselves. The market research norm, however, is to show the brand of interest, alongside other brands, so that customers do not get biased.

- Asking leading questions in qualitative research, e.g., 'Why do you think that electric cars are a better investment than gasoline cars?' The questions presuppose that consumers think that electric cars are better.

The list of such common mistakes is endless. There is no shortcut. We just have to learn the fundamentals.

Learning statistics and probability as a part of our basic knowledge skillset must be a priority. Uncertainty and probability are strongly related concepts, and one must learn to think in terms of probabilities, especially when dealing with questions with many unknowns.

## DISTINCT FAMILIES OF TECHNIQUES

In addition to mastering the basics, there are core families of techniques that can enrich our capacity to create great research designs that everyone should understand to a sufficiently deep level. To simplify the discussion, I will take one specific topic and explore how different techniques handle this subject.

One of the most common topics for exploration is identifying customer needs. It drives product and brand development, amongst other business actions. The table below summarises a few pivotal families of techniques that help understand different aspects of exploring customer needs. I believe any insights leader ought to be sufficiently well-versed, even hands-on, in applying these methods. Even if you are not specialized in insights, being aware of these families will make you think of methodologies more expansively. It is worth noting that I have not listed rating importance/agreement on a scale, or directly asking customers, a common approach to understanding customer needs, as these comprise the basics of market research.

The list above is not an exhaustive set, and they reflect my choice of essential families of techniques that can make us well-rounded. Knowledge of these techniques allows us

| | Family of techniques | Description | Assumptions underlying methods | Applications for Smart Phones |
|---|---|---|---|---|
| 1 | Enriched qualitative projective techniques used in traditional qualitative, design, or human factors research | These are focus groups or in-depth interviews with exercises such as collages, role-plays, and examining a critical incident that a customer has experienced. | Customers cannot articulate their emotional needs just by answering straight-forward questions and need alternative ways to elicit deep and rich responses. | Understanding what a 'smartphone' represents to people. For some, it might represent 'a lifeline' or 'connection' and for others, 'noise'. |
| 2 | Naturalistic methods, such as ethnographic methods, which enable research in realistic environments | Adapted from anthropology, these methods emphasize studying consumers in context and include methods such as living with consumers, observing them and undertaking activities such as shopping. | Culture and context shape individual needs that can be understood by interacting with people in their natural environment. | Nokia sent researchers to live with Indian consumers. Then they designed phones with a long battery life because of the limited supply of electricity in rural areas. |
| 3. | Semiotics | This is a method of studying signs, symbols and cultural codes to understand what consumers value. Semioticians analyse films, TV, advertisements, social media, and other media to arrive at their insights. | Culture codes can be understood by examining signs and symbols without interviewing people. | Conveying messages through packaging or design can be done through semiotic analysis, for instance, the usage of white by Apple to convey simplicity and elegance. |

| | | | |
|---|---|---|---|
| 4 | Heuristics and biases | Designing interventions based on heuristics and biases that people systematically use and then testing those in an experiment | People are not entirely rational in what they need, and they are affected by heuristics and biases, e.g., loss aversion. | Testing and offering a money-back guarantee as a way of mitigating losses or making it easy to upgrade to new models to minimise effort |
| 5 | Cognitive neuroscience-based methods | Uses insights from how the brain processes information. The main methods in use are eye tracking, fMRI, EEG, biometric testing, and Implicit Attitude Testing. | By analysing brain activity, eye movements, and other physiological responses, one can get subconscious reactions of people. | Testing alternative designs of a smartphone by scanning the brain through an fMRI and determining which designs are most emotionally engaging |
| 6. | Social Listening | It involves monitoring conversations happening over digital platforms such as social media sites and other forums. | Social listening enables us to listen to real conversations that are happening. | Discovering trends related to usage, e.g., remote working or features that are getting popular |
| 7 | Iterative prototype testing | This is a way of testing prototypes that vary in terms of the level of finish. To begin, one may test low-fidelity prototypes that might be sketches of the product. At the end, one might test high-fidelity prototypes that resemble the finished product. | It is easier to get useful feedback on design, layout, functionality, and performance by testing something concrete. | Giving people specific tasks such as taking pictures, navigating through different screens, making phone calls and getting feedback on the user experience |

| | | | | |
|---|---|---|---|---|
| 9 | Conjoint-based methods applied to surveys | It involves presenting respondents with a series of product profiles, each with different combinations of attributes and levels. Respondents rank or rate these profiles. The data is used to understand the trade-offs that the consumers make. There are many variants. | To ascertain the importance of an attribute, instead of asking for importance in the abstract, consumers must be made to choose between bundles of attributes with trade-offs built in in the choices. | Assessing the value of price, brand, operating system (Android/iOS), camera quality, storage capacity, design, and other features by presenting choices on these attributes with different levels |
| 10 | Supervised and unsupervised machine learning models | Supervised models are created to associate a certain output variable based on input variables. There are various algorithms, e.g., linear and logistic regression, support vector machines, and neural networks. | An outcome variable can be estimated by a set of input variables. For example, house prices can be predicted by inputs such as size, location, etc. | Delivering personalised offers based on user preferences, behaviour, and demographics |
| | | Unsupervised models are used to determine the natural structure of a data set without attempting to explain an outcome variable. There are various algorithms, e.g., k-means clustering, hierarchical clustering, and principal component analysis. | Underlying hidden patterns can be determined by these algorithms. | Developing a segmentation of customers based on attitudes and behaviour collected through a survey |

to combine methods and create hybrid approaches. It is important to grasp the principles underlying each family. For instance, conjoint-based techniques are essentially quantitative in nature. Yet, the idea of presenting customers with trade-offs, a fundamental principle about conjoint analysis, can be useful in qualitative settings. It is impossible to acquire deep expertise in all the families of techniques. Having access to a network of experts is beneficial. For instance, while I read a lot about semiotics and use it in my research, I always seek the help of a specialist semiotician. Conversely, for ethnographic work, I typically handle every aspect from beginning to end myself. Similarly, I would fully design and implement conjoint analysis-based studies for most projects. However, for more complex projects, I would consult a specialized expert.

## Knowledge Disciplines

There are many disciplines that affect the way we approach the field of customer insights. The typical courses that are taught in business schools, such as marketing, finance, and marketing research, are all relevant. When consulting companies hire people with a non-MBA background, they run a mini-MBA course to address that gap. For insights, the fields that continually impact our work are innovation, branding, segmentation, social sciences, statistics, machine learning, behavioural sciences, design, and cognitive neuroscience, and now, generative AI. Two fields that are becoming increasingly important, from my perspective, are philosophy of science and systems theory.

Philosophy of science gives us a perspective on how we gain knowledge, develop methods, and elicit truth – all of which are critical for insights professionals. Systems theory is an interdisciplinary field of study that examines complex systems such as climate change and is particularly relevant now. One need not be a master in any of these fields, but staying abreast of the latest thinking through papers, lectures, online courses, and books can enhance our ability to deliver practical insights.

## Programming

Programming is increasingly becoming a core skill. It enables us to experiment and play with many techniques. It enhances our ability to take advantage of AI.

## Global trends

Finally, given the changing trends that surround us, insights practitioners need to be abreast of global trends, whether these relate to technology, geopolitics, economics, climate change, or other aspects. This increases our ability to sense how the evolving environment may affect business and makes us insightful advisors to senior leaders. Reading books, journals, and research reports by think tanks are all good ways to stay abreast.

# MICRO-MASTERY IS A USEFUL PRACTICE FOR CROSS-POLLINATORS

To be true advisors to business leaders, insights practitioners must combine knowledge from different fields and be comfortable in designing hybrid approaches. This requires facilitating interactions between a variety of specialists. Equally, though, they need to be sceptical and be able to critique various methodologies. This ability becomes even more important while studying secondary research, such as academic articles or industry reports.

The challenge for insights leaders is to be able to develop sufficient intuition to get into the heart of a method and finally evaluate how the data that is being generated can be used effectively. Most of us with jobs do not have the ten thousand hours considered necessary to be a master in a single field, let alone in multiple fields. However, gaining a high level of competence in a single component of a discipline *can* be used in multiple fields.

The British author, Robert Twigger introduced the concept of micro-mastery[22], which he defined as 'a self-contained unit of doing, complete in itself but connected to a greater field'. He further clarified that 'you can perfect that single thing or move on to bigger things – or you can do both'. He gives an example of mastering making an omelette first, instead of trying to master cooking. The concept of micro-mastery is a simplifier for insights leaders who want to be authentic cross-pollinators. What would micro-mastery look like in practice for an insights practitioner?

We could start by specifying the different families of methods that are relevant to us. Instead of addressing the whole field, we can select a core set of methods as a starting point. For instance, for traditional supervised learning models, we could start by mastering correlation and regression – this would include different forms, e.g., linear and logistic regressions. A similar process can be followed for the other fields – for instance, Adaptive Conjoint Analysis (ACA) from the conjoint family, Implicit Association Testing (IAT) from cognitive neuroscience, designing and testing interventions based on behavioural economics, ethnography from qualitative research, and prototype testing from design research. For machine learning, we may choose to apply what we have learnt about logistic and linear regressions to bigger data sets. Or we may decide to learn something new, like running basic neural networks. Mastering any technique involves applying it in varied contexts and data sets, speaking to experts, and reading up on essential papers. All this will not happen overnight. But if we have a multiple-year plan, this is both achievable and rewarding. Building competency in just one or two techniques in each family of skills will significantly advance our intuition about the overall discipline. One can imagine creating sections or 'folders' for each discipline in our minds – a machine learning folder, an ethnography folder, etc. Having created the 'discipline folders', we will automatically know how to update knowledge through continuous learning.

There are two words[23] in Japanese for technique. Gi-Jitsu refers to a technique in a mechanical sense that may be applied in the context of industrial products. Waza, on the other hand, refers to technique as art. The human being is present in the technique. The application of technique is strategic and values the context. Waza is the approach to crafting methodologies that I am recommending. There is nothing mechanical about it.

Let us now look at how we can think in many ways to arrive at insights in the next chapter.

# 5

# Systematic Ways of Thinking Differently

'If you change the way you look at things, the things you look at change.'[1]

– **Wayne Dyer**

IN CHAPTER 2, WE EXPLORED THE CURIOUS WAYS IN WHICH insights emerge in our minds through various mechanisms – making connections, spotting dissonance, drawing analogies, and recognizing hidden patterns. The underlying workings of the mind are complex, involving multiple mental processes. One way to understand these processes is by examining how creative individuals generate novel ideas.

Robert and Michèle Root-Bernstein[2] have extensively studied this topic and identified 'thirteen thinking tools' that productive scientists and artists frequently use to develop groundbreaking contributions. Becoming proficient in these ways of thinking can enhance our ability to spot insights systematically.

This chapter focuses on *eight thinking modes* that are commonly used in developing insight:

1. Observing
2. Empathising
3. Imaging
4. Abstracting
5. Analogizing
6. Recognizing patterns
7. Playing
8. Modeling

Readers who wish to explore these concepts further are encouraged to delve into the original work of Robert and Michele Root-Bernstein. While they use the term 'thinking tools', I will refer to them as 'modes of thinking' or 'thinking processes' to avoid confusion with the term 'tools', which I frequently use to describe methods or techniques.

The first part of this chapter describes each thinking mode and its relevance. The second part outlines how to hone these skills. It is important to note that these mental processes do not operate in isolation – they occur simultaneously and dynamically.

For example, consider the scenario from Chapter 2 in which we discovered a segment of gynaecologists who favoured natural products, contrary to our client's expectations. At the interview site, we *observed* visual cues in their offices – product samples, informational leaflets, and other materials – suggesting that natural products were part of their daily practice.

By *empathising* with gynaecologists who acknowledged patient resistance to hormonal products, we understood their motivation for offering natural alternatives. As we conducted the interviews, we mentally contrasted this reality with our initial expectation that gynaecologists would view natural products unfavourably – this process involved *imaging* the shift in our understanding.

Rather than considering every possible factor influencing their choices, we *abstracted* the most salient dimension – their orientation toward natural products. Noticing this behaviour across multiple interviews allowed us to *recognize a pattern*. We then *analogized* by comparing this phenomenon to other industries where private practitioners cater to customer preferences.

All these thinking processes occurred rapidly and simultaneously.

## Honing These Thinking Skills

While we deploy these modes of thinking naturally, refining them requires deliberate practice.

> Without intentional training, we risk making snap judgments and missing key insights. To deploy these modes of thinking skilfully, we must first isolate them, practise them individually, and then integrate them seamlessly.

This approach mirrors the way top athletes develop fluency in complex skills. Learning a new skill initially requires slow, deliberate effort – a top-down process that overrides habitual patterns. However, with consistent practice, the skill becomes automatic and intuitive – a bottom-up process. By systematically improving each thinking mode, we develop the ability to combine them naturally and sharpen our insight-spotting abilities.

To simplify this learning process, I have grouped the eight thinking modes into three categories:

1. **Direct Experience** – Modes that help us engage with the world through our senses.
2. **Mental Visualization** – Modes that involve seeing and imagining in our minds.
3. **Thinking by Doing** – Modes that involve active experimentation and interaction.

By focusing on these categories, we can develop a structured approach to enhancing our ability to detect insights. The next section outlines practical ways to cultivate these thinking modes through deliberate practice.

# THE MODES OF THINKING

## Direct Experience

### 1. *Observation*

Before reading further, take a fresh look at your surroundings. Do you notice anything new about the space that you hadn't seen before? Has something revealed itself that you hadn't thought about before? Why?

Sherlock Holmes, the fictional detective created by Sir Arthur Conan Doyle, famously said, 'The world is full of obvious things which nobody by any chance ever observes.'[3]

Observation is the first step in developing insight, whether in science, business, or everyday life. Seeing is one of our most fundamental skills – so much so that even children begin making sense of the world through sight. However, when we talk about observation, we don't mean just seeing with our eyes. True observation involves all the senses – hearing, touch, taste, smell, and even intuition. It helps us detect hidden patterns, uncover unexpected insights, and spark innovative ideas.

Many breakthroughs in history – whether in science, art or business – began with a simple act of noticing something others overlooked.

In science, Alexander Fleming[4] discovered penicillin not through a planned experiment but by noticing something odd. While researching staphylococci bacteria at St. Mary's Hospital in London, he left a Petri dish open before going on vacation. When he returned, he found mould growing on the dish. More importantly, the bacteria around the mould had dissolved. Instead of dismissing it as contamination, Fleming examined the mould carefully, leading to the discovery of the world's first antibiotic.

In music, Dave Grohl from the Foo Fighters described how their hit song[5] 'Everlong' was born out of a moment of accidental discovery. Sitting in an isolation booth between recording sessions, he was casually strumming his guitar when he stumbled upon a few interesting notes. The sound reminded him of one of his favourite bands, Sonic Youth. Intrigued, he experimented further, eventually crafting the song's signature opening riff.

The business world, too, has benefitted from observation-driven innovation. Spencer Silver, a scientist at 3M, developed a low-tack, reusable adhesive but struggled to find a use for it. Years later, his colleague Art Fry realized its potential – not for industrial applications, but for something as simple as a bookmark that could stick to pages without causing damage. This insight led to the creation of Post-it Notes[6], now a global office staple.

Observation is just as valuable in understanding human behaviour as it is in scientific discovery. Often, what people say and what they actually do are very different. Psychologist Donald A. Norman[7] noted that when people struggle with poorly designed products, they often blame themselves rather than the product. If you ask them about their frustrations, they may not give meaningful feedback because they assume they are simply being clumsy. A trained observer, however, can see the design flaws in action.

For example, in our climate control device projects, we conducted usability testing and noticed that users struggled to figure out how to fill the water tank and were confused by the control panel buttons. Interestingly, none of them verbalised their frustration – but through observation, we saw the struggle. This allowed us to provide designers with concrete recommendations to improve the user experience.

At other times, people may not be comfortable telling the full truth. While working on a weight management innovation project for a consumer electronics company, we visited a woman in New York who expressed enthusiasm for calorie tracking. She claimed to follow a strict diet and exercise regimen and was excited about tools that could help.

However, while observing her home, we noticed a plate of chocolate doughnuts in the kitchen and a weighing scale hidden in a junk room. When we gently probed, she admitted that tracking calories felt like a reminder of failure. This shift in conversation revealed a deeper insight: out of all the things that she did to manage her weight, what she truly enjoyed was walking, because it freed her mind from fixating on weight. This realization led to the development of a product focused on enhancing the walking experience rather than just tracking calories. To be good at observing, we must first know where to look. This is a function of planning and design. For instance, if we really want to observe how people interact with a product in situ, it makes sense to do ethnographic work. We want the opportunity to observe the behaviours in the real environment. Second, we need to practise to be skilled at observation. This requires being in a receptive state and opening all of one's senses. We may pick up something unusual by a sight, a sound, a smell, a taste or a touch. We want to be mindful without distractions. We also cannot be narrowly focused, because that might blind us to what's happening in the here and now. Third, we must grasp the significance of the observation in the context of the purpose of the study.

Later in the chapter, we will cover methods for training these modes of thinking.

## 2. *Empathy*

Seeing the world from another's point of view is essential for developing insights. Empathy – the ability to understand and be sensitive to another's feelings, thoughts, and experiences – plays a fundamental role in developing deep insights.

> Empathy is a core human skill that enhances our interactions, communication, and relationships, and it has also been the foundation of countless innovations across industries.

Writers, actors, filmmakers, nurses, doctors, and many other professionals rely on it to connect with others. In business, empathy helps us tune into people's frustrations, uncover unmet needs, and develop solutions that truly enhance their experiences.

Many of the products and services that delight us today were born from an empathetic understanding of customer pain points. As an avid reader and traveller, I often felt frustrated by the glare of the sun when trying to read an e-book outdoors. Eventually, I started carrying paper books again, despite the inconvenience of their weight. Then came the Kindle, with its E Ink display – designed to reflect ambient light like paper, eliminating glare entirely. Overnight, my e-book collection grew significantly. Jeff Bezos[8], reflecting the customer empathy of the design team, stated that the goal of the Kindle was 'to disappear in your hands – to get out of the way – so you can enjoy your reading'. This is a powerful example of how understanding an unspoken frustration can lead to a transformational product.

For an insights professional, empathy is embedded in every aspect of a project. While scoping, one must tune into the needs of the project's key sponsors, as covered in Chapter 2. Empathy influences the choice of research methods – ensuring that they capture the most realistic and authentic responses. At the insight development and intervention design stage, it helps keep the user's perspective alive among stakeholders, ensuring that research translates into meaningful action.

A project we worked on for an HPV treatment illustrates how empathy can drive strategic decisions. Our client had recently acquired the rights to market a treatment in a European country. During an interview with the CEO, he revealed an aggressive sales target – an expected goal for any product launch. However, as the conversation progressed and trust was built, he shared something deeper. His true ambition for the project was to *demonstrate the company's superior insights capabilities,* strengthening collaboration with the licensor and paving the way for future acquisitions. This revelation changed how we approached the project. We ensured that the teams of both companies were immersed in the research process, allowing them to engage directly with insights as they emerged rather than merely receiving a final report.

The research itself was deeply emotional. We spoke to physicians and women diagnosed with HPV, choosing to conduct interviews in their homes to ensure that they felt comfortable. Many of them broke down during the conversations, revealing the immense psychological toll of the condition. Some key insights stood out[9]. The diagnosis often caught women by surprise – many saw their screening as a routine test, with little knowledge of HPV, and were suddenly confronted with an unfamiliar and distressing condition. After an abnormal smear test, they faced long waiting periods filled with anxiety and uncertainty, with some describing it as 'waiting to be sentenced'. Doctors tried to reassure them, but many patients remained confused, struggling to process the information they were given.

One of the most striking insights was the disconnect between doctors and patients in communication. For example, doctors often told patients that the virus was 'easy to catch', intending to explain its common nature. However, patients interpreted this as meaning they could easily pass it on to family members, leading to heightened anxiety for the patient. These misunderstandings were critical, as they shaped how patients perceived their condition and treatment. To bridge this gap, we brought these insights to life through videos and supporting materials, helping our clients see the condition from the patient's perspective. The resulting physician campaign shifted its focus – not just emphasizing the benefits of treatment but also addressing the emotional suffering and unanswered questions that patients faced. One of the most impactful pages of the campaign featured the very questions running through patients' minds after diagnosis:

- What is HPV?
- Do I have cancer?
- Why do I have a sexually transmitted disease?
- Will this affect my fertility?
- Do I have to tell my partner(s)?

By reframing the campaign around these concerns, our client strengthened their relationship with physicians and achieved remarkable results – securing an 18 per cent market share within a year. They credited this success to their empathetic understanding of the women affected by HPV, gained through the insights work they had engaged with firsthand.

While empathy is a fundamental trait of human beings, like any skill, it requires practice and refinement. There are different dimensions of empathy, each playing a role in insights work. Emotional empathy allows us to feel another's emotions deeply – when someone describes their suffering, we might choke up or shed a tear in response. Cognitive empathy provides an intellectual understanding of another's thoughts and feelings, essential for reading between the lines in discussions, emails, and online communication. Finally, empathic concern is what drives us to take action, turning understanding into meaningful solutions.

Balancing these forms of empathy is crucial. Daniel Goleman[10] has written extensively about these three forms of empathy. He notes that an excess of emotional empathy can overwhelm us, making it difficult to perform our roles effectively. Imagine interviewing a patient who suffers from chronic pain. If an insights professional lacks emotional resonance, the conversation may feel cold, weakening rapport. However, if they become too emotionally affected, it may hinder their ability to conduct the interview properly. Empathic concern – the ability to channel empathy into meaningful action – ensures that suffering is not just acknowledged but addressed through thoughtful solutions.

Another critical factor in applying empathy effectively is understanding the cultural context in which people operate. Anthropologist Gillian Tett[11] emphasizes that the behaviour and perspectives of individuals are shaped by the cultures they belong to, influencing their decisions in ways that may not be immediately apparent. Without recognizing these cultural factors, we risk misinterpreting what we observe. In her book *Anthro-Vision*, she shares examples of both successes and failures driven by cultural understanding. When Nestlé attempted to market Gerber baby food in Africa, they initially failed to recognize that in some cultures, product packaging typically features images of the ingredients – leading to confusion when parents saw a baby's face on the label. On the other hand, Kit Kat's success in Japan was fuelled by qualitative research that adapted the brand's 'have a break' concept to resonate with Japanese youth culture.

To develop stronger empathy in insights work, training should focus on several key areas. First, it requires a foundational understanding of empathy and its different forms. Second, practitioners must learn to monitor and regulate their own emotions so they can adapt to others' feelings while maintaining professional objectivity. Third, they must develop strong communication skills – reading facial expressions and gestures, conveying warmth through non-verbal cues like eye contact, and listening non-judgmentally, even in moments of silence. Lastly, they must cultivate cultural awareness, learning to decode the symbols, rituals, and myths that shape different worldviews.

Empathy, when harnessed effectively, transforms how we approach insights, innovation, and problem-solving. It enables us to move beyond surface-level understanding, uncover the deeper needs and emotions that drive human behaviour, and ultimately design solutions that truly matter.

## Mental visualization

3. *Abstracting*

One of the most invisible, subtle, and powerful sources of insight is abstracting. Unlike concrete thinking, abstraction allows us to engage with concepts that are not immediately accessible to our senses. Human beings naturally engage with abstractions all the time – our entire language and numerical systems, both fundamental to how we make sense of the world, are abstractions. Ideas, theories, works of art, and quantitative models are all examples. For the most part, abstracting happens automatically, but in this section, I want to describe the deliberate practice of abstracting for insight – the process of engaging with complex realities and distilling them into their essential essence. This is akin to a skilled programmer reducing many lines of code into a few elegant lines or an architect sketching an outline that captures the defining elements of a structure. It involves stripping away the non-essential aspects of a phenomenon and uncovering the core insight, which is often hidden beneath layers of detail.

Abstracting is central to the way we make sense of complexity in business. A clear example of this is customer segmentation[12] – a process that involves simplifying vast amounts of data into meaningful groups that marketers can act upon. When we worked on a climate control device project, our segmentation framework identified seven distinct groups, derived through a combination of qualitative and quantitative research.

See the figure below:

**Segmentation of Consumers for Climate Control Devices (Sanitized Example)**

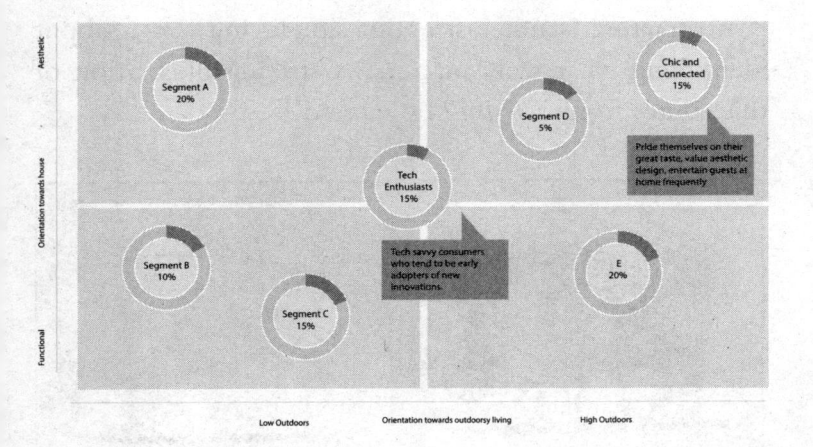

[Figure: A 2x2 matrix plot with y-axis "Orientation towards house" (Aesthetic at top, Functional at bottom) and x-axis "Orientation towards outdoorsy living" (Low Outdoors to High Outdoors). Segments shown: Segment A 20% (upper left), Segment D 5% (upper right), Chic and Connected 15% (upper right, "Pride themselves on their great taste, value aesthetic design, entertain guests at home frequently"), Tech Enthusiasts 15% (center, "Tech savvy consumers who tend to be early adopters of new innovations"), Segment B 10% (lower left), Segment C 15% (lower center), E 20% (lower right).]

These seven segments collectively represented approximately 160 million people. Naturally, within such a vast population, individual behaviours vary widely across numerous variables. Yet, through abstraction, we simplified this diversity into a meaningful framework that marketers could act upon.

That was the first level of abstraction. The next involved developing a **coherent portrait** of each segment – distilling their shared characteristics and naming them in a way that captured their essence, such as Chic and Connected. Another level of abstraction followed when we plotted these segments on a map using just two axes – functional versus aesthetic orientation and preference for an outdoor lifestyle. Each level of abstraction required analytical depth and imaginative thinking. Without strong abstraction skills, one might develop a segmentation model that is statistically robust but lacks a compelling narrative – one that inspires action.

Abstracting is not just about simplifying – it is about identifying what truly matters. A striking illustration of this comes from *The Bull* by Picasso[13].

Anti-clockwise: *The Bull*, stages second, fourth, eighth and eleventh © Succession Picasso 2025

In its final form, the drawing consists of nothing more than an outline – stark, minimal, and deceptively simple. Yet, this was not where Picasso began. He first rendered the bull in intricate detail, then worked through multiple lithographs, systematically removing layers until only the essence remained. This process mirrors the way abstraction functions in insights work.

While the final result may appear simple, it cannot be arrived at through shortcuts.

> Often, people see an elegant solution and assume they can recreate it without working through the details. This is a mistake. Just as Picasso started with a highly detailed drawing before reducing it, meaningful abstraction requires first engaging deeply with the granular reality.

In our segmentation study, we spent three weeks observing 35 consumers ethnographically, analysing their responses in detail. From this, we identified key variables that captured their behaviours and incorporated them into a structured questionnaire. Over 900 consumers participated in the survey, and through multiple rounds of analysis – both statistical and conceptual – we refined our model. This rigorous process ensured that our final segmentation was not just simple but also retained the underlying nuances of reality.

Picasso[14] once said, *'There is no abstract art. You must always start with something. Afterwards, you can remove all traces of reality. There's no danger then, anyway, because the idea of the object would have left an indelible mark. It is what started the artist off, excited his ideas, and stirred up his emotions.'* His insight applies directly to the practice of abstraction in insights work.

Selectivity is equally crucial in abstraction. It is not merely about simplification but about choosing the right elements to retain – those that are less obvious yet meaningful in solving the problem. The most valuable insights come not from simply reducing complexity but from identifying the hidden patterns that truly matter. A strong abstraction should feel intuitive yet reveal something new – something that makes us think differently and compels action.

This ability to extract the essential dimensions of a situation is what makes abstraction insightful. In our segmentation example, we could have categorised consumers based on any number of variables – the climate of their city, the size of their home, or other lifestyle factors that shape climate control needs. The requirements of someone living in Phoenix, Arizona, would differ significantly from those of a resident in Chicago. Similarly, the climate control needs of a person in a New York flat are vastly different from those of someone living in a 10,000-square-foot house with a large garden in Austin. All of these were legitimate segmentation dimensions. However, abstraction requires us to move beyond what is merely descriptive towards what is insightful. Our goal was to identify the handful of factors that best explained customers' motivations for choosing the client's three climate control innovations. That is what made the abstraction useful – it was not just a reduction of complexity but a meaningful distillation that drove strategic decisions.

Good abstraction creates something simple without losing essential nuance, ensuring that the final insight remains actionable. It enables generalization without oversimplifying. An abstraction that is too broad becomes an 'under-fitted' pattern – one that lacks enough depth to be useful.

This skill is not just relevant in segmentation – it is fundamental across all aspects of insights work. Decoding the core values of a brand from a complex array of symbols, distilling a brand proposition into a succinct tagline, or simplifying a product's interface by reducing it to its most essential features – all require abstraction. Steve Jobs recognized this, which is why he famously used Picasso's *Bull* in Apple's internal training sessions[15], demonstrating the principle of reducing a product to its purest form. Abstraction is also at the heart of building and applying quantitative models, which, by their nature, are simplifications of reality.

### 4. *Analogizing*

One of the most powerful ways to unlock insight is through analogies. The very foundation of deep learning – neural networks – was inspired by the way humans acquire knowledge. Terrence J. Sejnowski[16], a pioneer in deep learning, describes how clues from the human brain guided the invention of neural networks: our ability to recognize patterns, our reliance on practice to master difficult skills, our struggle with following strict rules or logic, and the billions of neurons in our brains that constantly communicate. Unlike earlier AI systems that relied on predefined rules, deep learning mimics the way children learn – by observing and experiencing the world. The story of neural networks is just one example of how analogies and metaphors have led to breakthroughs in science, art, and business.

Just as neural networks were inspired by the human brain, another revolutionary breakthrough – CRISPR-Cas9[17] – was born from nature itself. Jennifer Doudna and Emmanuelle Charpentier, who won the 2020 Nobel Prize in Chemistry for their work on CRISPR-Cas9 gene-editing technology, found inspiration in an unlikely source: the adaptive immune system of bacteria and archaea. The way bacteria defend themselves against viruses provided the blueprint for a gene-editing system that has transformed biotechnology.

In business, searching for analogous situations can often provide the best insights. When our climate-control client developed a proprietary cooling technology, they wanted to know whether to allocate significant resources to branding the technology itself. We examined analogous cases – Teflon, Dolby, Shimano, and Intel – where ingredient branding had succeeded. In each case, the technology was already established as distinctive in the marketplace, and multiple manufacturers using the technology contributed to marketing efforts. Since these conditions did not apply to our client's situation, we recommended against this strategy.

Analogies can also help us reframe a problem. When working on a women's sexual health product, we discovered that gynaecologists were forming judgments about patients based on non-clinical factors – such as whether they were in a new relationship or had a high-profile job. This suggested that the brand's communication was reinforcing a narrow stereotype, limiting its appeal to a small segment of women. The situation reminded us of Dove's 'Real Beauty' campaign, which successfully challenged conventional beauty standards. Inspired by this analogy, our client used data from a quantitative survey to show gynaecologists that a far broader group of women suffered from the condition than they had assumed.

Thinking in analogies and metaphors is second nature to us. But for an analogy to be truly insightful, it must, as Robert and Michèle Root-Bernstein describe, '... recognize a correspondence of inner relationship or of function between two (or more) different phenomena or complex sets of phenomena.'[18] The best analogies do more than highlight surface-level similarities; they reveal deeper, hidden relationships that might otherwise go unnoticed. Whether predicting the future of a technology, repositioning a brand, or developing a breakthrough innovation, the ability to think analogically remains one of the most powerful tools in an insights professional's arsenal.

## 5. *Imaging*

Many iconic products began as a simple sketch. From the classic Coca-Cola[19] bottle to the modern iPhone[20], each was first imagined, then sketched, before being engineered into a final product. In insights projects focused on innovation, imaging is just as essential.

Imaging is often associated with artists, photographers, designers, and illustrators – professions where visualization is an explicit skill. However, visual thinking is not limited to these fields. We all engage in imaging daily, whether picturing a scene from a story, recalling a holiday described by a friend, or planning a future event. For insights professionals, imaging is crucial not only for visualizing ideas internally but also for communicating them effectively to others.

> A skilled visualizer can listen to customer insights, translate them into mental images, and then sketch product or service concepts that bring those insights to life. Refining visual representations of ideas and prototypes significantly enhances the innovation process, which is why imaging and sketching are integral to design.

In ethnographic research, we often use films and photographs to vividly capture the product-use environment. Sharing these with engineering and design teams allows them to visualize customers' lives and develop ideas suited to their context. Imaging also plays a key role in mapping out processes. During interviews, customers frequently describe their journey of purchasing and using a product.

Insights often appear as visions, where seemingly disconnected information suddenly forms a coherent picture. When I worked at Pepsi in India, our challenge was to grow the soft drinks category, particularly for in-home consumption. While analysing vast amounts of data, I struggled to piece together disparate insights – the role of different consumers, marketing messages, packaging, promotions, and retail channels. Then, one morning in an empty office, everything clicked. I suddenly saw a complete mental image of how these elements needed to work together to grow the home consumption market. This vision informed our strategy. Clearly, my brain had been processing the data subconsciously for weeks, and the final insight emerged as a clear picture rather than a step-by-step deduction.

Imaging is also a powerful tool in quantitative analysis. Sometimes, just by eyeballing a few data points, we can anticipate broader patterns. Today, we have an array of tools that help visualize insights drawn from both qualitative and quantitative data. By developing our own imaging skills, we can take fuller advantage of these tools. Consider *Anscombe's Quartet*[21] – four datasets that share the same statistical properties but, when visualized, reveal entirely different patterns. The summaries alone can be misleading; it is how we visualize them that reveals their true meaning.

Summary for the four data sets:

N = 11, Mean of Xs = 9.0, Mean of Ys = 7.5

Equation of regression line = 3 + 0.5X

Stand error of estimate of slope = 0.118

T = 4.24

Regression sum of squares = 27.50

Residual sum of squares = 13.75

Correlation coefficient = .82

$r^2$ = .67

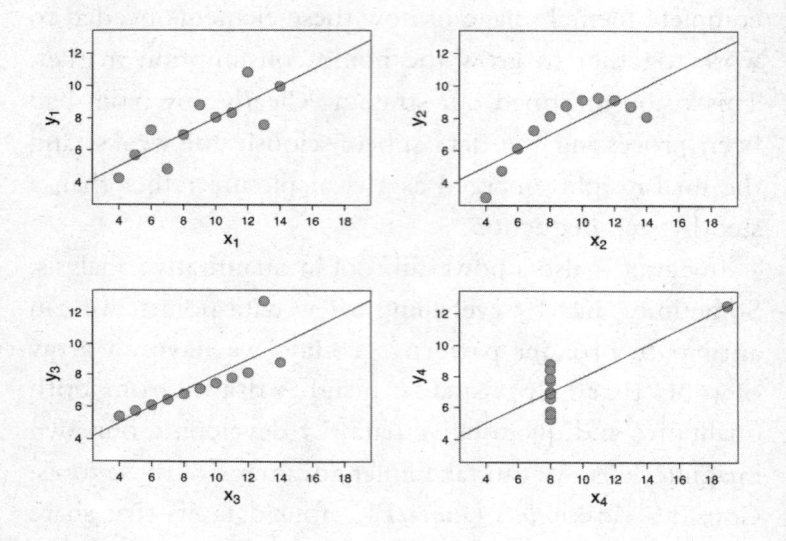

Beyond analysis, imaging plays a crucial role in performance. Sportspeople, actors, and dancers routinely imagine how their performance will unfold. Insights practitioners also engage in performance-based activities – conducting interviews, facilitating workshops, observing customers in their natural environment, and presenting findings. Visualizing how an interview might unfold – anticipating responses, participant engagement, or reactions to creative exercises – enhances research design and execution.

Perhaps one of the greatest benefits of imaging is in communicating insights. When presenting to clients, we often work with an expert sketch-note taker who visually maps insights in real time. By the end of the session, the client has not only heard the findings but also seen them come to life.

While imaging is a powerful tool, it must be used responsibly. As with abstraction and analogy, oversimplification can distort reality. Edward Tufte, in his book *Beautiful Evidence*[22], highlights common pitfalls in visualization – such as implying causation where none exists or selectively highlighting data to create a misleading narrative. For insight practitioners, this caution is especially important. Done well, imaging clarifies complex ideas, enhances communication, and unlocks new ways of thinking.

### 6. *Pattern recognition*

Patterns shape the way we function every day. They help us make sense of the chaotic mess of reality, guiding everything from our habits to our decision-making. We rely on patterns to predict, plan, and navigate the world efficiently. Given their significance in daily life, it might seem unnecessary to write about them explicitly. Yet, superior pattern recognition is highly valued across disciplines – whether in business, science, art, or sport – and is a defining trait of insightful thinkers.

In the world of customer insights, patterns are particularly valuable when they are hidden, unexpected, or reveal something new. Behavioural patterns – whether recurring within groups or individuals – help us understand how people interact with a product category and guide strategic decisions. Patterns can take different forms. The simplest type is the frequency of an occurrence within a population of interest. This becomes insightful when it is counterintuitive, challenges expectations, or leads to different strategic actions.

In the last chapter, we described how the market opportunity for a drug treating opioid side effects doubled when we discovered that physicians were also prescribing it for weak opioids. Simply quantifying the proportion of doctors who engaged in this unexpected behaviour revealed a much larger market potential than initially assumed.

A more complex pattern emerges when a relationship is identified between two or more variables. For example, an anecdote from Walmart[23] suggests that sales data revealed a surprising correlation between beer and diaper purchases. The explanation? Fathers, sent out to buy diapers, were treating themselves to beer at the same time. If true, this unexpected association could lead to tangible actions, such as placing beer near the diaper aisle to boost sales. Fortunately, Walmart collects vast amounts of purchase data, allowing them to test whether this pattern is real and whether marketing strategies based on this pattern are effective.

A hidden pattern can offer a significant competitive advantage. In our work on novel cancer treatments, conventional wisdom suggested that by the time patients reached third-line treatment – after failing two prior therapies – oncologists simply 'improvised'. It was assumed that no discernible treatment pattern existed, as physicians relied on their best judgment. However, our research uncovered a surprising insight. Rather than improvising, oncologists exhibited consistent, predictable behaviours shaped by the specific patient profile. Their treatment decisions were further guided by their overarching therapeutic mindset. 'Carers' prioritized quality of life, 'healers' focused on clinical efficacy, and 'innovators' pursued cutting-edge treatments. Recognizing this hidden pattern enabled our client to position their drug strategically, aligning with both the right patient types and physician mindsets.

Just as recognizing patterns can lead to breakthroughs, misidentifying them can lead to errors. False patterns, stereotypes, and cognitive biases can distort reality. We are prone to seeing connections where none exist, assuming randomness should be evenly distributed, or inferring causation from mere correlation. This challenge is particularly acute in qualitative research, where sample sizes are inherently small. Even with rigorous methodologies, the risk of drawing misleading conclusions remains. However, when applied carefully, pattern recognition remains one of the most powerful tools for generating insights, revealing hidden opportunities, and driving strategic action.

## Thinking by Doing

### 7. *Playing/improvising*

Playfulness and inventiveness are deeply intertwined. Musicians, jazz improvisers, and artists often create through play – exploring without rigid constraints and allowing unexpected ideas to emerge. Robert and Michèle Root-Bernstein[24] describe how various artists and scientists – including Alexander Fleming, Richard Feynman, Max Delbrück, and Escher – exhibited high degrees of playfulness, which translated into remarkable creativity in their work. Play is often pursued for enjoyment, without a clear goal, making it a natural enabler of serendipity – an essential ingredient for breakthrough insights.

While certain activities – such as brainstorming, concept development, and product prototyping – naturally benefit from playfulness, improvisation is valuable across all aspects of insights work. Whether analysing data, conducting qualitative research, or refining business strategies, a playful mindset fosters discovery and adaptability.

Experimentation in data analysis often leads to unexpected breakthroughs. In one project, we built a model to predict how likely women would be to purchase a new natural health product. A conventional approach would have been to use logistic regression – widely accepted for modelling binary outcomes – because of its simplicity and interpretability. However, my colleague, a curious learner, decided to experiment. Exploring different machine learning models, he discovered that a random forest algorithm revealed a hidden, non-linear pattern: moderate stress levels were associated with the highest likelihood of purchase, while those with either very low or very high stress were unlikely to buy.

This insight was surprising at first but became intuitive in hindsight. Further exploration revealed that women were using the product as a way to delay seeing a doctor – an unintended and potentially unhelpful behaviour. The non-linear relationship was quickly identified because my colleague enjoyed playing with different modelling techniques and had a habit of visually exploring data. The insight surfaced not through rigid adherence to standard practice but through curiosity-driven experimentation.

Improvisation is just as crucial in qualitative research. While conducting an interview to test a new technology concept, I noticed a sudden shift in the participant's attitude. He became highly critical, contradicting his earlier responses, and his body language changed – he leaned back, arms crossed in a defensive posture. As an interviewer, it was important to determine whether his critique stemmed from genuine concerns or was influenced by an emotional state. Instead of continuing with scripted questions, I improvised. I asked him to step over to a table and create a collage from magazine clippings that reflected his feelings toward the technology. The interactive nature of the task changed the dynamic. He became re-engaged and articulated both positive and negative views in a more thoughtful and balanced manner. This improvisation helped break his judgmental frame, leading to more authentic insights that would have been missed in a rigidly structured discussion.

One of the greatest values of playfulness, as noted in Chapter 4, is its ability to help us navigate uncertainty. Many insights projects involve working with incomplete information – our initial hypotheses often need to evolve as new findings emerge. Playfulness enables flexibility, allowing us to adapt dynamically. My background as a jazz piano student has reinforced a few key lessons that apply directly to problem-solving in insights. First, improvisation happens within a structure. Jazz musicians do not play randomly; they work within harmonic frameworks.

Likewise, in insights work, improvisation occurs within the structure of the problem. In the machine learning example, my colleague's experimentation with different models still adhered to statistical principles. The goal, the data, and the fundamental question remained unchanged – only the approach evolved. Second, one must master the rules before breaking them. Effective improvisation is not about disregarding structure but about understanding it deeply. Jazz musicians learn which notes fit harmonically and which create dissonance. Similarly, in insights work, one must first master the methodologies before intelligently deviating from them. The analyst who used random forest instead of logistic regression was still operating within the realm of supervised learning. Had he used an unsupervised method, such as k-means clustering, it would have been less suitable for the task. Finally, one must be comfortable with imperfection. When one improvises, mistakes are inevitable. The key is to embrace them rather than fear them. Often, what appears to be an error leads to creative breakthroughs. While conducting research on climate control devices, we accidentally recruited a professional installer instead of a regular consumer. Initially considered a mistake, this turned out to be a valuable opportunity – his expertise and deep customer interactions enriched our understanding of the market.

Improvisation also plays a crucial role in business strategy. In a study on pain medications, we were tasked with understanding how to improve the sales trajectory of a brand with low market share in Germany. As the study progressed, we noticed an interesting anomaly – the same product had been highly successful in the US. We decided to investigate further, despite the original project scope being limited to Germany. By interviewing leading physicians in the US, we uncovered a key driver of the product's success: it had been endorsed by cardiologists based on emerging evidence that it might be better for patients at risk of heart disease. This was an unexpected insight that had not been considered in the German market. While we did not have the budget to conduct a full-scale study in Germany, we formulated a hypothesis that cardiologist endorsement could influence adoption. This strategic improvisation – going beyond the initial research plan – generated a new direction for the brand's marketing strategy.

Improvisation is often seen as inefficient, but in reality, it creates space for unexpected insights and deepens our understanding. The ability to experiment, deviate from rigid processes, and adapt to new information is what separates routine analysis from breakthrough thinking. Whether in data science, qualitative research, business strategy, or the arts, the best insights often emerge from a combination of structure and play.

> As in jazz, good improvisation comes from knowing when to follow the rules – and when to break them.

## 8. *Modelling*

Models can be theoretical or representational, but in this section, I want to focus on the value of physical models in the insight development process. Physical models are widely used in science, design, architecture, sculpture, and the military. For insights professionals, modelling becomes particularly valuable because showing customers something tangible often reveals insights that would not emerge from verbal discussions alone. Among the many applications of modelling, prototyping is perhaps the most powerful for insights professionals. By building something tangible, we make our thinking concrete and test our assumptions in the real world. As discussed in Chapter 5, low-fidelity prototypes may be simple sketches, while high-fidelity prototypes closely resemble the finished product. There are many variants in between. Prototypes can be used to test nearly any product or service – whether a computer, phone, bank, or website. They are also valuable for communicating ideas. For example, pharmaceutical companies build models to illustrate a drug's mechanism of action.

Designers have a significant advantage over traditional market researchers when it comes to prototyping. Prototypes can take many forms – sketches, videos, paper mock-ups, or physical models. A growing range of tools enables rapid prototyping, but the core principle remains the same: quickly turn an idea into something tangible and gather customer feedback. By doing so, we identify blind spots early and at a low cost, making prototyping an invaluable tool for product development. Examples of innovations developed through prototyping abound. Any company renowned for its design excellence is also likely to excel at prototyping. The iPhone, Dyson vacuum cleaner, Post-it notes, and Tesla Roadster all went through extensive prototyping[25] before reaching the market. When we worked on climate control products, we uncovered far more than anticipated simply by showing prototypes to customers. For example, the material made the product look flimsy and not durable. The control panel was not well-lit, not intuitive, and the buttons didn't respond. The water tank was difficult to find, and water spilt when moving the product. The air throw was satisfactory indoors but ineffective outdoors. The aesthetic design didn't justify a premium price. Had these issues not been identified early, the product would likely have failed in the market. This highlights the importance of prototyping – not only to refine the product but also to avoid costly mistakes.

> Beyond gathering insights from customers, modelling offers additional benefits for insights professionals. First, working with our hands takes us out of an overly cerebral mode, stimulating creativity and fresh thinking – much like how playing with Lego or clay models sparked imagination in childhood.

Second, tangible outputs help align stakeholders within a company. When people can see and interact with a model, discussions become more concrete, and alignment is easier to achieve. Ultimately, modelling transforms abstract ideas into something real – helping both customers and organizations move from concept to action.

## TRAINING ON THE MODES OF THINKING

Having explored some of the essential modes of thinking, let's now consider how to improve them. Many of these skills develop naturally when one practises pragmatic polymathy, as discussed later in Chapter 8. In general, stimulating the brain in diverse ways – solving puzzles, doing crosswords, or learning new subjects such as languages – enhances our capacity to generate insights. However, there are also systematic ways to refine these modes of thinking. Two essential approaches to training can be particularly effective: the first involves expanding one's thinking by seeking inspiration from other disciplines, such as learning observation from detectives, artists, or photographers. The second focuses on developing these skills in the direct context of insights projects.

### Expanding Thinking through Other Disciplines

1. *Seeking Inspiration from Different Fields*

Learning directly from experts can provide deeper insight into the principles underlying each mode of thinking. For instance, to refine observation skills, one might seek guidance from a detective, a photographer or filmmaker, an artist, a writer, an anthropologist, or even a microbiologist. We once ran a session on observation using art and photography, where the participants were asked to recreate a specific shade of green using paints. This exercise made everyone realize how difficult accurate observation can be. They were also asked to take interesting photographs on their way to the office and explain what made each image compelling. After these warm-up exercises, they were trained in the principles of observation. A similar approach could be taken for listening, where musicians might serve as trainers.

Empathy, which is relevant in countless contexts, is approached differently across disciplines – anthropology, psychology, body language interpretation, cognitive neuroscience, communication, healthcare, mindfulness, and the arts, including creative writing and acting. We could deepen our understanding of empathy by taking separate courses. Personally, I have gained valuable insights into empathy through courses on non-directive executive coaching, mindfulness, and motivational interviewing. We could even attend or create a hybrid programme across disciplines. The Mayo Clinic[26], for example, runs a programme – aptly named the *Insights Series* – that incorporates theatre performances to help medical students develop empathy.

Any of the thinking modes can be developed through training programmes led by masters in their respective fields. Abstraction could be taught by mathematicians, physicists, abstract artists, poets, programmers, or designers – all of whom reduce complexity to its essence. Analogizing could be taught by polymaths, whose depth of knowledge in multiple fields makes them skilled at drawing connections. Pattern recognition and formation could be explored through mathematics, art, and music composition. Improvisation could be learnt from sketch notetakers, jazz musicians, and comedians. Modelling could be developed through sculptors and various craftsmen. In addition to structured training, reading books on these topics can be invaluable.

## 2. *Developing Skills through Hobbies*

Hobbies are powerful because they engage multiple modes of thinking simultaneously, often without conscious effort. A single hobby can develop a range of cognitive skills. For instance, playing jazz piano enhances listening skills, pattern recognition, abstraction, and improvisation. In a jazz piano transcription course, we listened to solos by famous pianists such as Keith Jarrett, played them on the piano, transcribed them onto sheet music, and analysed the patterns. My ability to hear and identify notes improved dramatically through this exercise. What struck me most was that even among professional pianists, there was uncertainty about the exact notes being played. Someone would claim to hear a faint F sharp, and after listening again, we would all hear it! This illustrated that no form of observation is easy, and there is always room for improvement.

Beyond listening, jazz musicians must also empathise with their fellow players to accompany them effectively. When soloing, they form patterns and improvise. Analysing a solo involves recognizing patterns and appreciating abstraction – Miles Davis[27], for instance, was known for his minimalist approach, distilling a tune to its essence. Similarly, writers train themselves to observe details in their surroundings and faithfully translate them into prose. They develop characters based on empathy and evoke empathy in their readers. They practise abstraction when crafting pithy sentences, employ metaphors and analogies to clarify ideas, and improvise as they refine their work. Sportspeople, too, engage in all these thinking modes. An ace batsman in cricket, for example, learns to see the ball as if through a magnifying glass, practises cognitive empathy by reading the bowler's intentions, visualizes field placements while planning a shot, improvises based on the game situation, and plays an unconventional stroke to secure the required runs.

Hobbies not only refine these skills but also make learning enjoyable, which accelerates the process. While we typically choose hobbies based on personal interest, we can also select them strategically to strengthen specific modes of thinking. If we want to improve modelling skills, for instance, building Lego structures can be a valuable exercise. Similarly, learning sketch note-taking can sharpen improvisational thinking.

### 3. *Sharpening Thinking with Puzzles and Paradoxes*

Solving puzzles and paradoxes sharpens our ability to reframe problems and challenge intuitive thinking. In Chapter 2, we noted that real-world insight problems are more complex than brain teasers, riddles, and puzzles. However, engaging with these regularly provides firsthand experience of the 'aha!' moment. Martin Gardner's *Aha! Insight*[28] is a collection of geometric, verbal, and procedural puzzles that are difficult to solve linearly but become easier once one grasps the underlying patterns. Similarly, counter-intuitive problems[29] like the Monty Hall Problem and paradoxes such as Simpson's Paradox teach us about flaws in our intuition.

For instance, the Monty Hall Problem presents a scenario where a contestant must choose one of three doors, behind one of which is a car. After selecting a door, the host – who knows what lies behind each – opens a different door to reveal a goat. The contestant must then decide whether to stick with their original choice or switch. The correct mathematical strategy is to switch, as it increases the probability of winning the car from one-third to two-thirds. This feels counterintuitive because it seems as though the two remaining doors should have equal odds, but in reality, the host's action of revealing a goat significantly alters the probabilities.

## Contextual Training: Applying These Modes in Insights Projects

### 4. *Classroom Training for Insights Professionals*

Classroom training focused on thinking tools should introduce principles and quickly move on to practical exercises. To train participants in observation, they might be shown the contents of a handbag and asked to infer the owner's attitudes. They could watch a video of a customer using a new phone and identify sources of frustration that the customer does not explicitly articulate. For empathy training, they might role-play as patients. For abstraction, they might be provided with extensive data and asked to construct a framework with only two dimensions to capture its essence. Another exercise might involve reviewing videos of customers making purchasing decisions in a retail store and distilling their decision-making process into a structured framework.

## 5. *On-the-Job Training and Practical Application*

The ultimate goal is for individuals to apply these thinking skills in their projects. Several key practices can facilitate this process:

- **Raising awareness of thinking modes** – Until these skills become second nature, deliberate practice is essential. Simply discussing the importance of observation, empathy, and abstraction at the start of a project can make a difference.

- **Establishing ways of working** – In qualitative research, we encourage team members to focus on what they see, hear, and feel without immediately jumping to conclusions. Similarly, in quantitative data analysis, we familiarise ourselves with the data first, browsing without a specific goal to allow ideas to emerge serendipitously.

- **Providing tools for creative thinking** – Supplying teams with resources such as Lego sets, journals, and coloured pens can encourage experimentation.

- **Coaching and feedback** – Constructive feedback is vital for refining how we deploy these modes of thinking. Working in teams helps avoid blind spots, challenge assumptions, and validate findings.

Having covered problem definition, methodology development, and different modes of thinking, we now turn to the five archetypes of unknowns. These represent some of the most challenging problems encountered in insights work. The ability to recognize, structure, and approach these unknowns effectively depends on how well we have trained ourselves in diverse modes of thinking. In the next chapter, we will explore how these thinking tools apply in practice, helping us navigate the uncertainties and complexities of real-world decision-making.

# 6

# Approaching the Five Archetypes of Unknowns

'There are three constants in life... change, choice, and principles[1].'

— **Stephen Covey**

I INTRODUCED THE FIVE ARCHETYPES OF UNKNOWNS IN Chapter 3. Solving these is immensely valuable for businesses. In Chapter 4, I described a general approach for dealing with unknowns; in this chapter I want to write about specific principles that are related to developing insight for each archetype of unknowns. For instance, using a bricolage of methods is generally good for all types of problems, but for preparing for the future, it is particularly useful. Similarly, all modes of thinking are relevant for each archetype. Yet, abstracting becomes especially useful for simplifying complexity. Therefore, I have highlighted it. The archetypes have been covered roughly in order of increasing complexity.

## REVEALING THE INVISIBLE IN A CONTEXT

Think back to the case example in Chapter 2, where we made an unexpected discovery: a segment of gynaecologists preferred natural products for treating menopausal symptoms – something our client had completely overlooked. This blind spot was not due to a lack of exposure. Most employees in the organization routinely interacted with gynaecologists as part of their jobs. However, they had formed an unquestioned assumption that medical professionals would be sceptical of natural treatments. In this context, that assumption was inaccurate. Their habitual ways of interacting had created a filter that prevented them from seeing the reality. It took our team – outsiders with fresh eyes and open-ended questions – to conduct ethnographic research and reveal this hidden reality.

### Making the Strange Familiar and the Familiar Strange

Anthropologists[2] often describe their role as making the strange familiar and the familiar strange. The first part – making the strange familiar – is intuitive. Imagine travelling to a distant country, immersing yourself in a new culture, and gaining an understanding of how people live. This deep knowledge often translates into business success. When PepsiCo entered India, for instance, its deep cultural understanding informed everything from advertising taglines and celebrity endorsements to its distribution strategy, allowing the brand to reach diverse town classes effectively.

What is less expected, however, is how often we fail to notice patterns hidden in plain sight, even in our own environments. This is where making the familiar strange becomes crucial. As discovered by Kahneman and Tversky[3], availability bias leads us to overestimate the likelihood of events that come easily to mind, distorting our perception of reality.

> Revealing what is truly happening in seemingly mundane situations is often the lowest-hanging fruit for insights professionals, yet it requires skilful observation.

Santosh Desai's book[4], *Mother Pious Lady: Making Sense of Everyday India*, is a masterclass in cultural observation. As I browsed through it, I was immediately captivated. The details evoked deeply buried memories, and the interpretations were both humorous and profound. One passage describes the ritual of families insisting on a 'just two-line postcard' confirming safe arrival – despite a large group of relatives seeing the traveller off, double-locking metal suitcases, and counting luggage pieces multiple times. The deeper insight is that the Indian psyche is shaped by a profound fear of separation, echoed in mythology and family structures. This is an example of making the familiar strange – turning an ordinary detail into a powerful cultural insight.

The actual distinction between strange and familiar is not always black and white in business contexts. When the anthropologist Margaret Mead[5] visited Samoa in the South Pacific, she was studying a culture that, as an American, may have felt distinctly 'strange'. However, in commercial insights work, the boundary between what is strange and what is familiar is often blurred.

Consider an ethnographic study I conducted in Chicago. I was staying at a downtown hotel and took an Uber for my first interview, which was 15 minutes away. Just before reaching the destination, the driver remarked, 'I hope you know someone here – this is the most dangerous neighbourhood in Chicago.' The woman I was interviewing had asked me to meet her at the local library, which had initially seemed like an odd choice; now, I understood why. Inside the library, I noticed a sign prohibiting guns. The experience was surreal but provided powerful insights. In large metropolitan areas like New York, London, Gurugram, or Paris, the character and culture can shift dramatically within just a few streets. Even within a single apartment building, the lives of people living there can be vastly different, yet we often fail to notice these hidden contrasts.

Regardless of whether we are making the strange familiar or the familiar strange, the overarching principle is to remain open-minded. The following approaches can be particularly useful.

## 1. Open-ended framing of questions

When attempting to uncover the invisible, it is essential to ask open-ended questions that encourage exploration and discovery. Suspending strong, hypothesis-driven questions allows for greater flexibility. When we were commissioned to develop the marketing strategy for three high-end climate control devices, our research effort began with broad questions such as:

- What are the needs of customers regarding climate control?
- How do these needs vary by context?

For many experienced insights professionals, such open-ended questions might seem naïve, even vague. However, questions framed in this way acknowledge a state of not knowing and foster the curiosity of a beginner. While hypotheses can be useful for ensuring actionability, in discovery-driven projects, it is important to hold them lightly. For instance, when we explored climate control needs, our broad questions led participants to describe areas in their homes where cooling solutions were inadequate, which would have been missed had we asked narrow, assumption-driven questions about room temperature preferences. As we learnt more, our questions became sharper and more hypothesis-driven.

## 2. Being an insider and an outsider

To shed light on the invisible, we need to engage with people who are part of the culture. At the same time, cultural norms often operate implicitly, making them difficult for insiders to articulate. This is where an outsider's perspective becomes invaluable. Insiders provide depth, but outsiders notice what has been normalised.

In a study on cultural archetypes, researchers Anjali Puri and Poonam Kumar[6] interviewed 'resident outsiders' – expats living in India – to uncover implicit cultural patterns. Similarly, commercial insights teams can balance insider knowledge with an outsider's ability to see what has been taken for granted. Involving cultural experts, semioticians, and ethnographers who can mimic an outsider's perspective can help highlight these blind spots.

Neerja Wable[7] shared a compelling insight based on her extensive international experiences. She cautioned against the common tendency to only focus on differences when working across diverse countries. Emphasizing the importance of identifying similarities, she argued that recognizing these commonalities and building empathy are essential for developing successful global brands.

## 3. Using methods that get us close to the context

To spot the invisible in a context, research should be conducted as close to the real environment as possible. Interviewing someone about their exercise routine in a focus group setting can yield useful insights, but observing them in a gym will reveal much more. If participants are asked to perform tasks – such as running on a treadmill or lifting weights – nuanced insights emerge.

While conducting ethnography for developing sports equipment, we discovered that users wanted focus-enhancing features for weight training but wanted to 'escape' during cardiovascular exercises. These findings were taken into account while designing the products. The elliptical machine, for example, was invented when Larry Miller[8] observed his daughter running and was inspired by the smooth, elliptical motion of her legs.

Similarly, in the study on climate control devices, we conducted ethnography for three weeks via the internet. Participants kept diaries and recorded videos of their homes, documenting their climate control needs. The research revealed 'dead spaces' – rooms such as home offices, studies, and exercise rooms, where air conditioning was inadequate, making them uncomfortable in summer. There were also outdoor situations, such as barbecues or gardening in the heat, where cooling solutions failed.

As evident from Santosh Desai's work, a semiotic lens can reveal unobvious insights. One example that Santosh[9] mentioned to me was that of Tanishq, a jewellery brand in India. At the time of Santosh and his team's involvement, Tanishq was a strong brand. However, it had not cracked the traditional jewellery market. People went to Tanishq for trinkets such as earrings, but not for wedding sets. Or they went to Tanishq if they were migrants in a city, so they did not know the traditional jewellers. The brand was characterised as a fashion brand that was led by design. Santosh and his team spoke to mythologists and jewellery historians and uncovered two crucial insights. The first insight was that in India, jewellery is about culture, not fashion. Santosh said, 'Fashion codes lead you astray. Fashion is about distinctiveness, about the individual coming first.' The second insight was that if you wanted to change something in India, you had to be an insider. So, the strategy recommended was to take traditional motifs and cultural ideas and infuse them with a sense of newness. The Tanishq team took the recommendations on board and changed the designs and names of products and launched a campaign with the tagline 'new tales of tradition'.

## 4. Being good at observing, empathizing, and abstracting

Whilst all thinking modes are relevant, being able to see and hear what is not obvious, feeling deep empathy for people, and being able to abstract are particularly important. Training to see and pick up cues in the context requires sharp observation. For instance, surveys often show that a high proportion of consumers are willing to pay for environmentally friendly products. That was an assumption that we had before we did our study. However, even before asking people, when one sees how people live and use energy, one gets a more realistic idea about their views about the subject. Empathy is another core skill since the point of such exercises is to create solutions that are in line with how people live. For instance, it is easy to be judgmental about a couple living in a house with an area of 10,000 square feet who have air conditioning switched on for the entire house 24/7. Yet, with cognitive empathy, one appreciates that they have always lived like that. Furthermore, they needed help in visualizing an alternative solution. When we conduct ethnography, we want to capture reality in its raw form. We encounter a barrage of unstructured stimuli. But to make sense, we need to move beyond the specifics to something generalizable. This requires abstracting. For instance, the notion of 'dead spaces' is an abstraction.

## 5. Communicating the richness while ensuring generalizability

Having discovered something invisible such as 'dead spaces' in US homes where people need a product or a hidden pattern that gynaecologists prefer natural products, one needs to communicate the findings in intricate detail. Using films, pictures, and raw material from projective techniques helps to ensure that the business leaders get close to a first-hand feel of the customer experience. The findings must also be generalizable. In ethnographic work, there is a great risk of 'over-fitting' where we describe the fine nuances of one specific customer that may not be generalizable at all. Quantitative research, informed by qualitative research, helps us achieve that.

## MAKING A CREATIVE IDEA RELEVANT

Throughout this book, we've explored how insights fuel innovation. But what about making an existing creative idea truly compelling for its intended audience? As insights practitioners, we're often tasked with assessing whether an idea – a new product, an advertisement, or a campaign – will succeed. Creativity delivers great returns on investment, and by helping bring creative ideas successfully to market, insights professionals add immense value. Take Pepsi's *Nothing Official About It!* campaign, for example. It showcased cricket stars in vibrant, playful settings – breaking away from the traditional image of cricket as a gentleman's game played in all whites. The campaign outperformed expectations. As PepsiCo India's insights lead, I rigorously tracked consumer metrics. Despite a significantly lower budget, Pepsi outperformed Coke on every measure. In an era when the internet was still nascent, the campaign went viral.

Yet, testing new ideas is not easy. Most of us struggle to recognize the value of a new idea. History is filled with groundbreaking innovations – like radars, digital cameras, and statins – that were initially dismissed. Safi Bahcall[10] coined the term *loonshots* to describe these big ideas that changed the world but had to endure multiple rejections before gaining acceptance.

This raises a critical question: Should companies ask consumers what they want?

## To ask or not to ask consumers

Many legendary business leaders are sceptical about relying on consumer feedback for innovation. Steve Jobs[11] famously argued that customers can only articulate what they already know, which is why he distrusted traditional market research.

Similarly, Nvidia founder Jensen Huang[12] ignored his customers when they asked the company *not* to double the speed of its graphics processors each year. Instead, Nvidia followed Moore's Law, believing that demand for 3D graphics would be insatiable – and they were right.

Nike's *Just Do It* slogan[13] provides another example. Inspired by the last words of a convicted criminal (*Let's do it.*), the tagline was launched on a leap of faith despite mixed opinions. Decades later, it remains one of the most powerful brand slogans in history.

However, while some of the most innovative ideas were launched without consumer validation, they all succeeded because they resonated deeply with their audience.

Even Steve Jobs, despite his disdain for market research, followed *The Apple Marketing Philosophy*,[14] developed by his mentor, Mike Markkula. The philosophy emphasized three points – the first was *empathy*, the ability to truly understand the customers' needs better than others, the second was *focus* so that they could eliminate anything that was unimportant, and the third was *impute*, which refers to the idea that every aspect of an Apple product, from its design and packaging to its marketing and customer service, communicates something important to the customer.

Nike's success, too, was rooted in its deep connection with athletes. Whether companies consult consumers directly or not, true insight into their lives increases the likelihood of creative success.

In general, the more innovative an idea, the harder it is for customers to imagine its value. In such cases, relying on futurists, early adopters, or highly creative consumers may be more effective than traditional research methods. Even when speaking to regular consumers, the goal should be to uncover *latent* needs – not simply to ask for their opinions.

## Two cultures

Often there is an adversarial relationship between industries that are seen as creative, e.g., advertising, and those that are seen as analytical, e.g., market research agencies. The source of the frustration for creative teams can sometimes be the tendency of customer insights people to reduce the appeal of creative ideas to responses to sets of simple questions while assuming the answers are sacrosanct. Customer Insights people might have the point of view that creative individuals are too detached from the target audience's preferences and needs.

The stereotype for market research groups is that they follow a linear, rational, evidence-based approach that relies on reductive methodologies and quantitative metrics seeking objectivity. The culture at creative agencies is stereotyped as non-linear, emotional, imaginative, non-rigorous, subjective, and more oriented towards qualitative work. The reality is more nuanced, and there is tremendous potential for great collaborations.

## Creativity at tension with business objectives

Creative ideas can emerge from various sources:

- A deep consumer insight (*e.g., Uber[15] – solving the pain of finding a taxi*)
- A technological breakthrough (*e.g., Google's search algorithm[16]*)
- A new business model (*e.g., Dell's direct-to-consumer strategy[17]*)

Regardless of the starting point, creativity must align with an organization's strategic goals. There is a school of thought that creative professionals, e.g., R&D teams or advertising creative teams, must be insulated from the harsh realities of business, as those could inhibit the flow of wild ideas. Often, scientists and engineers work in separate units. This is done to ensure a greater likelihood of generating breakthrough ideas through working in an environment that is more conducive to innovation. However, they may be far removed from the lives of customers and business strategy. This creates tension. As I am writing these lines, Apple is facing a major backlash from many quarters[18], including Hollywood, its strong franchise, for the dystopian 'crush' advertisement that shows a hydraulic press smashing musical instruments, including a guitar and a piano. This depiction of technology winning over human creativity is both a departure from Apple's brand strategy, which has creativity in its DNA. Apple has issued an apology for the advertisement.

There are substantial differences between the exact mechanics of testing a new product versus an advertisement; I have attempted to put down a few higher-order principles on how insights practitioners can add value.

1. **Being a bridge-builder with a focus on execution**

When I spoke with Vibha Rishi about PepsiCo's 'Nothing Official About It' campaign, what struck me was the number of hidden drivers of success[19].

- The birth of the campaign came as a response to a real obstacle. Vibha, the CEO, P.M. Sinha, and others in the Pepsi team recognized that having lost the sponsorship for the World Cup, a guerrilla marketing campaign was required.

- While it appears that the main story about the campaign is the brilliance of the creative idea, Vibha revealed that there was an equally powerful story about the use of media. Coke had struck a worldwide deal with ESPN, yet in India the most watched media channel was Doordarshan, India's national channel, which Coke ignored. Because of Coke's focus on ESPN, Pepsi had managed to proactively secure a favourable deal with Doordarshan. Through a series of negotiations and twists, Pepsi doubled the amount of television time for the same budget. Having access to such a lot of media time spurred Pepsi to come up with more creative executions.

- Vibha brought along a diverse set of people from within and outside Pepsi to make the campaign unfold flawlessly. She had meetings with Doordarshan, involved P.M. Sinha, the then Pepsi India CEO, in the negotiations, convinced the international team of Pepsico about the value of the campaign, and interacted with the ad agency. According to her, the creative part was easy because Anuja Chauhan came up with the winning idea after reading the brief, and that set the direction of the campaign.

Vibha, in this context, was a bridge-builder, engaging many people to ultimately make the campaign unfold flawlessly. This is an important lesson for any person who wants creative work to 'land' with people. It is easy to focus on the idea exclusively and to ignore the required collaboration between diverse groups.

The easiest way to break siloed thinking is to set up a small cross-functional team that works throughout a project. Thoughts related to strategy, insight, creativity, and execution flow seamlessly, connections are made, and the process moves along nicely. Also, small teams have skin in the game. They own the success of the innovation and commit to making it work. They are not detached observers.

John Copeland,[20] speaking of a branding boutique where he worked, emphasized the value of diverse skill sets: '*M was super right brain, incredibly creative... he would bring a very out-of-the-box way of thinking..., he would take it all the way to execution. You'd have to back him up, and then you could see the dots connect... that's really cool – there's value in bringing together someone who's super creative and super analytical, and we understood each other's roles.*'

In almost all my projects, I facilitate a series of workshops working between creative teams, e.g., designers/engineers/advertising creatives, and clients' commercial and technical teams. This is a practical way to become a bridge-builder.

## 2. Eliciting insight to connect with customers

Whether you do formal market research or not, you must attempt to build a relationship with the customers. Even if it's for a brief period, as is the case with many ads that have a short-term goal, forming a real connection increases the likelihood of success. Certain considerations to achieve this are outlined below:

### *A holistic view of customers*

The idea must reflect an insight into how people think, feel, and behave. What are their latent needs? What are their aspirations? What are they struggling with? How do they make decisions? How do they interact with their environment?

The questions don't have to be exhaustive and often will depend on the specific idea. For instance, in the

Pepsi campaign, there was a single, simple, and yet powerful insight. It was that 'official' in India had negative connotations. It was seen as boring and bureaucratic. Vibha[21] said to me, 'We told Anuja that this veneration of officialdom is contra to the youth, especially to Indians who had just emerged from the darkness of an over-officious government. What she came back with was a press ad. You could see how it could spin into a thousand different things... That got approved right away.' The Dove 'Real Beauty' campaign reflected a deeper and more holistic insight, in line with the longer-term business objectives of building the brand. Many product innovations are a result of looking at customers' holistic needs. Intuit's Quicken[22] was based on the insight that small business owners are not accountants and need a simpler set of features.

### Emotions, 'moments of truth', experiential benefits, and blind spots

Whilst testing ideas related to novel ads or products, emotional responses really matter. Mostly, these responses can be inferred from the body language of the respondents– they might laugh, get excited, look bored, or be irritated. They might make interesting gestures. When the Pepsi 'Nothing Official About It' ads were tested, it evoked laughter and mirth, and those were great signs about the receptivity of the audience. Even when we did quantitative research for Pepsi ads, we found that the best predictor of the ad's success was a metric that measures the extent to which someone liked the ad, called the 'likeability score'.

What must be avoided is giving consumers the role of an evaluator. That makes them either hyper critical, finding faults with random things, or sometimes they attempt to ingratiate themselves by praising everything about the idea.

One of the main benefits of testing novel ideas with customers is to understand what really sparks an insight amongst customers or what creates a 'moment of truth'. We were testing alternative mechanisms to explain to doctors how a particular drug worked. Across our qualitative sample, we found that doctors expressed their preference for one particular mechanism, gesticulating with their hands to indicate a wave and saying, 'I like the way this new drug builds the tissues like a wave.' This subtle movement was more telling than anything else that the doctors said. The campaign was launched. During in-depth interviews conducted after the launch, we discovered that most doctors mentioned that the conviction in the drug came from the 'miraculous' way it helped to build the tissue, once again mimicking a wave with their hands. Learning this, the salespeople spoke more about the mechanism in their calls, leading to greater success. For new products, ethnographic research reveals the experiential benefits for users. Often, instead of benefits, we discover blind spots. When we tested the climate control devices in the US, customers consistently said they would reject a product they liked a lot simply because there was no way to store the filter. That was great feedback for the design team.

## *Creative diversity, rapid prototyping, and iteration*

Often an idea needs to be explored through many executions. Customers cannot grasp the idea in its abstract form. The more executions one tests, the higher the likelihood of achieving a breakthrough. Iteration is essential, especially in the early stages of exploring the idea. The cost is low, and the value is huge.

## *Customer segmentation*

This is an overlooked aspect in assessing creative work. People have different drivers in terms of what appeals in relation to new ideas. Innovations should either be created with a clear segment in mind, or during post-hoc analysis, one must attempt to detect the variation in responses by segments. The absence of that can create a product that is sub optimal for everyone. There are rare situations, such as the development of smartphones, which provide a universal benefit and appeal to broad groups of people. In our case of climate control devices, the needs of the 'Chic and Connected' segment were very different from those of the 'Tech-savvy group', requiring different product features.

## 3. Seeking insights from creative professionals and intermediaries

Customers are central to an innovation. However, there are many other sources of insight. For someone writing a book proposal, it is very helpful to gain insights not only from the ultimate reader but from other authors, publishers, and agents. The lived experiences of each of these stakeholders are valuable for providing insight about readers. The analogy holds across industries. If you are an entrepreneur about to start your own tech company, speaking to VCs, other entrepreneurs, and tech experts can improve your chances of success. In the book *The Cooking of Books* Ramachandra Guha[23] gives numerous examples where his editor, Rukun Advani, transformed his writings into something more insightful and beautiful.

## 4. Leading with qualitative methods with selective use of quantitative research

As might be obvious from the discussion above, exploring ideas needs a lot of interaction and experimentation. Qualitative research is highly suited to such work because, by its very nature, it allows for greater subjectivity, flexibility and adaptation, which are essential for testing creative ideas. The techniques might vary; in certain cases, creative focus groups might be more appropriate, e.g., while evaluating an advertising tagline, and in others, ethnography, e.g., for testing a product. In either case, leading with qualitative research is a good idea. On the other hand, for sizing the market and optimising the product, e.g., prioritising between product features or determining prices, quantitative research is required.

## 5. Valuing creative judgment and intuition

Having done all the groundwork with customers, final decisions must be taken by leaders who understand the business and have good intuition. It could be a group of seasoned leaders, e.g., a marketing leader, an agency head, a design leader, or an entrepreneur. If someone has created many products or advertisements or companies and has lived with the consequences of their successes and failures, their intuition in such situations will be acute. Besides, they will understand the context of the business fully and consider all the subtle factors that are relevant. As I have argued, customers are not the best evaluators, even if their input is crucial. Jensen Huang spoke to his customers, considered their views, and decided to ignore them, ironically for their own good. That, too, is an insight-driven strategy. Customer research must be done for 'disaster-checks' or guarding against blind spots. We must acknowledge the difficulty in evaluating creative work and respect the judgment of seasoned professionals.

# CHANGING DEEPLY ENTRENCHED BEHAVIOURS

For most organizations, changing the behaviour of customers or other stakeholders is necessary for success. Apple is persuading iPhone users to upgrade or convincing Android users to switch. Amazon works to shift purchases online, while Costa Coffee aims to gain market share of the in-home consumption market. Beyond commerce, behaviour change is a core challenge in public health, sustainability, and social policy, encouraging people to eat healthier, exercise more, quit smoking, or adopt eco-friendly habits.

In recent years, behavioural sciences – drawing from behavioural economics, psychology, and neuroscience – have gained prominence in business. However, behaviour change is an age-old challenge, studied across multiple fields, from education and sports psychology to health interventions and wellbeing practices like yoga. Any approach benefits from integrating principles from these disciplines.

I had the opportunity to cofound the patient behaviour change service line at McKinsey & Company, working on projects related to smoking cessation, obesity management, healthcare utilization, and medication adherence. At Insight Dojo, I have continued this work. For instance, in Chapter 3, I discussed a project where we helped a private girls' school increase uptake of Physics as an A-level subject. In another case, we worked to change the behaviour of US oncologists who had stopped considering Radio Immunotherapy (RIT) for cancer treatment due to previous bad experiences.

Over the course of my work, I have reviewed theories, tested frameworks, and refined methodologies[24]. The following principles offer practical insights into changing 'sticky' behaviours in business and beyond.

## 1. Appreciating that behaviour change is a journey, not an event

It is important to acknowledge that change, mostly, does not happen overnight. Usually, people must first form an intention, then prepare to take actions, act to change behaviour, and then maintain it. There might be relapses along the journey if the change is particularly difficult. For instance, consider the journey of a smoker to quitting. Initially, they may have no intention to quit. They might eventually decide to give up smoking for a variety of reasons – a health condition, having a child, or a desire to do more sport. After that they might start acting on the intention, e.g., by going to a counsellor, getting information about nicotine patches, and eventually, they might quit. Or they may relapse and, after a few attempts, eventually succeed.

There is a model called the 'Transtheoretical Model' that captures such an approach in five stages – precontemplation, contemplation, preparation, action, and maintenance. Of course, this journey might be far more compressed. For instance, switching to a smartphone might take just one good experience to effect the change. In this case, the change is a single event and not a journey. But, in most cases, it is helpful to think of the change in terms of a journey for an insights project.

## 2. Inspiring the willingness to change

We see many services for changing behaviours, such as helplines designed to support those who want to quit smoking. Unfortunately, that leaves out a large proportion of people who will never pick up the phone because they have no intention of changing.

> Creating willingness is fundamental to effecting behaviour change. Many theories argue that a person's intention to act is the most important predictor of subsequent behaviour.

Therefore, it is essential to dig deep into what might inspire someone to begin the change journey. Often it is a slow process. At other times, it is a single experience that helps form the intention. Sometimes, the shift in intention may be a result of a change in life stage – getting a new job, getting married, or having a child. These types of events often serve as a 'wake-up' call to stop smoking.

When we were doing the work for the girls' school, we discovered a group of girls who were clear that they wanted to do physics because they would do engineering or a degree in physics. This group did not need any change in their behaviour. There were others who were passionate about art and found anything scientific less interesting. Again, there was no need to change their behaviour. However, there was a group in the middle who wanted to pursue social sciences in the university but loved solving problems in physics. It was this group, whom we called 'cross-pollinators', that we believed could be encouraged to take up physics. Often, girls in this group were unsure about how having physics as an A-level subject would affect their chances of getting admission for a social science degree. Helping them see that, far from being a barrier, the choice of physics could be seen as a strength was useful in having them consider the subject. Furthermore, there are courses that are more interdisciplinary in nature that would be in line with the needs of this group of girls. Providing such information was valuable for the cross-pollinators to consider physics as a choice for A-levels.

## 3. Focusing on four critical drivers of change

There are many factors that affect the behaviour change journey. I have listed four main drivers of change that are particularly important.

a. Benefit of change: We need to see the value of the change in their lives. In the case of the oncologists willing to consider radioimmunotherapies, the benefit was having satisfied patients; in the case of the 'cross-pollinator' girls, it was the enjoyment of problem-solving in physics without compromising the possibility of getting admission into the college of their choice; for the smokers, it could have been any number of benefits – better health, and being a better parent, being productive at work.

b. Losses due to change: Understanding what we give up because of our change in behaviour is essential. That is what gets in the way of change. The 'cross-pollinator' girls would have to give up some of their leisure time if they perceived that physics needed more time, being a difficult subject. For smokers, it could be giving up on rituals for relieving stress or giving up the benefit of a social activity with friends.

c. Ease of change: Self-efficacy, or one's perception of one's ability to change, is another important factor that is backed by a lot of evidence. Many clever girls, for instance, would simply lack confidence about doing well in physics, despite their teachers rating them highly. Similarly, there are smokers who would simply say they do not have the willpower. Providing support and structures to minimise effort becomes critical for changing behaviour. Many of the 'nudge'-based interventions are designed to make it easy for people to change. For instance, automatic enrolment into savings accounts has significantly increased employee contributions to savings simply by making contributions to savings a default option.

d. Social norms: We are strongly influenced by people around us and the norms of society. With the advent of social media, this phenomenon has become more prominent and explains the role that influencers play in our society. Even amongst physicians, we see that shared norms drive a lot of their prescription behaviour.

## 4. Recognizing the emotional nature of people's decision-making

We use many heuristics to make decisions which are not entirely rational. We prioritize short-term benefits and discount long-term dangers, e.g., the enjoyment of smoking versus the likelihood of getting cancer. We suffer from loss aversion, being far more concerned about losses, rather than gains, from a behaviour change. We seek choices that are convenient even if they are less than ideal on other dimensions. These seemingly 'irrational' heuristics must be understood well to design a behaviour change programme.

## 5. Segmenting people based on motivations and barriers to change

Many behaviour change interventions are not successful because they are designed to effect change amongst an entire population. People vary tremendously in terms of their drivers and barriers to change. For instance, for smoking cessation[25], we discovered that there was a 'hedonist' segment that sees smoking as an enjoyable activity and had no intention of changing. On the other hand, there was another segment which kept trying and failing and had no confidence to bin their ability to quit. Similarly, in the case of the girls' school, we found that there was a 'die-hard physics' segment, a 'cross-pollinator', and an 'artsy' segment. Whilst there can be certain interventions that work for all segments, there are others that need to be tailored to the specific facilitators and barriers of each segment.

## 6. Using ethnography, deep interviews, experiments and surveys to elicit insight

A combination of techniques is required for behaviour change. Ethnographic work helps us observe unconscious and in-context behavioural patterns, deep interviewing uncovers motivations and barriers, experiments allow testing of different interventions, and quantitative research to help identify and size segments

## 7. Designing interventions based on insight, evidence, and experimentation

First-hand insights that help us understand customers are powerful in creating change programmes. Equally, examining successful interventions in analogous situations can offer valuable insights. Running experiments allows one to fine-tune and refine these actions.

For instance, for smoking cessation, we were addressing a segment of smokers who were very hard to change. We reviewed the literature and found that general physicians (GPs) and nurses were successful in getting smokers to quit when they had brief conversations with their patients using an approach called 'motivational interviewing'[26]. It is a technique that involves empathetic listening, asking questions that make the person reflect on their behaviour, and gently nudging them towards the insight that might make a person want to change their behaviour.

Based on this, we created a motivational interviewing training programme for doctors and nurses that was tailored to the hard-to-change smoker segments that we had identified, since GPs and nurses were already doing it successfully. We piloted this programme and then refined it. The first-hand insight enriched the evidence-based intervention, which was further improved by piloting. In general, any behaviour change programme must be multi-pronged – it should provide a compelling narrative for change, create support and systems to make change easy, engage influencers to create a supportive social norm, and provide incentives to reaffirm positive change. All of these interventions must be designed considering the facilitators for change, and the barriers to change for each segment.

## The Kumbaya story[27]

On one of my field trips with my sister into the heartlands of Madhya Pradesh, India, she walked me through Kumbaya, a social enterprise that empowers women and people with disabilities through the art of stitching. Today, it is a well-known brand working on sustainable fashion and conscious design, retailing across India and manufacturing for designers in England, Germany, the Netherlands, Sweden, and Australia.

Kumbaya was started in 1994 by Nivedita Banerji, a founding member of Samaj Pragati Sahayog, one of India's largest grassroots organizations. In the communities they worked with, women were vital to the household's survival – cooking, collecting firewood, and tending livestock – but they remained invisible in decision-making. Any conversation about welfare was held with men. The first epiphany came when, as part of a watershed project, women started coming to the construction site in large numbers. For the first time, they could get regular work close to their homes and were paid wages equal to that of men. But even at these sites, it was unsettling to witness the gruelling manual labour that women had to do. At this point, Nivedita was actively looking for a solution that gave women economic stability. She also wanted to facilitate conversations amongst women on important issues such as health and land rights. Then a group of women visited Nivedita and her colleague, Shubha Pande, and seeing some patchwork in their home, the women asked to learn stitching. So they borrowed a few machines and began stitching.

The seemingly innocuous act of stitching became radical as it came face-to-face with patriarchal social norms. Men were angry that women were being taught how to stitch instead of the men doing this. They spoke disparagingly about the competence of women, especially about their ability to work with sewing machines. Women also had to make the time and be away from home to be available to learn stitching.

A critical challenge was building the self-efficacy of women. The women come from predominantly agrarian rural regions of India, where there were no traditional marketable crafts or any history of manufacturing. What was the best way to teach women who were used to moving all the time, from forest to field with headloads of firewood or fodder, to sit still and master the art of stitching? What products should be designed that were simple for them to make but could sell for high prices in urban markets? How could their confidence be strengthened? Through this period, the progress of women challenged the nexus of power and the patriarchy. In fact, their work shed was burnt down as the organization began gaining momentum. Yet, seeing that the income that the women were generating uplifted their households, the attitudes of the men began to change from antagonism to support.

Today over 100 women from marginalized communities are shareholders who own and work in Kumbaya Producer Company Limited, where employment is guaranteed for 300 days a year. Nothing is considered waste at Kumbaya. It sources fabric responsibly, uses dead stock, discarded by industrial fabric units, and buys hand-woven and other artisanal cotton fabric made by skilled master craftspeople across the country. Kumbaya specializes in crafting beautiful patchwork with every bit of waste leftover from production, revives unsold stock by stitching it into something else, and creates sustainable clothing using waste material from other allied industries as well.

The annual turnover exceeds $100,000. Kumbaya continuously works on skill development and has taught stitching to over 2500 women from 100 villages in the area. Many of these women have been able to use this skill from home to earn money as tailors in the local market. Most of these women had never stitched a garment before.

The Kumbaya Story was important to share because it's about transformation, and it highlights all the lessons we need to bear in mind while changing behaviour – having a long-term view, creating inspiration to change, overcoming obstacles, building self-efficacy, changing social norms, experimenting, building an immersive working style, etc. It made me think that businesses can learn from social enterprises about creating long-lasting change.

## PREPARING FOR THE FUTURE

In Chapter 2, we noted that one of the top concerns for CEOs is uncertainty about the future. Business leaders must make critical strategic decisions despite limited knowledge into what lies ahead. While forecasting models work well for stable, predictable environments, they become far less reliable when facing disruptive market forces, evolving technologies, or regulatory changes.

An insights practitioner, trained in diverse thinking skills, a wide range of methodologies, and the ability to process different forms of data, can help business leaders navigate uncertainty. By identifying key decisions, analysing trends, and building strategic scenarios, they can provide clarity where others see ambiguity, enabling leaders to make better-informed decisions.

Let us consider a few typical business situations involving different levels of uncertainty:

a. A soft drinks company launches a new flavour in an established and growing market. What will the sales be in the following year?

b. A biotech company has an innovative treatment for metastatic cancer that is to be administered immediately after surgery. Should it enter the market at all? The company's internal oncologists are sceptical about the number of surgeries being conducted and uncertain about whether their treatment should replace or complement a heated chemotherapy that is currently given to patients immediately after surgery. The company must determine how to position its drug, given a recent controversial trial questioning the efficacy of heated chemotherapy.

c. An insights and analytics firm faces the rise of generative AI. With predictions ranging from AI replacing human insights work entirely to views that these fears are vastly exaggerated, how should the firm prepare for the future?

As we move from Situation A to C, the degree of uncertainty increases dramatically. Each scenario requires different approaches to insight development – from traditional forecasting models to strategic scenario planning and horizon scanning.

The customer insights industry is good at dealing with Situation A. However, senior leaders are more likely to be concerned about situations such as B and C. I have outlined key principles designed to help business leaders prepare for the future, using Situation B to illustrate the principles. The same principles apply to Situation C, but with some variations that I have described at the end of this section.

## 1. Focusing on the critical decisions of business leaders

Reducing the vast uncertainty of the future to the main decisions that business leaders make is not only valuable but is also a simplification.

For instance, in Situation B, we started off with a broad business question about creating a commercial strategy for the new treatment that was consistent with physician and patient needs. As we got deeper and had numerous conversations, we identified the hard decisions that the company faced, which were:

- Would there be enough surgeries for the type of cancer to justify the client's entry into the market? Internally, there were many people who were opposed to the decision of entering the market at all.

- How should they position the treatment with respect to the heated chemotherapy, given its uncertain future after the controversial clinical trial that questioned the efficacy of that chemotherapy?

## 2. Analysing trends that matter

> Looking at the future requires a strong emphasis on understanding the entire ecosystem of the business – the economic climate, political environment, regulatory trends, technological shifts, socio-cultural forces, and industry trends.

Identifying trends, and linking these to what matters, is powerful in resolving uncertainties. Since most trends relate to the external environment of the business, there can be numerous ones. It is critical to prioritise those that have a bearing on the important decisions that were identified.

For Situation B, let's take a few examples of trends:

a. The state of the capital markets determines funding, which in turn affects the likelihood of completion of clinical trials. For instance, the recent Russia-Ukraine war affected the availability of capital and adversely affected the fate of many biotech companies.

b. The availability of new competitive drugs in the pipeline might affect the possibility of recruiting doctors and patients for the clinical trial.

c. The move towards surgeries being concentrated in centres of excellence, rather than being fragmented, would enable easier recruitment of doctors and patients for clinical trials in most countries.

d. Changes in the regulatory environment might affect the ease of approval of the drug. It may also affect aspects of clinical trial design requirements, such as the standards of safety and efficacy.

e. The likely impact of recent clinical trial results on the future behaviour of physicians.

f. Shifts in medical practices over time that might affect the adoption of the treatment. For instance, it is common to see certain types of treatments fall in or out of favour, and sometimes not because of clinical reasons. Similarly, the consensus on how certain patients need to be treated changes over time.

While monitoring most trends that are important for the biotech company, only the last two proved most important to answer the question. For instance, with respect to the question about whether there would be enough surgeries to justify entering the market, we first estimated the current number of surgeries, which were higher than our client's expectations. However, two trends were particularly helpful in establishing that the number of surgeries would grow. The first factor was a change in medical practices that expanded the range of patients eligible for surgery, creating significant potential for growth in this area. The second was that the clinical trial established that surgeries prolonged the lives of patients substantially, and that was likely to accelerate the growth of surgeries.

The next question was about how to position the treatment with respect to the heated chemotherapy. Here again, two trends were particularly helpful. First, the clinical trial showed no incremental efficacy for the chemotherapy relative to surgery alone. Although some surgeons who favoured the chemotherapy resisted accepting the results, it was unlikely to be part of the standard of care. Second, our research indicated that it was unlikely that another trial would be completed within the next 10 years that could challenge the results of the recent trial that had established the lack of incremental efficacy of the chemotherapy.

## 3. Diverse and selective interviewing – visionaries, sceptics and enthusiasts

To look at the future of any industry, we must speak to knowledgeable enthusiasts and sceptics. In the case of the biotech company just discussed, we spoke to 40 surgeons and oncologists across the US and Europe. Importantly, we spoke to those who favoured the heated chemotherapy, those who were neutral, and those who were outright rejectors. Speaking to people on the spectrum of scepticism-enthusiasm allowed us to identify the key variables that we needed to monitor.

It is also important to speak to people who are not only knowledgeable but are also more oriented toward thinking about the future. Future-oriented people are comfortable in visualizing the latent potential of a concept, can anticipate realistic barriers, and are good at drawing learnings from other analogous situations.

## 4. Triaging multiple methods and data points

Given that the future is ambiguous and multi-faceted, one needs to use hybrid approaches. A variety of methods need to be used. The common ones are scanning media reports, conducting primary qualitative and quantitative research with important stakeholders (these could be in-depth interviews, focus groups, or surveys), reviewing knowledge shared by thought leaders in interviews, books, and academic publications, reviewing secondary data, running quantitative models, or using theories. It's worth noting that models need to be used for gaining greater insight rather than for precise forecasting.

## 5. Future thinking for self and others

Whilst we may employ various methods to gather facts and elicit diverse opinions, there will always be significant gaps because the future ultimately needs to be imagined. The thinking skills that we described – imaging, abstracting, and analogizing – become essential in seeing what might happen. There are other exercises that can facilitate thinking about the future. One route is to start with the present and think of consequences, ultimately leading to a future scenario. This allows for second-order thinking, which helps us visualize the chain of consequences. For instance, imagine that the biotech company positions its treatment as a replacement for chemotherapy.

Some of the first-order effects could be:

- Some oncologists welcome the change as a safer and potentially more effective option.
- Others resist, citing a lack of long-term survival data.

The second-order effects may be:

- Regulatory agencies may impose additional approval hurdles due to the shift away from an established standard-of-care treatment.
- Surgeons may delay adoption until they see consensus among oncologists, slowing early market penetration.

- Patient advocacy groups may play a role, with some supporting a chemotherapy-free alternative while others raise concerns about removing an existing treatment option.

The other route is to write future histories, i.e., start from the future and work back into the present and imagine the conditions that would lead to the future.

For instance, imagine that in 10 years, the company's treatment has become the new standard of care (scenario three in the next section). Work backwards to determine the conditions required for this outcome:

- Clinical trials must demonstrate superior outcomes compared to chemotherapy.

- Early adopters among oncologists and surgeons must advocate for the treatment, influencing broader adoption.

- Regulatory bodies must be convinced of the treatment's efficacy and safety.

- Healthcare payers and insurers must be willing to reimburse the treatment, ensuring financial viability.

- The medical community's perception of chemotherapy must gradually shift, either due to new research or real-world evidence.

An important aspect for an insights professional is not just to think imaginatively but also to stimulate such thinking amongst others. For instance, when we interviewed the surgeons, we needed them to visualize how the client's drug would be administered in the operating room. Based on what they said, we had to imagine what might go wrong with the new treatment. Similarly, when we asked about their vision of how the future would unfold, we encouraged them to think of analogous case studies to bolster their arguments.

## 6. Creating plausible scenarios, assessing likelihoods, and drawing implications

The next step is creating scenarios for the future. Let us consider Situation B, about how to position the client's treatment with respect to the intense chemotherapy.

- **Scenario 1: Chemotherapy not relevant:** The chemotherapy does not provide significant survival benefits and may lead to higher toxicity. This leads to a re-evaluation of its role in the cancer treatment, given the added risks and the lack of improvement in long-term outcomes.

- **Scenario 2: Chemotherapy partially relevant:** The intense chemotherapy provides moderate benefits in specific patient subgroups. In this scenario, the treatment is selectively recommended for patients with specific characteristics. Clinical guidelines begin to endorse it for a few indications, where the benefits slightly outweigh the risks.

- **Scenario 3: Chemotherapy the standard of care scenario:** The chemotherapy leads to significantly improved outcomes in patients. Ongoing research and further refinements in the application of lead to better outcomes, without substantial decreases in adverse effects. It becomes a standard component of treatment for the type of cancer.

We ruled out Scenario 3 because, based on our research, we did not anticipate another clinical trial to be completed in the next 10 years, and that would preclude Scenario 3. Scenario 1 might have been a possibility; however, our primary research uncovered a segment of surgeons in every country who not only favoured the chemotherapy but had also invested years to become skilled at administering the treatment. In the US, in particular, these surgeons had a lot of autonomy and indicated that they would continue to use the chemotherapy, irrespective of the recent trials. There were other physicians who were not outright rejectors.

For the purposes of the clinical trial, we asked the clients to ignore the chemotherapy. Since its efficacy was in question, it would not be a good comparator. We also recommended to our client that their treatment could be positioned as a safer and more effective treatment.

## 7. Being flexible, updating predictions, and being transparent

Phillip Tetlock and Dan Gardner liken super forecasters[28] to foxes, who, unlike hedgehogs, are adaptable and flexible, look at diverse sources, and do not feel the need to have a unified and integrative view of the world. They frequently update their beliefs. However, while working with business leaders, it is essential to update them as well and ensure the assumptions and data underlying the perspective are transparent.

Let us briefly consider Situation C. The seven steps described above can be applied to that context as well. However, there are certain big differences given the higher number of uncertainties. First, the questions need to have a broader scope.

For the sake of illustration, these could be:

- What is likely to be the impact of generative AI on the product portfolio? Which products are likely to be replaced by AI, which will be enhanced, and which will be unaffected?

- What early initiatives related to generative AI need to be undertaken to prepare and adapt to the market in the next two years?

- What capabilities need to be built for the initiatives? Should the capabilities be built in-house or through outsourcing?

Second, the trends need to be scanned constantly. New risks and opportunities could emerge because of an entirely new disruption.

Third, a higher level of learning through experimentation is needed to assess what might be possible. For instance, developing possible applications of generative AI, by running and monitoring pilots, will produce a more concrete perspective. Fourth, these seven steps need to happen frequently and fast. There is a constant need for updating.

## SIMPLIFYING COMPLEXITY

Arriving at insights that simplify complexity while enabling actions that benefit both the customer and the business is simultaneously hugely valuable and deeply challenging. Simplifying complexity does not mean solving the problem in its entirety – rather, it is about reducing ambiguity and identifying the most critical factors to enable better decision-making.

This chapter approaches the subject from the perspective of an insights professional – someone who helps organizations navigate complexity by framing problems clearly, identifying the right disciplines, engaging experts, and synthesizing insights effectively.

A project we undertook for a genomics data provider serves as an example. Our task was to understand customer needs to shape product strategy. This case illustrates how complexity can be difficult to manage even in the present, without introducing the additional unknowns related to the future.

### 1. Reducing ambiguity by focusing on the critical decisions of business leaders

As with preparing for the future, tackling complexity begins with clarifying the core business decisions that need to be made. Complexity is inherently overwhelming because of the sheer number of variables involved. By anchoring insights work to a specific business decision, we reduce the ambiguity.

In the genomics case study, our primary task was to help our client determine which customer segments to prioritise for migration from an on-premise system to a cloud-based system, ensuring a seamless transition without compromising customer satisfaction.

This single business decision served as a focal point for all our research and analysis, preventing us from being overwhelmed by the vast complexity of the genomics ecosystem.

## 2. Identifying the unique dimensions of complexity and the relevant disciplines

The first step is to appreciate the nature of the complexity. This is not a trivial point. In the real world, relevant knowledge is highly context-specific and is unlikely to be found neatly organised in textbooks. You don't know what you don't know. It is easy to get lost in irrelevant topics and, conversely, have a blind spot with respect to something critical.

In the genomics project, our initial assumption was that the most relevant expertise was in molecular biology. However, as we immersed ourselves in the field, it became evident that several other disciplines were equally critical, including:

- Bioinformatics – The computational methods used to analyse genetic data.

- Machine learning – Algorithms that detect genetic patterns.

- Computing infrastructure – The storage, processing, and security of large-scale genomic datasets.

To illustrate, consider a researcher conducting a Genome-Wide Association Study (GWAS) to identify genes associated with ALS (Amyotrophic Lateral Sclerosis). Their work involves the following multiple complex stages:

- Storing large-scale genetic data in specific formats.

- Accessing, analysing, and visualizing data through specialized software.

- Utilising the latest R and Python libraries for coding.

- Relying on high computational power for data processing.

- Exporting results securely to maintain data privacy.

Any disruption at any stage – such as a system update or an outdated software version – can severely impact the entire process.

Additionally, complexity was further heightened by the diverse use cases in genomics. Scientists had different workflows depending on their area of research, and their needs varied based on whether they worked in commercial organizations or academic institutions.

To determine which aspects of complexity matter most, insights professionals must immerse themselves in the organization's ecosystem. This involves:

- Speaking with internal experts to understand the product.
- Studying competitors, manuals, and technical papers.
- Observing customer workflows through demos and, where possible, using the product firsthand.

Walking in the shoes of the customer ensures that complexity is simplified in a way that is useful and actionable.

### 3. Deploying interactional expertise

Interactional expertise[29] is a concept developed by sociologists of scientific knowledge, Harry Collins and Robert Evans. It refers to the ability of a person to understand and communicate the language and concepts of a specialized group, typically a scientific or technical community, without necessarily having practical skills in that field.

Ed Fidoe[30], the founder of the London Interdisciplinary School (LIS), emphasized the value of people with interactional expertise in solving complex problems: *'So when they are dealing with climate change, they are not worried about staying in a box of chemistry or biology. We need people who function as connectors with interactional expertise who can move between subjects and talk to deep experts and make connections.'*

This form of learning, where the purpose is to understand a scientific field better without trying to build one's own expertise, is quite distinct from typical expertise-building programmes. Developing expertise in any discipline is inherently a sequential and slow process where one needs to master basics before proceeding further to advanced concepts. The type of learning described here is less rigorous, fast, and non-linear. The learner has to grapple with a set of both basic and advanced concepts with the ultimate objective of building a bridge between experts and non-experts. Despite significant gaps and blind spots in acquiring such knowledge, it remains highly valuable, even though the learning process is likely to be somewhat chaotic. Below are some helpful guidelines:

- **An agile, curious, and gritty mindset:** Diving into a field in which you are a novice needs a high degree of intellectual agility. Loving learning makes the process easy. Curiosity provides the inspiration and energy, along with the constant receptivity needed to internalise new information. We need grit to persevere through the difficulties, the periods of confusion, and the feeling of getting stuck. Grit also provides the courage and humility to ask novice questions repeatedly.

- **Explicit time for learning:** We need to allocate a phase just to immerse ourselves in the relevant disciplines. We cannot simply begin executing the project without investing time to learn the basics. This is particularly important when the project involves speaking to highly specialized experts for whom time is scarce. Internalising fundamental concepts from diverse knowledge areas is necessary preparation to be able to ask the right questions.

- **Diverse sources and testing knowledge:** As previously mentioned, the starting point is to learn from internal sources. From there one must zoom out and use a wider range of sources – engaging with external experts, reading scientific publications and textbooks, and exploring online resources, including attending short courses. When we are trying to learn something new rapidly, it is very easy to have an illusion of understanding. One helpful practice is to externalise the knowledge by getting all one's learnings on a physical medium and organizing it on a communal site, e.g., sharing all presentations, handwritten notes, drawings, Excel sheets, and interview recordings on a cloud-based system. Other ways are explaining concepts to others in the team and periodically checking with internal experts.

**4. Eliciting knowledge from deep experts:** The interaction with the expert customers is an important determinant of the quality of the project. Having done the knowledge gathering, one must allow it to settle in the background and be completely focused on understanding the expert's perspective. For that, we must do a few things:

- **Get into an approach mindset before the interview:** We need to be excited about discovering the fascinating new world of the expert.

- **Be comfortable with the asymmetry of knowledge:** The expert customer will always know a lot more. It is alright to ask basic questions to clarify our understanding. Clients often tell us that at the beginning of projects, they believed that we were asking questions to which the answers were already obvious, only to later be surprised to find that their assumptions were completely wrong. Their lesson was that they should ask many more questions than they were currently doing.

- **Probe experts on how they make decisions in real situations:** To inject fresh thinking and get contextually relevant knowledge in an interview, it is important to ask experts how they make decisions in actual practice. This could be done by asking about a past situation, e.g., asking a doctor about a patient they found difficult to manage, or by asking them to react to a hypothetical yet realistic scenario, e.g., how they would treat a specific type of patient.

- **Follow the expert's lead:** Experts will often go on unplanned digressions. These might be sources of new breakthrough insights. Often one cannot follow everything that an expert says. It is important to accept the ambiguity and keep the conversation going. We can listen to the interview later and research the ideas that we didn't understand.

## 5. 'Physicist' and 'biologist' thinking to simplify without losing nuance

Samuel Arbesman[31] contrasts two approaches to complexity:

- Physicists seek unifying theories and elegant simplifications.
- Biologists embrace messiness, exceptions, and system diversity.

   In insights work, both approaches are essential:

- Physicist-thinking helps create useful simplifications. For instance, in our work on genomics, despite the wide variety of use cases, we were able to develop a common framework – both for the user journey and for customer segmentation – by abstracting the underlying patterns.
- Biologist-thinking ensures that important exceptions are not lost – for instance, a surgeon's need for specific procedural tools or a scientist's need for a unique database structure.

Whilst the objective of simplification is to make it useful for non-expert audiences, a good way to test whether the solution you've arrived at is insightful or superficial is to test it with an expert.

Inspired by biological thinking, one must capture details that do not fit in a simplified version. Certain needs of experts are unique and highly technical in nature. These must not be simplified. Examples include a surgeon anticipating specific complications while using a therapy, a scientist requiring a different structure of a database or an analyst needing specific types of data or analytical software. Recommendations related to these can have a huge impact. It is important to represent what the expert said faithfully, without adding your own interpretation, and check in with internal experts to clarify the significance of the recommendation.

## 6. Engage experts whilst crafting and communicating recommendations.

Complex situations, such as the one just discussed, have an 'entanglement' problem[32] – some people understand parts of the system, others understand the whole system in an abstract manner, but no one understands the full system in detail. In such a situation, it is essential to draw in experts from different disciplines to create and communicate recommendations. In particular, the audience may comprise many non-expert stakeholders, and we find that often the simplified recommendations gain more salience rather than the specific technical recommendations. It is important to elicit the support of internal experts to counter this bias.

Having covered all the approaches for the five archetypes of unknowns, let's look at how we can create an environment that is conducive to generating insights in an organization.

# 7

# Getting the 'Insight Wheel' in Motion: Embedding Insights

'It's not about ideas. It's about making ideas happen.'[1]
— Scott Belsky

THIS BOOK HAS EXPLORED THE IMPORTANCE OF CREATING A conducive environment for perspective-shifting insights to take place in a sustainable manner and on a large scale. But what should this environment look like? An ideal setting enables creative and robust thinking, facilitates learning and experimentation with different knowledge areas and methods, and sets up processes for better proliferation of insights throughout the organization. Creating such work surroundings is achievable but difficult. This chapter will address how one can build an organization driven by insights and well-considered decision-making.

## BARRIERS TO INSIGHT

I have mentioned many barriers to insight throughout the book. It is worth summarising the ones that relate to how organizations operate. Appreciating how these factors impede the path to insight and action is the first step for creating the right environment. Addressing these barriers can unleash the power of insight in an organization and catalyse actions that lead to business success.

1. Lack of conviction of senior leaders in customer insights: This gets reflected in the organizational design in which we see that the insights department is far removed from the C-suite and the strategic decisions related to the company. Insights people become executors or validators of small parts of strategy, largely focusing on repetitive tactical work instead of proactively shaping a strategy. Disempowered, the learning agenda of the team weakens, and the focus shifts to procedural work. This, in turn, makes them less suitable to serve the C-suite, which reaffirms the scepticism.

2. Organizational silos that prevent cross-fertilization of knowledge, methods, and insight: Business problems need a diverse set of people across different functions to collaborate seamlessly. In general, insularity of different groups creates a myriad of problems. As noted in Chapter 4, for insight and creativity, it is particularly detrimental to have siloed working, especially if there

are tensions between these teams. The silos might be based on function, e.g., marketing vs engineering; subspecialties, e.g., market research vs design research; hierarchical, e.g., headquarters vs business units; or geographical, e.g., US vs Europe. Managing the tension between silos drains away precious energy that is required to develop breakthroughs.

3. A culture that values predictability and control: Powerful insights are unexpected and may be in dissonance with the existing beliefs in the organizations. This is disruptive to an organization's sense of stability and control and may lead to a reversal of strategy. The need for predictability and control negatively influences the ways of working for insight generation.

4. Human bias that affects adoption of Insight: Behavioural sciences have revealed several biases that affect our decision-making. These can hinder progress in developing insight. These might prevent us from accepting dissonant information that could have triggered an epiphany or make us select information that makes us look good.

5. A mechanical, formal, and cerebral view of insight development: One of the biggest barriers to nurturing insights within an organization is mistaking factual or dry outputs from a market research project as insight. Such a perspective fails to recognize that insights, by their nature, have a vitality which ultimately motivates people to act. Communication becomes formal, cerebral and lifeless.

Vibha Paul Rishi[2] captured some of these barriers best when she said to me, '*The world rewards you for being uber-logical, focused, and linear. So thinking about insight as a living/breathing thing is frightening... because it makes you feel out of control.*'

## SIX INSIGHTS ARCHETYPES OF BUSINESS LEADERS

Leaders shape the culture of an organization, influencing not just strategic priorities but also the value placed on customer insight. A leader's approach to insights determines how deeply insights are embedded into decision-making, how resources are allocated, and how insights drive competitive advantage. Over the years, our team has worked across multiple industries, geographies, and organizational levels, systematically analysing how different business leaders interact with insights. From this work, we identified six recurring leadership archetypes, each reflecting a distinct mindset toward insights and decision-making. These archetypes help us answer a crucial question: How do different leaders engage with insights, and how can we work effectively with each type?

Why does this matter? The way leaders engage with insights directly impacts business outcomes. Organizations led by archetypes that value insight tend to innovate faster, adapt to market shifts, and make customer-driven decisions. On the other hand, companies dominated by those who inhibit or undervalue insight often miss critical opportunities, struggle with alignment, or fail to act on valuable insights.

## Archetypes that value insight

### 1. *Insights Visionaries*

Seeing it as a source of differentiation and innovation, they believe that insight is fundamental for business success. When a country head of business said to us, '*Let's show our partners what a big difference distinctive insights can make to a launch*', they were displaying the *insights visionary* archetype. Insights visionaries are interested in discovering what is hidden or unknown and translating it into creative business strategies. They are always looking at business activities from the customer's perspective. When they encounter a challenge, they want to see if superior insight into their customers can help them solve the problem or come up with a strategy that is more cost-effective.

Given their strong orientation to use insight for developing innovative business actions, they value integrative problem solving and are open to unconventional methodologies. They are less concerned about what is methodologically 'pure'. They are likely to reject findings from market research if they do not pass an intuitive sense check.

They are likely to personally get involved with anything related to customers. Even if they are the CEO, they will look for opportunities to see customers directly themselves. A dominantly 'insights visionary' CEO, Takashi Takenoshita, would insist on being there for any major customer insights brainstorming session or debrief. He would attend qualitative fieldwork when he could and routinely accompany salespeople when they visited customers.

Such leaders evangelise customer centricity across the organization and create values and rituals to encourage that. For instance, Takashi also insisted that unless a person had first-hand experience with a certain number of customers, they were not allowed to voice strong opinions in executive meetings. Vibha Paul Rishi[3], who exemplifies this archetype, said, '*The receiver of insight must be immersed in the situation. It's not like insight comes to you wrapped in a box. Immersion will allow you to recognize insight when it comes.*' She later said, '*People should not make the mistake of thinking that the customer is not the centre of your universe.*'

The insights visionary archetype is a powerful facilitator of making insights an integral part of the workings of an organization. This is especially so if the person is in the C-suite. They can accelerate the adoption of insights across an organization and create a transformation. However, there are a few drawbacks that need to be managed. This archetype might have a tendency towards idealism and may be frustrated by conventional, though tried-and-tested, approaches. Being maverick-like, their working style may lead to certain groups of people feeling disempowered. But, on balance, if these drawbacks are managed, this is a highly desirable archetype.

It is worth noting that in defining these archetypes, we are focused on the extent to which leaders value insight, not on how much conviction they have in market research.

It is well known that Steve Jobs was sceptical about market research. Yet, it is hard to argue that he was passionate about customer insight and saw its role in driving Apple's innovation. In fact, Takashi Takenoshita[4] said he made a distinction between insight and market research. 'As a CEO, it's a priority for senior leaders to deeply engage with insights projects. For market research projects, they can delegate the work.'

### 'Insights Visionary' Summary

| Dimensions | Characteristics |
| --- | --- |
| Orientation towards insight | • Perceive insight as a core aspect of business operation<br>• Believe it is a source of differential advantage and innovation for business<br>• View all business decisions from a customer point of view |
| Approach to insight | • Focus on relevant link to business decisions<br>• Appreciate creative and unconventional methods<br>• Frustrated by mechanical application of conventional approaches |
| Personal involvement with insight development | • Highly involved, especially in developing insights and actions<br>• Attempt to get 'first-hand experience by seeing customers |
| Role in disseminating in organizations | • Evangelists for insight<br>• Facilitator of a conducive environment |
| Opportunity | • Ideal archetype to creatively deploy across an organization |
| Watchouts | • At times, maverick-like and disruptive to routine processes and to the workings of people |

## 2. Seasoned Insights Practitioner

The *seasoned insights practitioner*, like the insights visionary, believes customer insight is core to doing business. The main difference is that their conviction comes from years of doing insights work and having seen its value in driving business forward. For instance, if you have spent your career doing marketing in an organization such as Unilever, P&G, or Amgen, it is likely that you have used insight for many past decisions and have reaped the benefits. Eliciting customer insights well is seen as a best practice for business.

In terms of approach to insights, they are likely to have strong views and better than average knowledge of methodologies, especially if they have worked in organizations where customer insight capabilities are excellent. For instance, they are less likely to save on research costs by lowering sample sizes. Their convictions are based on what they have tried and tested. Marco Renoldi, being a predominantly seasoned insights practitioner, had a view that there should be a maximum of three customer segments when a product was launched, because beyond that, the salesforce would find it too complex. This was based on years of business experience. Such heuristics are useful in directing insights work.

They will not hesitate to share their perspectives on methodologies. It is important to involve this group at an early stage of insights work because they are likely to have strong opinions on methodologies.

They influence the organization by establishing systems, such as allocating sufficient resources and setting up internal insights teams and partners who are skilled.

People with this dominant archetype are likely to ensure that insights are systematically integrated in business operations with robust methodologies. Marco Renoldi, as a senior leader in pharmaceuticals, presented frequently to various senior audiences, e.g., the board of directors and investors, and customer insights formed the foundation of his presentations. He said to me, '*The fact that I have had direct experience of watching customers gave me an understanding of why what we were doing was appropriate, and I also knew what we needed to change. It also increased my confidence when I spoke to investors.*'[5]

For certain people with this archetype as a dominant one, a watchout is that they may be less open to new methods and may be overly attached to what they have done in the past. This becomes a problem if the context of their past experience was different from their current one.

Both *insights visionaries* and *seasoned insights practitioners* are excellent archetypes to ensure that insights are embedded in an organization. In fact, a combination of the two can be ideal for instilling both creativity and rigour.

The next two archetypes are more difficult to deal with and are likely to represent large groups of leaders.

## 'Seasoned Insights Practitioner' Summary

| Dimensions | Characteristics |
|---|---|
| Orientation towards insight | • Perceive insights as a core aspect of business operation<br>• Conviction in the value of insights is based on positive experiences<br>• Feel confident about decision-making with insight |
| Approach to insight | • Value actionable business recommendations<br>• Belief in best practices for Insight<br>• Rely on tried and tested approaches<br>• Value pragmatism |
| Personal involvement with insight development | • Prefer to get involved in critical meetings |
| Role in disseminating in organisations | • Establish systems by making insights part of business processes, allocating resources, and setting up the right team and partner network |
| Opportunity | • This archetype can ensure that insights are systematically integrated in business processes |
| Watchouts | • May be less open to new and unconventional approaches |

## Archetypes that undervalue insight

### 3. 'Show Me the Value'

This is an archetype that does not consider customer insights to be central to the success of a business. The CEO of a consumer goods company once said to me, '*I have no need for consumer insights now. I have a clear idea on what makes us money. As long as we make our product available, we will sell. Maybe at a later point, I'll need customer insight.'* I convinced him that there were significant opportunities he was missing by not focusing on the consumer, and he agreed to work with us. At the end of our work, he was so pleased, he got me to present the work to the entire global leadership team with the brief that I should teach them what good insights look like.

This type of initial resistance is common amongst many leaders. Often, they do not have a good understanding of the power of insights to create substantial business impact. Most of the barriers we highlighted, such as a lack of conviction, a mechanised view, or human bias, are present in this group. They will justify business decisions based on superficial market research, e.g., a few focus groups, when the work needed was quantitative research or vice versa. Their intentions are good, but they have limited knowledge of the opportunity cost of doing mediocre insights work. Personally, they might get involved in insights meetings, but they tend to express scepticism. If they are in a senior position, they may even pose a barrier to an organization doing insights work.

Given the potentially large number of C-suite leaders with this archetype present, one needs a strategy to convince them of the value of insight. It is worth mentioning that converting this archetype is both possible and a valuable endeavour. It involves creating the Aha! insight about the value of insight. At various points, I have changed the perspective of such people and made them champions of insight.

I learnt that lesson early on in my career. I met a C-suite leader who was deeply troubled by the slowdown of the growth of the category. He called other C-suite people to a meeting to discuss the possible reasons. My boss could not attend, so I was sent to help. I had prepared for the meeting by reviewing all our primary research and looking at the macrotrends. When he asked for opinions, I offered my hypothesis on the reasons for the slowdown. He snapped, 'Give us the data that we ask for, not your opinion.' The following day, I put the data in charts and took him through those before communicating the same hypothesis that I had shared the day before. As I presented, I could see from his expression that his attitude towards me was changing. In fact, he subsequently requested my presence in every strategy meeting. I have seen this pattern repeat itself many times. The principle is to focus on an issue that really matters, make links to business outcomes such as profitability and sales, and provide insight backed by evidence.

### 'Show Me the Value' Summary

| Dimensions | Characteristics |
| --- | --- |
| Orientation towards insight | • Do not believe customer insights is core for business<br>• Sceptical of its value<br>• Need to be convinced of its potential impact with evidence |
| Approach to insight | • Not particularly knowledgeable about the value of insights or methodologies, though not bothered by it |
| Personal involvement with insight development | • Prefer not to get involved or accept with scepticism |

| Role in disseminating in organizations | • Might prevent the active dissemination |
| --- | --- |
| Opportunity | • Addressing their criticisms can sharpen the insight, and if convinced, they can become champions |
| Watchouts | • Can lower the energy of insights teams |

## 4. Insights Delegator

These are leaders who believe that the field of customer insights is meant for people who are junior to them or for another part of the organization. They are not likely to be involved with the development of insights. Often CEOs who have a strong background in finance or operations may exhibit this archetype. They believe insights is part of the marketing black box. Sometimes even people in roles such as the head of marketing or head of strategy may delegate the customer insights to a junior person. Whilst the *Show me the value* and *Insights Delegator* archetypes do not believe customer insights is core to business operations, the former archetype nurtures an active scepticism, whilst the latter archetype is just not thinking about insights. The barrier to reach these people is much higher. They need a complete shift in perspective. The headroom for impact through insights will be limited. It is frustrating to work with this archetype. Attempting to engage them is challenging. Even the most talented insights manager will find it difficult to achieve the desired impact with leaders with this as a dominant archetype. In such organizations, one needs to look at leaders with more receptive archetypes.

### 'Insights Delegator' Summary

| Dimensions | Characteristics |
|---|---|
| Orientation towards insight | • Delegate insights to some other person or department<br>• Customer insights are not part of their consciousness. |
| Approach to insight | • Delegate to others<br>• Do not have a point of view |
| Personal involvement with insight development | • Detached from these processes |
| Role in disseminating in organizations | • Have no role |
| Opportunity | • Limited opportunity |
| Watchouts | • In senior positions, they can significantly limit the headroom for impact. |

The last two archetypes are somewhat different and can be inhibitors of impact through insights if not managed appropriately.

## Archetypes that inhibit insight

### 5. Insights Controllers

These people see the field of insights as part of their turf and a source of power in their organization. They view customer insights as their functional area and want to exercise control over it. Such leaders can be hierarchical and somewhat insular. For instance, they may not want junior people within their departments to interact with people in other functional areas or 'go over them' to interact with senior people. They also want to maintain control over insights agencies. We are hired mostly by the C-suite teams. If we encounter this specific archetype, we know we have to tread carefully. When these leaders are talented, this mentality can result in a positive outcome. Such people would be good at creating centres of excellence for insight in an organization, especially if they have high standards of quality with respect to methodology. Insight, however, is multi-faceted, and it's about fostering connections. A controlling mentality will eventually get in the way of insights development and dissemination. People in this archetype must be coached to be open and collaborative.

### 'Insights Controller' Summary

| Dimensions | Characteristics |
| --- | --- |
| Orientation towards insight | • Perceive insights as a core part of the business, but it is an area that they need to control |
| Approach to insight | • Use agencies and methods that they can control<br>• Prefer to use tools they have developed internally |
| Personal involvement with insight development | • See insight development as a core part of their function<br>• Would ideally like to micro-manage all processes<br>• Need credit for all successful insight projects |
| Role in disseminating in organizations | • Like to control the dissemination<br>• Tend to be hierarchical and do not like sharing of insights in a manner that breaks hierarchy<br>• Not easy cross-functional collaborators as they might view other groups as competitors |

| Opportunity | • If they have high standards of quality, they can create a centre for excellence. |
| --- | --- |
| Watchouts | • Controlling can have a negative effect on insight development and dissemination. |

## 6. Politicians

Their approach to insights is driven by what makes them look good. Whilst this is a problem for any function, it is a killer of good insights. Uncovering truth requires purity of intent. Without such an intent, a self-serving bias can distort the perception of reality. We have encountered countless situations where clients have held on to studies whose results show them in a good light or used agencies that are willing to accommodate any request from them. In one such study, we found that in a survey, our client was getting the highest possible customer service ratings despite having a low market share. While this is a theoretical possibility, examination of the survey revealed that the initial questions were not framed in an unbiased manner. It was easy for the customers to know who the sponsors were, which in turn biased the customer satisfaction question in our client's favour. Although we pointed out this flaw to the client, they continued to use the same questionnaire and methodology. The business lost out. The organization did not learn the truth about customer service. They also lost the opportunity to increase sales through better execution. While having a negative influence on the insight development and embedding process, in certain difficult political situations, this archetype might be quite helpful because they are astute at understanding the motivations of stakeholders and can help present insights accordingly.

**'Politician' Summary**

| Dimensions | Characteristics |
|---|---|
| Orientation towards insight | • Varies, however, the important driver for them is what makes them look good |
| Approach to insight | • Use agencies and methods that they can control and that make them appear competent<br>• Self-serving bias gets in the way of eliciting truth |
| Personal involvement with insight development | • Involvement is often based on power dynamics. If someone they perceive as powerful is a sponsor, they would like to be in the limelight.<br>• Choose activities that make them conspicuous |
| Role in disseminating in organizations | • Likely to be enthusiastic in disseminating if the results make them look good |
| Opportunity | • Can be valuable in providing input on how to disseminate insight in a politically charged environment |
| Watchouts | • Have a destructive effect on insight development and embedding<br>• Have a demoralising effect on teams |

## Applying the Insights Archetypes Framework

Every leader has a dominant insights archetype, shaped by their experiences, biases, and organizational culture. Recognizing our own tendencies – and those of our colleagues – can help us leverage strengths, mitigate weaknesses, and improve how insights drive decision-making.

Certain key questions for reflection are given below:

- Which archetype best describes my approach to insights?
- How does my perspective on insights shape decision-making in my organization?
- What can I do to strengthen my ability to act on insights more effectively?

The most effective organizations are those where leaders not only value insights but also embed them into the fabric of decision-making. By understanding these archetypes, we can work towards building a culture where insights thrive, guiding the organization toward smarter, more customer-centric choices.

## FIVE PRACTICES TO CREATE A CONDUCIVE ENVIRONMENT

When a visionary CEO is replaced by a delegator, what happens to the role of insights in decision-making? A single leadership change overnight altered the way insights were valued. The values that underpin the culture in such circumstances become meaningless statements.

In this chapter, I outline five key practices to create an environment where insights can flourish, regardless of leadership changes. In a boutique firm like ours, which is specialized in insights, one must strive to create a suitable culture. But if you are a large organization with many functions, it can be difficult to make the case for and create a conducive culture for insights. Besides, it takes many years of sustained effort to build such a culture.

> Practices are more concrete than culture, allow for training, and can be implemented more easily.

## Mindfulness Practice

Mindfulness is our ability to stay present. It is a very simple idea. Yet, the benefits it brings for insight are profound. It ensures that we are in a receptive and curious state. It activates our right hemisphere and activates all the modes of thinking that may lie dormant within us – it makes us more relaxed, creative, playful, observant, empathetic, and intuitive. It helps us overcome various biases – confirmation, availability, and being self-serving. It engenders a genuine desire for truth.

Lack of mindfulness can block insight. We were conducting a patient immersion session with a client team and showing them videos from the ethnographic work that vividly portrayed the suffering of the patients and the extent to which their lives had been disrupted by their health condition. Most members of the cross-functional team were completely absorbed in the experience and were feeling a little low. Suddenly, a member of the marketing team beamed at the entire group and said, 'Our target segments are happy, confident and optimistic', as if they weren't seeing what was transpiring right in front of their eyes. In their eyes, the segments described in a black-and-white manner in the original presentation were frozen. In business, we often fall into the trap of clinging to a framework, technique, or concept that prevents us from getting real insight. This rigidity can lead our business in the wrong direction, especially in a world that is rapidly changing. Conversely, when we are being truly mindful, we are on a path to discovering something new.

Being sensitive to what is happening requires constant practice. We implement mindfulness in different ways described below:

- *Develop awareness of its importance:* The first step to change is often having awareness of a problem. All of us are susceptible to being distracted. At a first level, if we become aware of this tendency, we are likely to be more receptive to practising mindfulness.

- *Integrate mindfulness in every step of a project*: Mindfulness requires being in a receptive state, both in the way we conduct ourselves individually and in the way we interact with others. This may include modifying our physical space to remove clutter, following exercises such as meditation, or setting guidelines for team interactions, e.g., on how to listen. Also, it is worth ensuring that mindfulness is customised to each step of the research process. For instance, during fieldwork, we switch off all devices when observing qualitative research, maintain a level of silence, and spend time noticing what is happening, e.g., listening for specific sentences or looking at facial expressions, rather than trying to come to conclusions during the interaction. While doing analysis, we may do a short meditation so that we are able to analyse data with a clear mind. We also use metaphors to help us. For instance, when we are preparing a presentation, we use a metaphor from music that musicians should practice slowly to ensure that they have complete control over the phrasing, the dynamics, and other aspects of producing the music. With an approach like that, we do not rush the process and ensure that we enjoy it.

Mindfulness practices help address the specific challenges of each stereotype, e.g., they can make an 'insights visionary' focused and calm, a 'seasoned insights practitoner' open to new approaches, an 'insights controller' more relaxed, and a 'politician' less self-serving.

## Receptive Mastery Practice

Valuing mastery means going deep with constant practice, being grounded in the enduring basic principles, and pushing the boundaries of a field. Yet, mastery cannot be dogmatic and must avoid the 'I know best' trap. In fact, mastery allows one to be more receptive – hear better, see better, and feel better. Many of the methodological problems that I wrote about in Chapter 5, e.g., mistaking abstract measurements for truth, or conflating correlation with causation, are a result of a lack of mastery.

I was serving a leading telecom provider in Seattle. The Head of Insights was a very good problem solver and business thinker. He had credibility with the C-suite, and that made it easy for insights to reach the top management. However, he lacked experience and expertise in quantitative research related to innovation. For instance, while testing new product ideas, he was strongly in favour of poor product concepts being pursued further just because they ranked highest in a set of inferior product concepts tested. Any savvy expert would have rejected all the concepts and gone back to the drawing board to develop new product ideas.

Not everyone can be a master in every field, but collectively an organization must strive to develop mastery in different disciplines related to insight. Apart from actively investing in training of employees, an organization must create a culture with the following characteristics:

- *Enable continuous learning and skill development*: Companies should provide access to both internal and external training programmes on relevant disciplines. Furthermore, coaching and mentoring, by more experienced people, needs to happen routinely. In the McKinsey Customer Insights and Analytics practice, individuals had to choose the area where they wanted to become experts and were then provided opportunities to build mastery. For example, if someone wanted to become an expert in a conjoint analysis, they would be actively staffed on projects that were particularly suited to the technique, e.g., product/service design or pricing. They would be mentored by senior people who had the expertise and were encouraged to attend internal and external training programmes.

- *Allow deep experts to make decisions related to a domain:* For instance, if a decision is being taken on how to forecast demand for a product, the relevant forecasters must lead the decision. If prototypes of a product are being tested, the design team must lead.

- *Value fundamental principles even while innovating with the most advanced techniques:* People who lack mastery are swayed by every new approach. Those who have mastery evaluate the approach rigorously, look at its strengths and weaknesses relative to available methods, and then decide whether to use it and how best to use it.

- *Take time to develop insights:* Mastery requires dedicating significant time to each project and thoroughly analysing details following a deliberative System Two approach. This not only safeguards against biases but also helps practitioners develop intuition, which is a big advantage in the long run.

- *Bring expertise from outside the organization:* Those who value mastery do not hesitate to invite deep experts from the outside world. They proactively build a partner network that provides the requisite mastery.

At Insight Dojo, we regularly collaborate with experts in fields where our own expertise is not as deep.

## Pragmatic polymathy practice

While mastery is about going deep, polymathy is about breadth of interests and cross-pollination. I have dedicated Chapter 8 to the practice of polymathy at an individual level. Additionally, organizations can help in encouraging polymathy by doing the following:

***Invest in Employee Development through External Expertise, Experiential Learning, and Cross-Disciplinary Training***

To strengthen employee capabilities, companies should tap into external networks that include seasoned practitioners and academic experts from relevant fields. Launching pilot initiatives aimed at addressing real business challenges – while deliberately combining varied methodologies – can encourage innovation and practical learning. Furthermore, designing training programmes that blend elements of the arts and sciences can expand how employees approach problems, helping them think more creatively and generate unconventional insights. These programmes are particularly effective when tied to solving concrete, real-world issues.

***Broaden the Talent Pipeline***

Organizations should widen their hiring lens to include candidates from diverse disciplines such as computer science, design, and journalism, as well as those with interdisciplinary academic paths. Casting a wider net increases the likelihood of discovering unique skill sets and hybrid thinkers. Beyond formal credentials and job experience, exploring a candidate's broader range of interests – such as hobbies or side projects – can uncover individuals with polymathic potential. It's especially valuable to consider whether these pursuits have resulted in meaningful outputs like published work, performances, inventions, training initiatives, or impactful problem-solving efforts.

## Co-creation Practice

Co-creation improves the quality of insights, makes them more contextually relevant, allows people to experience insights first-hand, and raises the chances of insights being implemented.

- *Diversity in views enriches insight development*: When people from different functions and knowledge areas collaborate, the quality of insights improves.

- *Experienced insights are remembered for a long time*: Co-creation allows for insights to be experienced. Those tend to be remembered for a long time. We find it striking when clients recall specific insights from projects they did many years ago. Often, it's because they were directly involved in a workshop where the insight was shared.

- *Action always requires cross-functional co-creation*: Many functions need to come together for most significant decisions. Cross-functional co-creation insights allow us to bypass bureaucratic processes and implement actions quickly.

Running co-creation sessions with various stakeholders, across functions and levels, must be the default in every project. Such sessions require imaginative communication, interactive workshops, and different ways to make the insights vivid.

## Link with Strategy and Tactics Practice

Insight needs to be inextricably linked to strategy and action. This seems like a basic requirement, and the statement above seems like a truism. However, the connection of insights with strategy and action is so deep that these two aspects can never be too far away from the insight development process. Strategy frames the context and focuses insights. Similarly, potential for action serves as a test that ensures the insights are implementable. Also, in our increasingly dynamic world, the relationship is not so linear.

However, we often find that in actual practice, companies follow a linear model, with these three aspects being run separately and sometimes even by different people.

To implement this practice, insights people should build strong capabilities in strategic thinking and be cognizant of how each function works. They can then facilitate the engagement of the relevant stakeholders.

## BEGINNING THE CHANGE JOURNEY

How do you spark an insights transformation in an organization that doesn't yet value insights? The journey isn't easy. In previous chapters, I introduced key ideas to enhance insight development. But how do we begin making real change? This section outlines a stepwise process to help us initiate that transformation.

1. *Find a champion*: It might be you or someone else. Somebody needs to feel passionate about driving business impact with insight and want to lead the change. In terms of archetypes, the most suitable ones are visionaries or seasoned practitioners. Many years ago, I was the market research manager at Pepsi in India. Despite being the insights lead, I was junior in the organization. Looking back, I can see that I was influenced by two archetypes within myself. The *insights visionary* in me could see the headroom for the impact of insight across the whole organization. I was also influenced by the *seasoned insights practitioner* archetype. Having served Pepsi as an agency person, I was deeply anchored in the robust methodologies that worked well for soft drinks. That gave me credibility. Over a period of 20 months, I managed to increase the utilisation of insights significantly, for both strategic and tactical decisions, to the extent that the role of head of insights became significantly elevated.

2. *Create a narrative with the 'Why' for insight*: In PepsiCo, it was very easy. Our CEO had focused the

entire organization on the goal of driving growth. I could frame insight as a way of helping growth happen. Before my time, employees viewed research positively or negatively, based on what it implied about their performance. If the brand preference or share dropped in a market, people would challenge the result defensively. I repeated the mantra that insights were to identify and realize growth opportunities and are not meant for performance evaluation. Aligning insights to a concrete goal is a strong way to galvanise an organization to support an insights effort. Another way is to emphasize the value of customer centricity for business. The 'insights visionary' CEO referred to earlier used the rationale that one cannot implement a value such as 'putting the customer first' without being good at insight. Another framing can be about gaining a competitive edge. Creating a narrative helps align people, irrespective of their archetype.

3. *Enrol other influencers and role models*: Role modelling is a powerful means of bringing about change. In most organizations, there are individuals who are particularly excited about insight. They can be in the C-suite, marketing team, or engineering team. These are powerful allies in diffusing insights across the organization. It helps a lot when senior leaders serve as influencers and role models. During a pharma project, I was conducting an insights training session with the sales and medical teams on how to tailor their conversations to physician segments. The CEO

of the company attended. He felt that he had learnt a great deal that would help him communicate more effectively with key opinion leaders he was meeting. He asked me to run a training session for all the board members. Since the CEO acted as a champion, the insights got communicated to the entire organization fast. Interestingly, this CEO had a predominantly *Show Me the Value* archetype, but having been convinced, he became a champion. The influencer does not have to be a senior person. For one client, a middle-level member of the engineering team of a technology company attended one of our presentations and got excited about the depth of insight. He then invited us to work with the engineering team to help develop certain new innovations.

4. *Identify 'hot' contexts and create small wins for insight-driven impact*: The C-suite are constantly faced with hard problems such as drops in market share, lower category growth, or the launch of a competitive product. Proactively identifying these situations and developing insights to solve these problems builds credibility fast.

5. *Build your capability with training and partnerships*: Insight development, as advocated here, is a cross-fertilization of skills, knowledge, and methods – business problem solving, thinking skills, the ability to deploy different modes of thinking, learning complex matter rapidly and basic knowledge of certain core

disciplines and techniques. A critical decision is to identify what skills need to be developed internally versus skills to be outsourced. For instance, in Insight Dojo, we train ourselves in most of the areas. However, we selectively use other partners. A classic example is our approach to machine learning – we are proficient in using basic machine learning algorithms such as linear regression, logistic regressions, support vector machines, basic neural networks, or k-means cluster analysis. But, for sophisticated deep learning algorithms, we use more specialized partners. Such clarity ensures that we are not constrained by our capabilities, even in the short term.

6. *Develop long-term partnerships whilst ensuring innovation*: True long-term partnerships are beneficial because organizations get to know each other, allowing them to share implicit knowledge that improves the quality of insight and saves time and cost. However, it is important that this does not get in the way of innovation and that people do not fall into a comfortable inertial pattern. One must always be on the lookout for new innovative partners.

7. *Codify what you have done and create training material*: Having done one or more pilots, organizations must codify the methods and ways of working and create training material which needs to remain relevant and up to date.

I have seen some organizations go through a transformation following such a process.

> It improves the business performance, unifies the organization by connecting its people to the needs of its customers and stakeholders, and provides them a certain *joie de vivre*. It inspires people and raises their energy.

# 8

# The Practice of Pragmatic Polymathy

'Originality depends on new and striking combination of ideas. It is obvious therefore that the more a man knows, the greater scope he has for arriving at striking combinations. And not only the more he knows about his own subject but the more he knows beyond it of other subjects[1].'

– **Rosamond E. M. Harding, An *Anatomy of Inspiration***

MARCH 2013 WAS A TURNING POINT. SEVEN MONTHS AFTER leaving McKinsey & Company, I was exploring new directions in my career when a friend invited me to speak at a pharmaceutical company's senior team meeting. What started as a simple presentation on insight turned into a moment of profound personal and professional clarity.

They asked me to talk about insight broadly, without focusing on marketing or customer insights, as the audience would include people from other functions, namely medical, finance, regulatory affairs, and HR. It was an interesting challenge. To engage this diverse audience, I framed insight development principles using examples from science, art, jazz improvisation, and martial arts. But I also grounded each principle in real-world business applications – product innovation, customer segmentation, and brand differentiation. The interaction was surprisingly inspiring for both the audience and me. At the end of my presentation, I spoke about a portrait by Picasso of himself drawing Marie-Thérèse. I felt my presentation had a similar recursiveness to the depiction in the drawing. The principles that I was speaking about were integral to the construction of the presentation. That thought, and the analogy with the Picasso drawing, triggered an epiphany. Developing insight to solve practical problems by cross-pollinating ideas from diverse fields was what I enjoyed most. This was my art form – not market research, music, martial arts or any other discipline that I was pursuing. Taking myself outside the customer insights and marketing context clarified to me that insight is a phenomenon that we experience in our minds and bodies, and the process through which we arrive at it is common across science, art, business, and other fields. I had connected different parts of me and found my mission. In less than three months, I started my company, Insight Dojo.

The idea appeared in a flash, but it had been incubating for many years. I had coined[2] the term 'pragmatic polymath' to describe people characterised by an openness to learning new things, who immersed themselves in new disciplines, and cross-pollinated ideas, methods, and knowledge to drive innovations.

I practised what I preached. I got into various disciplines related to insight – traditional qualitative and quantitative research, anthropology, design, behavioural economics, cognitive neuroscience, and health psychology. I also drew inspiration from my two main hobbies – playing jazz piano and karate. But on that day in 2013, during the presentation, I managed to connect my varied interests in a single unifying idea. It all came together. In the past 11 years, I have made pragmatic polymathy one of the core practices in Insight Dojo that is implemented in all our projects to create better value for our clients.

The idea of a polymath being creative is not new. It has existed for as long as anyone can remember. Specifically, in the Renaissance period, dating from the 14th to the 17th century, the ideal was the 'universal' man who developed holistically and was skilled in multiple fields related to science and art, with Leonardo da Vinci or Michelangelo exemplifying this ideal[3]. There are many famous artists and scientists who were polymaths. For instance[4], Samuel Morse, who invented the Morse code, was trained as an artist; prolific novelist William Somerset Maugham studied medicine; and Rabindranath Tagore was a poet, composer, philosopher, social reformer, and painter.

Yet, we encounter people every day who are neither famous nor geniuses who love learning and go deep in different fields, e.g., poetry and computer science, to generate new practical ideas. Instead of taking their creativity for granted, businesses could actively seek them out for creative projects and change the way they hire people.

In today's complex world, where challenges span industries and disciplines, polymathy is not just an intellectual luxury – it is a necessity. Insights professionals must think flexibly, absorb knowledge from many domains, and break traditional boundaries. The polymathic approach is not about being a genius; it's about cultivating curiosity and openness and drawing inspiration from many fields. Businesses that recognize and nurture this mindset will unlock deeper insights, foster innovation, and stay ahead in an ever-changing landscape.

## PRAGMATIC POLYMATHY AS A PRACTICE

The problem of defining generalists, specialists, and pragmatic polymaths

There are many debates about the value of specialists versus generalists, with the two groups often pitted against each other. Specialists are known for producing excellence in a single field but are criticised for being siloed in their thinking, which is problematic in a world that needs an interdisciplinary perspective. Generalists are commended for their integrative thinking skills but may be scratching the surface with respect to the relevant knowledge domains and may not be able to create anything distinctive. The reality is that most people are multi-faceted and engage with different domains of activity in unique ways with various levels of depth.

Classifying people into neat buckets of specialists and generalists often proves to be difficult. How we describe ourselves does not help either. In a genomics organization, I recently encountered a person with a PhD in bioinformatics who had done years of scientific research but described himself as a generalist. From his vantage point, there were others who had much deeper knowledge than him in the field. From my perspective, he was a specialist. On the other extreme, you have people who are considered deep functional specialists, despite limited expertise, because the base level of knowledge in that organization is low. Additionally, context really matters. A general practitioner in a medical setting, by definition, is valued for their breadth of knowledge and, for complicated illnesses, must refer patients to specialists. However, when they switch careers and choose to work in a commercial setting, as sometimes people do, they are more than qualified to contribute as deep experts in medicine.

When it comes to developing insight, there is another complication. Most categorizations of specialists and generalists are based on what they do professionally or the disciplines they studied formally in their education. For developing insight, however, activities that we undertake in a personal capacity – DIY, art, gardening – can be hugely enriching.

A pragmatic polymath, in a sense, is a hybrid of a generalist and a specialist. Aspects that might characterize them are given below:

- Loving learning and having a wide set of interests, both professional and personal, that they pursue to achieve competence, even if not mastery.

- Implicitly or explicitly cross-pollinating ideas, methods, and knowledge to achieve their purpose.

- Having an overarching purpose in the real world. In the case of insights practitioners, this purpose is to develop insights which help organizations achieve positive impact.

Range is important. Yet, for generating creative and insightful ideas, depth in multiple fields enriches our capacities. That is why the conflation of generalists with polymaths, which happens often, can be problematic. Depth is a key aspect that differentiates a polymath from a generalist. But what is the level of depth required in a field? That again varies by context. As an example, consider doing market research in healthcare; you need a strong grounding in biology, especially related to diseases, health systems, mechanism of drugs, and knowledge of clinical trials. You do not need a degree in medicine. If you have one, that can be a bonus. On the other hand, you should aspire to achieve sufficient expertise in most qualitative and quantitative disciplines.

While the idea of pragmatic polymaths may be clear, they are hard to define precisely – as in the case of generalists and specialists. After reading the ESOMAR paper in which I introduced the concept of a 'pragmatic polymath', some people, often generalists, assumed they were pragmatic polymaths and were pleased at being part of an exclusive club. At other times, genuinely polymathic people, e.g., someone who was an accomplished violinist, a Pilates instructor, and a TV presenter, once asked me if I thought they were a pragmatic polymath. In both cases I realized it was not for me to judge and classify people into categories. Attempting to create an exclusive club was precisely the opposite of what I was trying to accomplish. I want to democratise the act of accessing different pools of knowledge and creating practical value. Furthermore, people are constantly in a state of flux, and there is no need to freeze people into these profiles. We keep changing and growing, so perhaps it's more important to think of pragmatic polymathy as a practice that most people can adopt.

> Pragmatic polymathy is a practice that helps us break boundaries within ourselves.

It is true that certain people are more drawn to a polymathic life. I keep encountering people who immerse themselves in multiple fields, e.g., serious practitioners of one or more sports, accomplished in an art form, and having a career in a completely unrelated area such as finance or technology. They love learning and become good at it by learning to learn. Their social media timelines, personal or professional, will reflect the diversity of their interests and communities. Certain people live a polymathic life even without realizing it. They are phenomenally good at DIY, gardening, or activities related to childcare that might be seen as part of routine living. Yet, these require tremendous skill acquired through practice and are building rich neural pathways in our brains that are waiting to be accessed for insights. The practice of pragmatic polymathy is a natural way to embrace and evolve our multi-faceted selves and bring that creatively to our work. It is about breaking boundaries within our own selves. Anyone can do it with awareness and effort.

A salient example that comes to my mind is that of a physics schoolteacher who took up running as a hobby late in life. Soon the interest extended to cycling, and she began taking part routinely in long races. She was surprised by the increase in her fitness levels, but even more so in her levels of confidence and enjoyment of the sports. She began thinking of how to increase the confidence and enjoyment of physics amongst girls in her school. That is what got Insight Dojo to undertake a qualitative and quantitative study to increase the engagement level and uptake of physics in the school. The recommendations are being implemented. The original insight here came in the form of an analogy from long-distance running and cycling.

The essence of the practice is to pursue multiple activities or disciplines, chosen out of love or necessity, to a certain level of depth. Thereafter, we connect ideas in order to develop innovative practical ideas. If boxes represented disciplines, the practice involves opening the boxes, playing with the content inside, mixing it all up, and creating something new. The pursuits might be long term, e.g., becoming a deep expert in machine learning over many years or pursuing an art form, or they might be short term, e.g., doing a course on cloud-based systems for a project, running a 10K race, or building a ChatGPT-based model. There are many ways to choose the activities and disciplines that may be particularly useful for insights professionals, though it is counterproductive to be too prescriptive. So many fields intersect that are of direct relevance to insights work, e.g., theories of innovation, statistical techniques, programming skills, and subject matter relevant to an industry such as telecommunications. Hobbies, too, offer many metaphors and help us think in varied ways.

> Pragmatic polymathy is about 'how' and not just 'what' we learn.

One might imagine that anyone who is a super-achiever in multiple fields – a national sports player, a grade 8 pianist – and ranking in the top 5 per cent of their academic class qualifies as a polymath and must, therefore, exhibit a capacity for creativity and for developing wonderful insights. This is not necessarily true. Passing a high-grade exam in piano requires talent and discipline, and it's a remarkable achievement. However, certain people can succeed by exclusively focusing on practising the skills needed to excel in the exam – the musical pieces, the scales and the arpeggios, and other tests. You can even succeed without being passionate about music. Others may only reach grade 5 while deeply enjoying the music, figuring out why a composition works, learning musical patterns that enrich their own compositions, or seeing parallels between classical music and other genres of music or even domains other than music. If I were attending a concert, I might prefer listening to the grade 8 pianist, but if I had to hire someone, and all other things were equal, I would choose the grade 5 person as described above. The latter type of learning is more likely to blend with other fields and spark insights. An interesting aspect of insights is they often appear when you relinquish focus and control.

People who are curious, who like playing with ideas and seeking truth, are more likely to stumble upon an insight. If the appearance of an insight is more mediated by the right hemisphere of the brain, as suggested by Iain McGilchrist[5], creating conditions that are congruent with it, i.e., being present, engaging with emotions, being relaxed rather than focused, and being willing to lose self-centredness, are likely to be helpful.

We encounter these contrasting ways of working in customer insights. Certain people and companies like to develop a 'best practice' method and apply those across a wide set of problems. It allows one to gain scale rapidly, train others, and build norms. It is an efficient way of working. The alternative way is that of curiosity and creativity. As shown in Chapter 5, my colleague who was playing with machine-learning models, only to discover a U-shaped pattern, illustrated this manner of working. We experiment, customize, and create methods based on the situation. Other than curiosity and playfulness related to the discipline, this example illustrates the importance of taking the knowledge and applying it in a real-world situation. My colleague was studying machine learning deeply in his own time; when they were assigned to the client project, they immediately saw the opportunity to experiment.

Real-world situations make us accountable and solidify our knowledge into something useful. There is a paying client on the other side whom we must convince about the truthfulness and usefulness of our work. Getting back to a music analogy, I have noticed that often even intermediate-level jazz players internalise knowledge of advanced music theory well. This is because they must get to grips with the theory to work out their improvisations.

### Why we need both breadth and depth for insights.

Since insights appear by connecting ideas from different fields, or in the form of analogies, thinking in terms of metaphors and analogies or exposure to a wide range of activities and disciplines increases the likelihood of making these connections.

But why is depth required? For several reasons. First, going deeper develops thinking skills. Robert Twigger[6] describes the 'rub-pat' barrier that you must overcome when you are learning a new skill. The name comes from the difficulty of patting your head and rubbing your stomach simultaneously. It is about coordinating two separate skills, which is not easy. Even for a linear regression model for a very large dataset, apart from the knowledge of statistics related to the model, one must know programming and the basics of operations of vectors and matrices, because that is how the data is stored. We could make errors if our understanding of the concept of regressions is poor, if we do not know about matrix operations, or if our programming skills are weak; or it could be a combination of these factors. Even if we do implement the model, the programme might be inelegant because we may end up writing many lines of code which a better coder could reduce to a few lines.

Let's imagine that we persist and create an elegant model. We have overcome a rub-pat barrier and created new neural pathways that will help us in insights work in completely unrelated fields. Apart from strengthening our logic, the exercise would build our ability to integrate separate concepts. It would develop our visualization skills, as good programming requires us to imagine how the model will interact with the data and create the output. It will make us better at abstracting because that's what we would have done to simplify the code.

Second, pursuing a field deeply helps us internalise the metaphors from that field. The act of reducing a programme to its essence, through simplification, will serve as a metaphor for many other activities, e.g., helping simplify a product design based on customer feedback or reducing a brand to its essence. Going deep, in a hands-on manner, to simplify the programme would make the metaphor more implicit, allowing it to be accessed faster in another situation.

Third, we would develop a broader intuition of what it takes to create a good algorithm. If we had a highly specialized expert in the team, who built more complex deep learning models, the ability to learn from the person, by asking more nuanced questions, would be enhanced.

Fourth, being competent in multiple knowledge fields allows us to build innovative and effective hybrid methodologies quickly. As mentioned in Chapter 4, hybrid methodologies help in getting sharp insights. Creating these needs an understanding of how to extract the essential elements of each method, e.g., conjoint analysis, ethnography, and designing prototypes, and being able to combine these to solve the business problem. This requires expertise, or at least competence, in multiple areas. A generalist approach will not work, and combining many specialists is both expensive and time-consuming. Fifth, as noted in Chapter 6, in order to solve complex problems, we need interactional expertise, and we need to gain knowledge about the relevant subject matter, e.g., oncology, cloud computing, and molecular biology. Interactional expertise is easier with the practice of pragmatic polymathy.

## NAVIGATING THE TENSION BETWEEN WIDTH AND DEPTH

Once we accept the premise that pragmatic polymathy boosts our capacity for insights, we encounter the fundamental barriers of balancing breadth and depth. Curious people will naturally gravitate towards new subjects. They need to go deep and explore them from the inside.

> Feeling the tension between breadth and depth of interests is perhaps a defining characteristic of a polymath.

How should one choose what to pursue at a given time? Say you have just finished an inspiring project on generating innovative ideas for mobile phones by conducting ethnography with young early adopters in Tokyo. You hung out with them in stores in Ginza and Akihabara, travelled on various metro lines, watched how they used the phone in crowded spaces, spent evenings at their home, talked about their influencers, and watched their rituals as they interacted with the packaging. The sponsors of the project are impressed by the richness of your recommendation, and you by the power of ethnography. You realize you have only scratched the surface and must go deeper. You also realize that the next stage involves quantitative testing, and there is a master course being run by Sawtooth Software on advanced conjoint analysis. How should you allocate your time in the next few months? Such trade-offs are faced in the practice of pragmatic polymathy on a routine basis.

This applies to your hobbies as well. You are training for a tennis championship in the club, but your team at work decides to run a 10K race as a bonding exercise, which requires you to spend time preparing. What do you do? Polymathy involves juggling depth across different fields, based on the context, interest, and purpose at hand. This is not easy. At one level, there is a risk that far from being energized, you fragment and exhaust yourself and become a dabbler in everything. You also feel frustrated that you are progressing slowly on a journey of excellence in each individual field because you are not as focused as others. For instance, I have seen people who were once my peers, or juniors, in karate working towards their 3rd Dan as I reached my 2nd Dan. Should I not have been more single-minded rather than pursuing other interests simultaneously? Navigating this tension between breadth and depth is not trivial. We need to organise our minds and activities to learn how to learn. One can learn to resolve this tension by following the five suggestions below:

1. **Seeing insight as an assimilative field that is worth mastering.**

Being clear about the end is important. As practitioners in this field, our purpose is to create insights that lead to impact. That is the art. That is where we want to achieve mastery. The potential for impact is huge. As we have observed, insight, by its very nature, is intricate and multi-dimensional, and even more so when solving real-world problems where contextual factors are critical and boundaries between knowledge disciplines become less clear. So even if you are slower in achieving mastery in individual disciplines, it is the combinatorial power achieved by studying diverse subjects that makes you a master in the field of insight.

This also means treating insight as an assimilative field. Thinking of jazz again; it is an art form that can assimilate ideas from anywhere. It is an open framework. You can integrate ragas from Indian classical music, syncopated rhythms from Latin music, or harmonic ideas from Western classical music. Any material can be used to serve the purpose of improvising and creating music. Insight can be viewed as a field of mastery which is open and fluid, that can absorb ideas from anywhere and can create practical value.

Wallace and Gruber[7] created the term 'network of enterprise' as a concept to describe the pattern of work of creative people. They defined the term enterprise as '*a group of related projects and activities broadly enough defined so that 1) the enterprise may continue when the creative person finds one path blocked but another open toward the same goal and 2) when success is achieved the enterprise does not come to an end but generates new tasks and projects that continue it*'. They also described how the network structures a polymathic life – '*In the course of a single day or week, the activities of the person may appear, from the outside, as a bewildering miscellany. But the person is not disoriented or dazzled. He or she can readily map each activity onto one or another enterprise.*' We can imagine a similar 'network of enterprise' for us where the overarching purpose is developing breakthrough insights, but with different enterprises – human behaviour, innovation and creativity, applied mathematics, mind-body well-being, etc. Explicitly thinking about such a 'network of enterprise' can provide cohesion over our varied pursuits over time and help us feel less fragmented.

## 2. Use five considerations to design your portfolio of interests.

How should we choose our portfolio of activities to undertake? This is perhaps the most challenging decision. It isn't just about choosing to do what you want. It involves saying no to many things that you like. There are five considerations that I have found helpful.

a. **Purpose:** Immersing oneself in disciplines that are directly relevant to the objective at hand is an obvious thing to do. This could be a short-term project, or it could be related to the long-term purpose of our organization or our career. For instance, at the time of writing, I am keen to serve a global technology company based in the US. I have made it a priority to learn about servers, storage, and networking industries. I am attending courses, speaking to people in the industry, reading articles, and watching online videos to increase my knowledge.

b. **Enjoyment:** We should always prioritize disciplines, whether related to our work or hobbies, that we enjoy. We will go deeper, learn more, and be happier. We will effortlessly spot connections within a field and naturally transfer them to other domains to create insights. It is no surprise that the metaphors that most help me in my work are from music, specifically jazz. I am deeply immersed in the field, and analogous connections keep appearing.

c. **Independence (orthogonality) of activities:** After accounting for importance and enjoyment, if one has a choice, we should pick activities that are orthogonal or sufficiently different from each other, for instance, a quantitative area such as segmentation analysis and a qualitative one, such as semiotics at work, or a sport and an art as a hobby. This is one way to exercise one's mind and body by challenging it in many ways. One can seek inspiration from Howard Gardner's categories of multiple intelligences[8], e.g., musical, bodily-kinaesthetic, logico-mathematical, etc. Using this as a guide, we can pick up activities that utilize distinct categories of intelligence that are independent from each other. It makes learning fun and easy. Also, it creates less confusion. Learning two fields that are very similar can cause confusion. This is best exemplified with languages. Learning French and German simultaneously is less likely to be confusing than French and Italian, which share the same Latin roots. Similarly, learning karate and kung fu simultaneously, which are both 'striking' and 'hard' martial arts involving a lot of punching and kicking, can be confusing. On the other hand, learning judo and karate can work because judo involves mastering throws and locks, which are only a small part of karate.

d. **Complementarity:** Certain fields have a synergistic relationship. Studying machine learning algorithms, probability, and a programming language simultaneously is an example of complementarity. Advancing in any of these disciplines will make us more competent machine learning practitioners.

e. **Novice activities:** Cultivating a beginner's mindset is perhaps one of the most valuable ways of looking. Often, the best way is to become a beginner. I took a course[9] in drawing and painting called 'Drawing and Painting for the Terrified Beginner'. Not only was it an incredibly relaxing and enjoyable experience, but the course also taught me that drawing and painting regularly improves one's observation skills. I have used some of the exercises to train my team on observation skills for ethnography.

## 3. Practising 'micro-mastery' and learning to learn.

I introduced Robert Twigger's concept of micro-mastery in Chapter 5. Practising micro-mastery is a great way of navigating the depth versus breadth tension. It allows us to take up a small unit of a field and develop great depth in it. In martial arts, a 'kata' is a sequence of techniques that is meant to be practised alone whilst visualizing being attacked by imaginary opponents. The performance of each kata lasts only a few minutes, but training regularly provides a strong foundational knowledge of essential principles of the martial art. One might imagine constructing 'katas' for different customer insights fields, say, for example, 'a behavioural economics kata' that allows one to study heuristics and biases in the context of customer decision-making or a 'conjoint kata' to imagine how customers trade-off different product features.

## 4. Cross-pollinate deliberately.

A lot of cross-pollination happens implicitly. Metaphors and analogies appear automatically. You see connections across disciplines subconsciously. However, it is also worth proactively combining practices from separate domains. Santiago Ramón Y Cajal[10], a Nobel laureate who is considered the father of modern neuroscience, used to prepare and observe cross-sections of the brain or spinal cord each morning. Being an accomplished artist as well as a surgeon, he used to draw sketches of the preparation from memory in the afternoons. Later in the day, he would compare his drawings with the preparations. He repeated the process until he felt that he had captured the essence of the anatomical structure accurately. He was less interested in the particularities of a specific cross-section. Instead, he wanted to capture the generalizable essence that would hold good across many cross sections.

The power of deliberate cross-pollination is best illustrated by the insight underlying the founding of the radically innovative university, London Interdisciplinary School (LIS). I was curious about the insight that led Ed

Fidoe[11], the founder, to take such a big risk. He told me that he got the insight to found LIS at School 21, which he has also founded. He said, *'We were doing lots of interdisciplinary projects at school – we could combine music and science or history with drama and art. We created an immersive experience for the local community to learn about World War I... and the students were acting within it in character, and this blew people away.... My view on this was that the students aged 12 learnt a small number of topics, but they would remember them for the rest of their lives...I remember thinking when these students choose their A-levels they will stop doing art and drama, and what was driving this. I realized it is the university sector... so the idea of LIS came from solving a problem – how do you change the way universities do entrance admissions? You can't really do it centrally because it's controlled by the faculties who are looking for how good you are in physics or history. The university system drives school behaviour. I thought maybe if we started something outside of the system – a new kind of interdisciplinary institute... that made me think of the argument that increasingly the complex problems that we face are interdisciplinary.'*

The CEO of a company I was serving asked me to run a workshop with the theme 'What it means to have a black belt launch'. The idea was to use the metaphor from martial arts to see if we could get new insights on launch excellence. The big idea that came from the workshop was to see the consumer as the 'sensei' or teacher. The notion was that in a martial arts place, students diligently listen to the teacher and learn to put their teaching into practice.

If we treated the customer as a teacher (not a king), we would be more likely to listen harder to their needs and respond accordingly. It was a subtle but significant shift in the team's mentality.

## 5. We must create insight with *joie de vivre* (joy of living).

Insight and happiness are closely related. The experience of gaining insight is a euphoric feeling. Also, being relaxed and joyful creates a welcoming environment for insights to appear. We must actively cultivate a feeling of harmony while developing insight. Remembering to do that helps us engage with our multiple interests with lightness. We avoid rigid definitions of ourselves and remain open and adaptable. That allows for a more fluid integration of knowledge and maintains the joy of learning. This also means that we must take care of our own well-being, e.g., maintain a healthy lifestyle by ensuring we get sufficient sleep, do activities that make us mindful – meditation or taking a walk, eat well and exercise.

A polymathic approach is not without difficulties. I often find people writing about the topic, but their focus is on the 'poly' part or having a range of interests rather than the 'math' part, which is about having sufficient depth. They underestimate how difficult it is to achieve competence in a single field, let alone multiple ones, especially since we have such busy lives. Richness, in any field, lies in depth. It surfaces in the daily grind of practising scales, doing crunches or writing code. Also, pragmatic polymathy is not everyone's cup of tea. Many people prefer to be more single-minded in their pursuits, and there is a lot to be said for that type of focus. In any case, the motivation must be intrinsic and cannot be imposed top-down. Furthermore, when you pursue many interests, you are less likely to define yourself by any one of those. I personally love this aspect, yet it creates confusion for many people. My company Insight Dojo has been variously called a firm that focused on design, strategy, segmentation, innovation, qualitative research, behaviour change, data analytics or conjoint depending on the background of the person. This is especially problematic in a world with a low attention span. It is easier to convince someone that you are great at segmentation if that is the only thing you do rather than when it's just one of the multiple things you do.

Fourth, making pragmatic polymathy work to deliver insights takes effort. I have met people who excel in multiple fields but possess only an average ability to generate truly novel insights. I have also seen the reverse situation many times, where people aren't particularly committed to any field and are simply brilliant at coming up with breakthrough ideas.

Due to my deep involvement with this topic, I come across many debates on the value of generalists versus specialists. From my point of view, these discussions have limited value given some of the challenges in defining generalists and specialists as argued in this chapter. The discourse on polymaths has been focused on geniuses and is too restrictive. The idea of pragmatic polymathy has been my humble attempt to offer a way forward that is inclusive and allows vast numbers of people to get better at developing insights.

Ultimately, in a complex world, to make sense of what's going on, one must be a genuine truth seeker, be humble, think flexibly and creatively, and absorb knowledge from many disciplines. We need to master technology and adapt to complex changes in the world. Henry Kissinger, Craig Mundie, and Eric Schmidt[12] have asserted that AI will be the ultimate polymath in its ability to integrate vast amounts of knowledge from diverse fields fast. The world will not be constrained by the number of polymaths. Even in that world, human beings who practise pragmatic polymathy will be able to work better with AI to craft insights. The devil is in the details.

# 9

# A Checklist for Building Your Aha! Insight Quotient

THROUGHOUT THE BOOK, I HAVE SHARED THE PRINCIPLES essential for developing breakthrough insights.

To facilitate your insight development capability, I am listing below a set of questions that can help boost the Aha! Insight Quotient of your organization or for you as an individual. This is a subset of a much longer list, but it can help you get started.

## Solving the right problem

1. Are you or your team solving the hard problems that the C-suite faces?
   1.1 Will solving the problem unlock substantially positive outcomes?
   1.2 Is there sufficient uncertainty in the questions you are addressing?

1.2.1 Which types of uncertainties are you solving for – revealing hidden patterns in a context, bringing a creative product to the market, changing deeply entrenched behaviours, shedding light on the future or simplifying complexity?

1.3 Do you routinely syndicate your views with the senior leadership team?

1.4 Do you always write a clear problem statement?

1.5 Do you break down the problem further into components? Do you have hypotheses about the answers?

1.6 Are you clear about your organizations' resources and capabilities at the outset?

1.7 Do you have a clear idea of the strategic and tactical levers available to you at the problem-solving stage?

## Generating Aha! Insights

2. Are you or members in your team developing Aha! insights to solve these problems?

    2.1 Do you or your team members experience and recognize the Aha! moments frequently?

    2.2 Are you aware of the mechanisms through which the insight is generated? Do you connect disparate elements? Do you spot observe dissonant counter intuitive patterns that lead to insight? Does analogical thinking lead to insight? Does overcoming obstacles lead to insight? Do you uncover new variables or patterns?

2.3 Are there mechanisms of insight that you use more often? Are there mechanisms that you can consciously attempt to deploy more?

## Being a multi-modal thinker

3. Are you and your team training yourselves to use multiple modes of thinking?

   3.1 Are you training both your analytical and intuitive thinking skills? Does one need to be developed more?

   3.2 Can you simultaneously be anchored in the reality of the situation and make imaginative leaps?

   3.3 Are you comfortable with subjective interpretation whilst recognizing the value of objective facts?

   3.4 Do you regularly undertake activities that strengthen your mind-body connection – exercise, yoga, sports, meditation, practice an art, DIY, etc.?

   3.5 Do you try to develop awareness about your biases, such as confirmation bias?

   3.6 Do you actively take steps to overcome your biases?

   3.7 How good are you at different modes of thinking – observing, empathising, abstracting, analogizing, imaging, recognizing patterns, playing or modelling?

   3.8 Which of these modes of thinking need more work?

3.9 How will you approach training to get better at these modes of thinking?

3.10 Do you actively create space for serendipitous insights to appear – take breaks for insights to incubate, go to museums, or take walks in nature?

## Being an experimenting craftsman

4. How do you and your team approach knowledge and methods necessary for insight?

4.1 Are you or others in your team on a path of mastery in the main disciplines related to insight?

4.2 How good are you at cultivating a beginner's mind that is fresh and receptive when it comes to learning?

4.3 How often do you experiment with new methods?

4.4 How often do you learn new disciplines/get inspired by new fields?

4.5 How good are you at cross-pollinating across different disciplines?

4.6 How would you rate yourself on interactional expertise, i.e., the ability to understand and communicate competently in the language of a specific domain or field of expertise without being a practitioner in that field?

4.7 How would you rate yourself on making your methods analytically robust, e.g., in drawing better causal inferences?

4.8 How strong are your basics related to qualitative and quantitative research?

- 4.9 How deep is your understanding of the 10 families of techniques?
- 4.10 How strong is your understanding of concepts related to business such as strategy, innovation, and marketing?
- 4.11 Do you look at future trends on a routine basis?
- 4.12 How good are your programming skills?
- 4.13 Do you have extra-curricular interests and hobbies? To what extent do they provide inspiration for creating insights?
5. How do you and your team go about embedding insights in your organization?
    - 5.1 Do you routinely support the leaders in the C-suite about what's on their minds?
    - 5.2 Do you routinely interact with leaders of different functions and elicit their support?
    - 5.3 Do you routinely support the frontline in their activities?
    - 5.4 Do you work to support different countries and regions in your organization?
    - 5.5 Do you feel a strong ownership for your organization's goals?
    - 5.6 How often do you challenge decisions made by leaders based on your insight?
    - 5.7 How easily can you switch from big-picture thinking to detailed executional thinking?
    - 5.8 Do you know your own profile in terms of the insight archetypes?
    - 5.9 Do you recognize the archetypes for the leaders in your organization?

5.10  Do you recognize the champions for insights in your company? Do you elicit their support?

5.11  Do you have a set of practices in your company to ensure that breakthrough insights are generated routinely?

5.12  Are you attempting to create a centre of excellence for insights?

5.13  Do you have a system that captures your knowledge and past insights so that it can be shared with others?

5.14  How good are you at coaching people on the value of insights?

5.15  Do you break silos and collaborate with other departments to develop insights?

# Notes

## Introduction

1. Jeff Howe, 'Clayton Christensen Wants to Transform Capitalism.' Wired, 12 February 2013. https://www.wired.com/2013/02/mf-clayton-christensen-wants-to-transform-capitalism/, last accessed March 2025.

## Chapter 1

1. Arno Penzias – Biographical, www.nobelprize.org/prizes/physics/1978/penzias/biographical/, last accessed 16 May 2025.
2. Carolyn Dewar, Scott Keller, and Vik Malhotra, *CEO Excellence: The Six Mindsets That Distinguish the Best Leaders from the Rest*, John Murray Business, March 2022.
3. 'MasterCard's Ajay Banga: Why "Yes, If" Is More Powerful Than Saying No', *Knowledge at Wharton*, 24 July 2014, last accessed 16 May 2025.
4. Richard Haythornthwaite and Ajay Banga, 'The Former and Current Chairs of Mastercard on Executing a Strategic CEO Succession', , last accessed January 2025.
5. 'MasterCard's Ajay Banga: Why 'Yes, If" Is More Powerful Than Saying No', *Knowledge at Wharton*, 24 July 2014, last accessed 16 May 2025.

6. Alan Wheatley, 'Cash is Dead, Long Live Cash', IMF, June 2017, https://www.imf.org/external/pubs/ft/fandd/2017/06/wheatley.htm, last accessed 27 May 2025.
7. Steve Jobs, Calligraphy and Mackintosh, www.youtube.com/watch?v=zOlRWg_iyWY, last accessed 16 May 2025.
8. 'What is Uber about, 6 fun facts to benefit our reader', *Uber Blog*, https://www.uber.com/en-AE/blog/dubai/uber-fun-facts/, last accessed May 2025.
9. Joel Garfinkle, 'Netflix CEO Reed Hastings' Big Idea – How Netflix Got Started', YouTube, www.youtube.com/watch?v=Hs2fgh5FvDw. last accessed 16 May 2025.
10. Hites Ahir, Nicholas Bloom, and Davide Furceri, 'The World Uncertainty Index', Discussion Paper, *World Economic Forum*, April 2025.
11. ⸺ 'The World Uncertainty Index', Discussion Paper, *World Economic Forum*, April 2025.
12. Horst W.J. Rittel, Melvin M. Webber, 'Dilemmas in a general theory of planning' *Policy sciences* 4.2 (1973): 155–169.
13. 'AIF: Ajay Banga & Indra Nooyi on her book *My Life in Full: Work, Family, and Our Future*', www.youtube.com/watch?v=On26m71QXrY, last accessed 16 May 2025.
14. Richard Rumelt, *Good Strategy, Bad Strategy: The Difference and Why It Matters*, Crown Business, 2011.
15. HPCwire. "Meta's Chief AI Scientist Yann LeCun Questions the Longevity of Current GenAI and LLMs." *HPCwire*, February 11, 2025. https://www.hpcwire.com/2025/02/11/metas-chief-ai-scientist-yann-lecun-questions-the-longevity-of-current-genai-and-llms/.
16. Martin Gardner, *Aha! Insight*, W.H.Freeman & Co Ltd, 1978.
17. Devjyot Ghoshal, Chayut Setboonsarng, 'Southeast Asia prepares for factories fleeing Trump tariffs on China', *Reuters*, https://www.reuters.com/world/asia-pacific/southeast-asia-prepares-factories-fleeing-trump-tariffs-china-2024-11-08, last accessed January 2025.
18. Robert Tait, 'US pollsters taking heat – again – for failing to predict Trump triumph', *Guardian*, https://www.theguardian.com/us-news/2024/nov/06/trump-presidential-election-polling, December 2024.

19. Salsa Della Guitara Putri, et al, 'Echo Chambers and Algorithmic Bias: The Homogenization of Online Culture in a Smart Society.' *SHS Web of Conferences*, vol. 202, 2024, 05001, https://doi.org/10.1051/shsconf/202420205001.
20. Jeanne Nakamura, Mihaly Csikzentmihalyi, 'The construction of meaning through vital engagement,' 2003.
21. Steve Jobs, 'Steve Jobs' 2005 Stanford Commencement Address', YouTube, https://www.youtube.com/watch?v=UF8uR6Z6KLc., June 2011.
22. Shani Harmon, Renee Cullinan, 'Connecting the Dots – A Vital and Neglected Capability.' *HuffPost*, www.huffpost.com/entry/connecting–the–dots_b_5102403, April 2014.
23. Arnold Toynbee, *A Study of History*, Oxford University Press, 1934–1961.
24. John Copeland Interview conducted on Zoom for 60 minutes, 17 October 2024.
25. Michael Lewis, *The Undoing Project: A Friendship That Changed Our Minds*, W. W. Norton & Company, 2016, p. 250.
26. Jeremy Adelman, *Worldly Philosopher: The Odyssey of Albert O. Hirschman*, Princeton University Press, 2013, p. 116.
27. 'Introduction', *The Essential Hirschman*, edited by Jeremy Adelman, Princeton University Press, 2013, p. viii.

## Chapter 2

1. Osho, *Osho on Zen*, St. Martin's Griffin, 2001.
2. 'Darwin's Finches', *Encyclopædia Britannica*.
3. Barry Miles, *Paul McCartney: Many Years from Now*, New York: Henry Holt and Company, 1998.
4. Vibha Rishi Interview conducted on Zoom for 60 minutes, 13 September 2024.
5. Iain McGilchrist, *The Master and His Emissary: The Divided Brain and the Making of the Western World*, Yale University Press, February 2009.
6. Jacques E. Rossouw, et al, 'Risks and Benefits of Estrogen Plus Progestin in Healthy Postmenopausal Women: Principal Results from the Women's Health Initiative Randomized Controlled Trial', *JAMA*, vol. 288, no. 3, 2002, pp 321–33.

*eScholarship*. escholarship.org/content/qt3mr6f93p/qt3mr6f93p.pdf?t=prll4c.
7. 'Thirty Years Later, the Women's Health Initiative Provides Researchers with Key Messages.' *National Heart, Lung, and Blood Institute (NHLBI)*, National Institutes of Health, www.nhlbi.nih.gov/news/2024/thirty–years–later–womens–health–initiative–provides–researchers–key–messages, May 2024.
8. Richard E Mayer, 'The search for insight: Grappling with Gestalt psychology's unanswered questions', 1995.
9. Webster's New World College Dictionary (7th ed.), Houghton Mifflin Harcourt.
10. Janet E Davidson, 'The suddenness of insight', 1995.
11. Janet Metcalfe, David Wiebe, 'Intuition in insight and noninsight problem solving.' *Memory & Cognition* 15.3 (1987): 238–246.
12. Thich Nhat Hanh, *The art of power*, Harper Collins, 2007.
13. Janet E Davidson, 'The suddenness of insight.'
14. Gary Klein, *Seeing What Others Don't: The Remarkable Ways We Gain Insights*. PublicAffairs, 2013.
15. Ruchir Sharma, 'Investor & Author Ruchir Sharma Talks to Prannoy Roy on the 10 Economic Trends For 2025', YouTube, uploaded by *NDTV*, https://www.youtube.com/watch?v=hYVJl9AcKd0., March 2025.
16. Thomas S Kuhn, *The Structure of Scientific Revolutions*, 3rd ed., University of Chicago Press, 1996.
17. Gary Klein, *Seeing What Others Don't: The Remarkable Ways We Gain Insights*, Public Affairs, Hachette Book Group, 25 June 2013.
18. Steven Johnson, *Where Good Ideas Come From: The Natural History of Innovation*, Riverhead Books, 2010.
19. *Suits*, Created by Aaron Korsh, performances by Gabriel Macht, Patrick J. Adams, and Meghan Markle, Universal Cable Productions, 2011–19.
20. *Dangal*, Directed by Nitesh Tiwari, performances by Aamir Khan, Fatima Sana Shaikh, and Sanya Malhotra, Aamir Khan Productions, 2016.
21. 'Darwin and Malthus', Evolution, WGBH Educational Foundation, https://www.pbs.org/wgbh/evolution/library/02/5/l_025_01.html., 2001.

22. Janet E Davidson, 'The suddenness of insight', 1995.
23. Gary Klein, *Seeing What Others Don't: The Remarkable Ways We Gain Insights*, Public Affairs, Hachette Book Group, 25 June 2013.
24. Vibha Rishi Interview conducted on zoom for 60 minutes, September 13, 2024
25. Malcolm Gladwell, 'The Gift of Doubt.' *The New Yorker*, June 2013.
26. Gary Klein, *Seeing What Others Don't: The Remarkable Ways We Gain Insights*, Public Affairs, Hachette Book Group, 25 June 2013.
27. Rita Banerji Interview conducted on zoom for 60 minutes, March 14, 2025.
28. Iain McGilchrist, *The Master and His Emissary: The Divided Brain and the Making of the Western World*, Yale University Press, February 2009.
29. Iain McGilchrist, *The Master and His Emissary: The Divided Brain and the Making of the Western World*, Yale University Press, February 2009.
30. John D Norton, Chasing a Beam of Light, https://sites.pitt.edu/~jdnorton/Goodies/Chasing_the_light/, accessed March 2025
31. Bahadur, Nina (21 January 2014). "Dove 'Real Beauty' Campaign Turns 10: How A Brand Tried To Change The Conversation About Female Beauty". *Huffington Post*. Archived from the original on 29 October 2015. Retrieved April 2025.
32. Christoph Molnar, *Modeling Mindsets: Many Cultures of Learning*, Independently, 28 April 2022.
33. Richard Rumelt, *Good Strategy, Bad Strategy: The Difference and Why It Matters*, Crown Business, 1 January 2011.
34. Adam Webb, "Harnessing the Power of Your Reality Distortion Field," *Forbes*, October 4, 2021. https://www.forbes.com/councils/forbesbusinessdevelopmentcouncil/2021/10/04/harnessing-the-power-of-your-reality-distortion-field/, April 2025
35. John Kay, Mervyn King, *Radical Uncertainty: Decision-Making Beyond the Numbers*, W. W. Norton & Company, 5 March 2020.

36. Hitendra Wadhwa in-person interview conducted in London, August 26, 2024
37. Robert Scott Root–Bernstein, Michele Root–Bernstein, *Sparks of genius: The thirteen thinking tools of the world's most creative people*, Houghton Mifflin Harcourt, 9 August 2001.
38. Shunryu Suzuki, Edited by Trudy Dixon, *Zen Mind, Beginner's Mind*, Weatherhill, 1970.
39. Richard E. Mayer, 'The search for insight: Grappling with Gestalt psychology's unanswered questions', 1995.
40. Thomas Gilovich, Dale Griffin, Daniel Kahneman, *Heuristics and biases: The psychology of intuitive judgment*, Cambridge University Press, 2002.
41. Kevin Dunbar, 'How scientists really reason: Scientific reasoning in real–world laboratories.' *The Nature of Insight* 18 (1995): 365–395.
42. Steven Johnson, *Where Good Ideas Come From: The Natural History of Innovation*, Riverhead Books, 1 October 2010.
43. Graham Wallace, *The Art of Thought*. Harcourt, Brace and Company, 1926.

# Chapter 3

1. G.K. Chesterton, *The Scandal of Father Brown*, Dodd, Mead and Company, 1935.
2. ‹The power of partnership: How the CEO–CMO relationship can drive outsize growth›, *McKinsey & Company*, (n.d.), https://www.mckinsey.com/capabilities/growth–marketing–and–sales/our–insights/the–power–of–partnership–how–the–ceo–cmo–relationship–can–drive–outsize–growth, March 2025
3. John Forsyth interview, conducted on Zoom for 60 minutes, October 24, 2024.
4. Insight Dojo, Customized Research for a Client.
5. 'Why 95% of New Products Miss the Mark—And How Yours Can Avoid the Same Fate', *MIT Professional Programs*, professionalprograms.mit.edu/blog/design/why–95–of–new–products–miss–the–mark–and–how–yours–can–avoid–the–same–fate., 2024, last accessed March 2025.
6. Safi Bahcall, *Loonshots: How to Nurture the Crazy Ideas That Win Wars, Cure Diseases, and Transform Industries,* St. Martin's Press, 19 March 2019.

7. 'What Do A–Level Results Tell Us About Physics?', *Institute of Physics*, www.iop.org/about/blogs/what–do–a–level–results–tell–us–about–physics#gref., August 2023.
8. 'It's Different for Girls: The Influence of Schools', *Institute of Physics*, www.iop.org/sites/default/files/2019–04/its–different–for–girls.pdf., October 2012.
9. Insight Dojo, Customized Research for a Client.
10. 'What Do Graduates Do? 2024/25', *Prospects Luminate*, https://graduatemarkettrends.cdn.prismic.io/graduatemarkettrends/Z0Sn968jQArT1SXd_what–do–graduates–do–202425.pdf., 2024, last accessed Feburary 2025.
11. John Kay, Mervyn King, *Radical Uncertainty: Decision–Making Beyond the Numbers*. W. W. Norton & Company, 5 March 2020..
12. Nassim Nicholas Taleb, *The Black Swan: The Impact of the Highly Improbable*, Random House, 2007.
13. Paul J.H. Schoemaker, 'Scenario planning: a tool for strategic thinking.' *MIT Sloan Management Review*, 1995.
14. Benjamin Hale, 'He "Was Struggling Not to Laugh": Inside Netflix's Crazy, Doomed Meeting with Blockbuster', *Vanity Fair*, www.vanityfair.com/news/2019/09/netflixs–crazy–doomed–meeting–with–blockbuster., September 2019.
15. ——'He "Was Struggling Not to Laugh": Inside Netflix's Crazy, Doomed Meeting with Blockbuster'
16. 'David Cameron: Brexit is a Risk We Can Avoid – BBC News', YouTube, uploaded by BBC News, www.youtube.com/watch?v=HO6MZcOQH0g., June 2016.
17. Tim Bale, 'Why David Cameron Called the 2016 Referendum – and Why He Lost It,' *UK in a Changing Europe*, ukandeu.ac.uk/why–david–cameron–called–the–2016–referendum/, October 2022.
18. 'PwC's 26th Annual Global CEO Survey', *PwC*, www.pwc.com/gx/en/ceo–survey/2023/main/download/26th_CEO_Survey_PDF_v1.pdf., 2023, last accessed December 2024.
19. 'Procter & Gamble: Swiffer', *Continuum*, www.continuuminnovation.com/what–we–do/case–studies/swiffer., last accessed March 2025.
20. Samuel Arbesman, *Overcomplicated: Technology at the Limits of Comprehension*, Current, 2015.

21. Clayton M. Christensen, *The Innovator's Dilemma: When New Technologies Cause Great Firms to Fail*, Harvard Business Review Press, 1997.

## Chapter 4

1. Richard Sennett, '*The Craftsman*', Allen Lane, 2008.
2. 'Exit Poll 2024 Frenzy Could Be Followed by Profit Booking After Results; Focus to Shift on Budget, Say Experts.' *Livemint*, HT Media, www.livemint.com/market/stock–market–news/exit–poll–2024–frenzy–could–be–followed–by–profit–booking–after–results–focus–to–shift–on–budget–say–experts–11717397025638.html., March 2025.
3. M.K. Venu, 'The 'Exit Polls and Stock Market' Imbroglio Could Have Far Reaching Consequences.' *The Wire*, thewire.in/economy/exit–poll–stock–market–scam–allegations, March 2025.
4. Vasudha Mukherjee, 'Lok Sabha Elections: What Do Yogendra Yadav and Prashant Kishor Predict?', *Business Standard*, Business Standard Ltd., www.business–standard.com/elections/lok–sabha–election/lok–sabha–elections–what–do–yogendra–yadav–and–prashant-kishor–predict–124053001154_1.html., December 2024.
5. 'Center for Contemporary South Asia. "Yogendra Yadav." *Watson Institute for International and Public Affairs, Brown University*. https://watson.brown.edu/southasia/people/yogendra-yadav.March 2025.
6. Mahesh Avadhutha, 'Yogendra Yadav on How He Got 2024 Polls Predictions Right, Why Opposition Needs Coherent Agenda.' *NewsMeter*, newsmeter.in/top–stories/yogendra–yadav–on–how–he–got–2024–polls–predictions–right–why–opposition–needs–coherent–agenda–733114.,December 2024
7. Yogendra Yadav, 'Yogendra Yadav Interview: How He Got the Lok Sabha Elections Predictions Right?', YouTube, uploaded by NDTV, www.youtube.com/watch?v=g7pfa5MuF7Y., May 2024, last accessed March 2025.
8. Steven Johnson, *Where Good Ideas Come From: The Natural History of Innovation*, Riverhead Books, 2010.
9. Nassim Nicholas Taleb, *The Black Swan: The Impact of the Highly Improbable*. Random House, 17 April 2007.

10. Brian M. Hughes, *Psychology in Crisis*, Palgrave, 2018.
11. John PA Ioannidis, 'Why most published research findings are false.' *PLoS medicine* 2.8 (2005): e124.
12. Gerd Gigerenzer, *How to Stay Smart in a Smart World*, MIT Press, 2022.
13. Steven Sloman, Philip Fernbach, *The knowledge illusion: The myth of individual thought and the power of collective wisdom*, Pan Macmillan, 2017.
14. Judea Pearl, Dana McKenzzie, *Book of Why: The New Science of Cause and Effect*, Penguin, 2 May 2019.
15. Nassim Nicholas Taleb, *The Black Swan: The Impact of the Highly Improbable*. Random House, 17 April 2007.
16. Nassim Nicholas Taleb, *The Black Swan: The Impact of the Highly Improbable*. Random House, 17 April 2007.
17. Leo Breiman, 'Statistical modeling: The two cultures (with comments and a rejoinder by the author).' *Statistical science*16.3 (2001): 199–231.
18. Richard Sennett, *'The Craftsman'*, Allen Lane, 2008.
19. 'Tate Modern: Olafur Eliasson Exhibition Guide', [specific exhibition dates if available, e.g., 11 July 2019 – 5 January 2020], *Tate*, www.tate.org.uk/whats–on/tate–modern/olafur–eliasson/exhibition–guide.
20. Judea Pearl, Madelyn Glymour, Nicholas P. Jewell, *Causal Inference in Statistics: A Primer*, Wiley, March 2016.
21. Clayton M. Christensen, *The Innovator's Dilemma: When New Technologies Cause Great Firms to Fail*, Harvard Business Review Press, 1997.
22. Robert Twigger, *Micromastery: Learn Small, Learn Fast, and Unlock Your Potential to Achieve Anything*, Penguin Random House, 17 May 2017.
23. Kenji Tokitsu, *Katas: The Meaning Behind Movements*, Inner Traditions, 2010.

## Chapter 5

1. 'Success Stories', *Wayne's Blog*, https://www.drwaynedyer.com/blog/success–secrets, Feburary 2010, last accessed December 2024.

2. Robert Scott Root-Bernstein, Michele Root-Bernstein, *Sparks of genius: The thirteen thinking tools of the world's most creative people,* Houghton Mifflin Harcourt, 9 August 2001.
3. Arthur Conan Doyle, *The Hounds of Baskerville,* 1902.
4. 'Discovery and Development of Penicillin- International Historic Chemical Landmarks', *American Chemical Society,* www.acs.org/content/acs/en/education/whatischemistry/landmarks/flemingpenicillin.html, last accessed November 2024.
5. David Grohl, 'Introduction and Performance of Everlong (Accoustic)', YouTube, www.youtube.com/watch?v=vLkBybsH73k, last accessed December 2024.
6. Post-it Brand Site, post-it, 3m.co.uk/3M/en_GB/post-it-notes/contact-us/about-us, last accessed November 2024.
7. Donald A. Norman, *The psychology of everyday things,* 1988.
8. 'Introducing Kindle', Amazon Press Centre, press.aboutamazon.com/2007/11/introducing-amazon-kindle, last accessed November 2024
9. Genevieve Hall, Vivek Banerji, Angelo D'Alessandro, Dan Atkins, Daniel Raynier, 'Rapid Impact, Creating a market leader in a year through machine-learning, ethnography and psychology', *ESOMAR,* Congress, 2019
10. Daniel Goleman, *Focus: Hidden Drivers of Excellence,* Bloomsbury Publishing PLC, 9 October 2014.
11. Gillian Tett, *Anthro-vision: A new way to see in business and life,* Simon and Schuster, 8 June 2021.
12. Anonymized and disguized example from Insight Dojo Customomized Research in 2020
13. Robert Scott Root-Bernstein, Michele Root-Bernstein, *Sparks of genius: The thirteen thinking tools of the world's most creative people,* Houghton Mifflin Harcourt, 9 August 2001.
14. Dore Ashton, *Picasso on Art: A Selection of Views, Da Capo Press,* First Edition (22 Aug. 1988), Page 64.
15. John Brownlee, 'How Apple Uses Picasso To Teach Employees about Product Design', *Fast Company,* www.fastcompany.com/3034240/how-apple-uses-picasso-to-teach-employees-about-product-design, November 2014.
16. Terrence J. Sejnowski, *The deep learning revolution,* MIT press, 2018.

17. Jennifer A. Doudna, S. H. Sternberg, *A Crack in Creation: Gene Editing and the Unthinkable Power to Control*, Boston, MA, USA: Houghton Mifflin Harcourt, 2017.
18. Robert Scott Root–Bernstein, Michele Root–Bernstein, *Sparks of genius: The thirteen thinking tools of the world's most creative people*, Houghton Mifflin Harcourt, 9 August 2001.
19. 'From AT–Ats to iPhones: Early Sketches of 10 Iconic Products', *Wired*, www.wired.com/2012/10/early–sketches–of–iconic–objects, October 2012, last accessed November 2024.
20. 'From AT–Ats to iPhones: Early Sketches of 10 Iconic Products', *Wired*, October 2012, accessed November 2024
21. F. J. Anscombe, Graphs in Statistical Analysis. *The American Statistician*, 27(1), 17–21, 1973.
22. Edward Tufte, *Beautiful Evidence*, Graphics Pr, 2006.
23. 'Diaper–Beer Syndrome', *Forbes*, https://www.forbes.com/forbes/1998/0406/6107128a.html, 1998, last accessed November 2024.
24. Robert Scott Root–Bernstein, Michele Root–Bernstein, *Sparks of genius: The thirteen thinking tools of the world's most creative people*, Houghton Mifflin Harcourt, 9 August 2001.
25. 'Case Studies of Successful Engineering Prototyping', *Emergent Design Lab*, emergntdesignlabs.com/blog/new–blogs/5–the–ultimate–guide–to–engineering–prototypes/#tesla–roadster, last accessed January 2025.
26. Mark A. Warner, 'You trained at mayo clinic? wow!.', *Mayo Clinic Proceedings*. Vol. 89. No. 3. Elsevier Limited, 2014.
27. Ashley Kahn, *Kind of Blue, Miles Davis and the Making of a Masterpiece*, Grant Books, 2001.
28. Martin Gardner, *Aha! Insight*, W.H.Freeman & Co Ltd, 1978.
29. Judea Pearl and Dana McKenzie, '*Book of Why: The New Science of Cause and Effect*', Penguin, 2019.

## Chapter 6

1. '7 Habits of Highly Effective People', *Private Security Professionals of America*, www.mypspa.org/article/more/the–7–habits–of–highly–effective–people, last accessed November 2024.

2. Gillian Tett, *Anthro–vision: A new way to see in business and life*, Avid Reader Press, Simon & Schuster, 8 June 2021.
3. Thomas Gilovich, Dale Griffin, Daniel Kahneman, eds, *Heuristics and biases: The psychology of intuitive judgment*, Cambridge University press, 8 July 2022.
4. Santosh Desai, *Mother Pious Lady: Making Sense of Every India*, HarperCollins, 14 April 2015.
5. Margaret Mead, 'The Role of the Individual in Samoan Culture.' *The Journal of the Royal Anthropological Institute of Great Britain and Ireland* 58 (1928): 481–495.
6. Anjali Puri, Poonam Kumar, 'From Intuitive Knowledge to formal cultural knowledge, Reading Culture Through Archetypes', *ESOMAR Qualitative*, 2010.
7. Neerja Wable Interview on Zoom for 60 minutes, February 6, 2025.
8. Tom Kelley with Jonathan Littman, *The Art of Innovation*, Profile Books, 2001.
9. Santosh Desai interview conducted in-person in Gurugram for 120 minutes, July 15, 2024.
10. Safi Bahcall, *Loonshots: How to Nurture the Crazy Ideas That Win Wars, Cure Dizeases, and Transform Industries.*
11. Lucy Handley, 'Steve Jobs disliked market research – but it is essential', *Marketing Week*, https://www.marketingweek.com/steve–jobs–disliked–market–research–but–it–is–essential/, May 2012, last accessed in November 2024.
12. Jensen Huang, 'Jensen Huang–Favoring Moore's Law Over Customer Feedback', YouTube , https://www.youtube.com/watch?v=6Uc–EiQ2xnU, August 2013, last accessed in December 2024.
13. '02: Nike (1987) – Just Do It', *Creative Review*, www.creativereview.co.uk/just–do–it–slogan, last accessed December 2024.
14. 'The Apple Marketing Philosophy', *Steve Job Archives*, stevejobsarchive.com/artifact/the–apple–marketing–philosophy, last accessed December 2024.
15. 'What is Uber all about? Fun facts about Uber's history', *Uber*, www.uber.com/en–ZA/blog/what–is–uber–facts', last accessed December 2024.

16. 'Our Story: From the Garage to the Googleplex,' About Google, https://about.google/company-info/our-story/.
17. Sissi Cao, 'Michael Dell Shares His First Lesson of the 'Dell Direct Model' When He Was 16', *Observer*, observer.com/2024/03/michael–dell–interview–sxsw/, March 2024, last accessed December 2024.
18. João da Silva, Tom Gerken, 'Apple apologizes after piano crushing ad backlash', *BBC*, www.bbc.co.uk/news/articles/cld0rxlqgggo, May 2024, last accessed May 2024.
19. Vibha Rishi Interview, conducted on Zoom for 60 minutes, September 13, 2024.
20. John Copeland Interview, conducted on zoom for 60 minutes, October 17, 2024.
21. Vibha Rishi Interview, conducted on Zoom for 60 minutes, September 13, 2024.
22. Tom Kelley with Jonathan Littman, *The Art of Innovation*, Crown Currency, 16 January 2001.
23. Ramachandra Guha, *The Cooking of A Book: A Memoir*, HarperCollins, 29 January 2024.
24. Mark Conner, Paul Norman, *Predicting Health Behaviour*, Open University Press, 2005.
25. Vivek Banerji, Takashi Takenoshita, Berangere Braggard, 'Planting a Seed for Behaviour Change: Shaping the Future Now', *ESOMAR QUALITATIVE*, 2011.
26. Nicola Lindson, et al, 'Motivational interviewing for smoking cessation.' *Cochrane Database of Systematic Reviews*, 2019.
27. Nivedita Banerji Interview, conducted on zoom for 60 minutes, 8 February 2025.
28. Philip Tetlock, Dan Gardner, *Superforecasting: The Art and Science of Prediction*, Random House Books, 13 September 2016.
29. Harry Collins, 'Interactional expertise as a third kind of knowledge.' *Phenomenology and the cognitive sciences* 3 (2004): 125–143.
30. Ed Fidoe Interview, conducted in-person in LIS, October 2, 2024.
31. Samuel Arbesman, *Overcomplicated: Technology at the Limits of Comprehension*.

32. Samuel Arbesman, *Overcomplicated: Technology at the Limits of Comprehension*, Current, 2015

## Chapter 7

1. Scott Belsky, 'It's not about ideas. It's about making ideas happen', *Recruit Ventures*, https://www.recruitventures.com/blog/its–not–about–ideas–its–about–making–ideas–happen, December 2024.
2. Vibha Rishi Interview, conducted on Zoom for 60 minutes, September 13, 2024.
3. Vibha Rishi Interview, conducted on Zoom for 60 minutes, September 13, 2024.
4. Takashi Takenoshita Interview, conducted on Zoom. For 60 minutes, October 10, 2024.
5. Marco Renoldi Interview, Conducted on Zoom for 60 minutes, Feb 6, 2025.

## Chapter 8

1. Rosamond Harding, *An Anatomy of Inspiration*, 1942.
2. Vivek Banerji, 'Do We Need Pragmatic Polymaths to Boost the Qualitative Research Industry', *ESOMAR QUALITATIVE*, 2008.
3. The Art Story Foundation. n.d. "Renaissance Humanism." *The Art Story*. Accessed May 13, 2025. https://www.theartstory.org/definition/renaissance-humanism/., March 2025.
4. Samuel F.B. Morse. *Encyclopaedia Britannica*. https://www.britannica.com/biography/Samuel-F-B-Morse, March 2025
   Boyd, William. 'The Secret Lives of Somerset Maugham by Selina Hastings.' *The Guardian*, 13 September 2009, https://www.theguardian.com/books/2009/sep/13/secret-lives-somerset-maugham., March 2025.
   Rubin Museum of Art. 2018. 'Rabindranath Tagore: An Indian Polymath.' *Rubin Museum of Art*. 3 August 2018, https://rubinmuseum.org/rabindranath-tagore-an-indian-polymath/, March 2025.
5. Iain McGilchrist, *The Master and His Emissary: The Divided Brain and the Making of the Western World*, Yale University Press, February 2009.

6. Robert Twigger, *Micromastery: Learn Small, Learn Fast, and Unlock Your Potential to Achieve Anything*, Penguin Random House, 17 May 2017.
7. Doris B. Wallace, Howard E. Gruber eds, *Creative people at work: Twelve cognitive case studies*, Oxford University Press, 3 September 1992.
8. Howard E. Gardner, *Intelligence reframed: Multiple intelligences for the 21st century*, Hachette UK, 18 September 2000.
9. Art Course in Guilford by Kim O'Neil, Jan–May 2012.
10. Robert Scott Root–Bernstein, Michele Root–Bernstein, *Sparks of genius: The thirteen thinking tools of the world's most creative people,* Houghton Mifflin Harcourt, 9 August 2001.
11. Ed Fidoe Interview, conducted in-person in LIS, 2 October 2024.
12. Henry A Kissinger, Eric Schmidt, Craig Mundie, *Genesis: Artificial Intelligence, Hope, and the Human Spirit*, Little Brown and Company, 19 November 2024.

# Index

**Symbols**

7-point scale 150

**A**

ABCD ('Always Be Connecting Dots') 24
Abstract
   Insight, lived experience in 34
Abstracting
   thinking mode, mental visualisation 174, 175, 176, 177, 178, 179
abstraction 209
Abstraction
   selectivity in 178
A/B tests 144
Adaptive Conjoint Analysis (ACA) 159
Adelman, Jeremy 30
Advani, Rukun 220
'Aha!' 14
Aha! insight 263

Aha! Insight Quotient 308
   checklist for building 308
      experimenting craftsman being 311, 312, 313
      generating 309, 310
      multi-modal thinker being 310, 311
      right problem solving 308, 309
Aha! insights
   generating 309, 310
Aha! moment 12, 45, 46, 47
   creating an environment 46
Akihabara 297
A-level subject 222
   physics, as 224
Aligning 280
ALS (Amyotrophic Lateral Sclerosis) 245
Analogies 50
   sources of insight 50
Analogising
   thinking mode, mental visualisation 180, 181

Analogizing
  thinking mode, mental visualisation 179
Analytics practice 274
Anscombe's Quartet 183
Anthropologists
  role as making strange familiar and familiar strange 202, 203, 204, 205
    being an insider and an outsider 206
    methods that get us close to context 207, 208
    methods that get us close to the context 206
    observing/empathising/abstracting, being good at 208, 209
    open-ended framing of questions 205
    richness while ensuring generalisability, communicating 209
Antioco, John 88
Arbesman, Samuel 91, 250
Archetypes
  applying insights framework 269, 270
  Insights Visionaries, value to 257, 258, 259
  seasoned insights practitioner 262
  Seasoned Insights Practitioner 260, 261
  that inhibit insight
    Insights Controllers 266, 267
    politicians 268, 269
  undervalue insight
    Insights Delegator 265, 266
    'Show Me the Value' 263, 264
    'Show Me the Value' 262
art 159, 298
Art
  jazz, form 299
Artificial intelligence (AI)
  transforming world 17, 18, 19
Artist
  imaging, associated with 181

## B

Bahcall, Safi 210
Banerji, Nivedita 5, 229
Banerji, Rita 6, 52
Banga, Ajay 11
  insight and vision for MasterCard 12
  Mastercard transformation 29
  vision fro cashless economy 13
behavioural economics 89
Behavioural economics 19
Behavioural patterns 185
behavioural sciences 222
behaviour change 222
Behaviour change
  benefit of 225
  ease of 226
  losses due to 225, 226
  self-efficacy 226
  social norms 226
'Benign' problems 16
Bezos, Jeff 169
Bioinformatics 245
Bird's eye view 71, 72
black swan events 87
Blockbuster 88, 92

Books
   "Mother Pious Lady" 6
Branson, Richard 24
Breiman, Leo 123
BREXIT 31
Business leaders
   six insights archetypes of 256, 257
Business macro environment important than past 16, 17
Business question 79, 80, 81, 82
Business success 97

## C

Cajal, Santiago Ramon Y 303
Cameron, David 31, 89
Carers 187
Causal inference
   difficult to drawing 142
   making right 140
   methodological guidelines 142, 143, 144, 145, 146, 147, 148, 149
      building causal maps and using counterfactuals 145
      confounders and identify variables, analysis to control for 146
      C-suite and cross-functional teams, engage 147, 148, 149
      do not reinvent wheel 146, 147
      practise thinking differently 147
      right test and control groups, stratifying study with 142
      running experiments 144
      understand sequence of events, longitudinal data to 143, 144
Causality 119
Causation 140
Centre for the Study of Developing Societies (CSDS) 108
CEO of Europe 43
Change
   create narrative with 'Why' for insight 279, 280
   journey beginning 279, 280
      codification 282
      enrol other influencers and role models 280, 281
      find champion 279
      identify 'hot' contexts 281, 282
      long term partnerships, develop 282
      training and partnerships, build capability 281
Charpentier, Emmanuelle 14, 180
Chauhan, Anuja 215
'Chic and Connected' segment 219
Chouinard, Yvon 14
Christensen Clayton 8
Christensen, Clayton theory 91
Christensen's insight 92
Classroom training
   insights professionals for 198, 199
Clayton Christensen's theory 91, 147

Co-creation 277
　action and cross-functional co-creation 278
　diversity in views 277
　experienced insights 277
Cognitive empathy 172
Collins, Harry 246
Complementarity 302
complexity 75
Complexity 244
　business problems 93
　contrasts approaches 250
　not confined to industries, technology's widespread 92
　simplifying 91
Components
　disaggregating problems into 100, 102
Computer Revolution 19
Computing infrastructure 245
Conducive environment creating 270, 271
　mastery practice 273, 274, 275, 276
　mindfulness 271, 272, 273
　pragmatic polymathy practice 276
Confirmation bias 66
connecting the dots 48
Consumer insight 26
Consumer tracking study (CTS) 37
Contextual training
　applying thinking modes in insights projects 198, 199
Control
　desire, reduce insight 25
Conversations 29

Copeland, John 5, 28, 216
correlation 119
Correlational data
　problems related to 119, 120, 121, 122, 123, 124, 125
Counterfactual questions 145
country head 43
COVID-19 pandemic 15
craftsman 125
Craftsman
　experimenting 64, 65
　　beginner's mind – master perspective 65, 66, 67
　　serendipity-purposeful 69
　　serendipity-purposeful enquiry 68, 70
　　single domain expertise 67, 68
Craftsmanship
　in designing methods 125
　　be analytically robust 138, 139, 140, 141
　　be flexible/iterate/combine 130, 133, 137, 138
　　mindset first, truth always 126, 127, 128
　　problem determines method 128, 129
　　stakeholders not just customers, think ecosystem of 129, 130
craftsmen 126
Creative agencies 212
　stereotype for 212
creative desperation route 52
creative marketing campaign 83
Creative thinking
　providing tools for 199

Creativity
　at tension with business
　　objectives 213
　bridge-builder with a focus on
　　execution 214
　bridge-builder with focus on
　　execution 215, 216
　connect with customers,
　　eliciting insight to 216,
　　217, 219
　　　emotions and blind spots
　　　　217
　　　holistic view of 216
　creative professionals and
　　intermediaries, seeking
　　insights from 219, 220
　customer segmentation 219
　diversity and iteration 219
　emotions and blind spots 217
　hiding hand 52
　making, idea relevant 210
　novel ads
　　emotional responses 217
　qualitative methods with
　　quantitative research,
　　leading with 220
　valuing creative judgement
　　and intuition 221
credit cards 11
CRISPR-Cas9 180
cross-pollination 303
cross-pollinator 225
cross-pollinators 224
Cross-pollinators
　micro-mastery, useful practice
　　for 157, 158, 160
crush advertisement 213
Csikzhentmihalyi 23
C-suite 27, 78, 281

Cross-functional teams 147
culture
　analytical, facts-driven 58
　evidence-based objective 58
Customer experience 35
Customer insights
　development, mechanical/
　　formal/cerebral view of
　　255
　human bias 255
　lack of conviction of senior
　　leaders in 254
　marketing silo 28
　organizational silos 254, 255
　values predictability and
　　control, culture related 255
Customer Insights 212
Customer insights practitioners
　custodians of methodologies
　　28
Customers
　appreciating, a journey 223
　changing deeply entrenched 226
　changing deeply entrenched
　　behaviours 221, 222, 223,
　　224, 225, 226
　　　designing interventions
　　　　228, 229
　　　ethnography 228
　　　motivations and barriers,
　　　　segmenting people
　　　　based on 227
　creativity and emotions 217
　critical drivers of change,
　　focusing on 225, 226
　diversity and iteration in
　　creativity 219
　eliciting insight to connect
　　with 217, 219

creativity and emotions 217
creativity and holistic view of 216
Kumbaya story 229, 230, 231, 232
people's decision making, emotional nature of 226, 227
segmentation 219
willingness, inspiring to 223, 224
customer segmentation 80
Cutting-edge area
industries at 92
CX KPIs 35

## D

Dangal movie 49
Darwin's insight 50
Davidson, Janet E. 4
da Vinci Leonardo 286
Davis, Miles 14, 196
dead spaces 207, 209
deep learning 179
Delbrück, Max 187
Democratic Party 22
Depth 289
Desai, Santosh 6, 15, 203, 207, 208
Designers
prototypes 192
Digital environments 144
digital ethnography 137
Directed Acrylic Graph (DAG) 145
Discipline 156, 157
divided brain 53
Doudna, Jennifer 14, 180
Dunbar, Kevin 69
Dyson 100

## E

EEG (electroencephalography) 19
einstellung 65
Eliasson, Olafur 128
elliptical machine 207
Emotional empathy 172
Emotional responses
novel ads 217
Empathic concern 172
Empathy 208
approach in different disciplines 195
cognitive 172
defined 168
dimensions of 172
emotional 172
thinking mode
direct experience observation 168, 169, 170, 171, 172, 173
thinking mode, direct experience 168, 169, 170, 171, 172, 173
Empowering disrupter 70
bird's eye view 71, 72
exclusivity-inclusiveness 72, 73, 74
skin-in-the-game/witnessing like outsider 72
enquiry 69
enterprise 299
Escher 187
ESOMAR paper 290
Ethnographic work 228
ethnography 10, 35, 64, 297

Ethnography
  changing customer deeply
    entrenched behaviours 228
  for developing sports
    equipment 207
  specialism 122
European Medical Agency (EMA) 77
Evans, Robert 246
Exclusivity-inclusiveness 72, 73, 74
Exit polls 107
Experimentation
  in data analysis 188

## F

False patterns 187
Families of techniques
  creating great research
    identifying customer needs 152
    knowledge of 152
    my choice of essential 153, 154, 155
Fashion 208
Fernbach Phillip 113
Feynman, Richard 187
Fidoe, Ed 4, 246
Fivethirtyeight Interactives 21
Fleming, Alexander 165, 187
fMRI (functional magnetic resonance imaging) 19
Foo Fighters 166
Forsyth, John 5, 75, 78
Friedman, Milton 61
Fry, Art 166

## G

Gardner, Dan 241
Gardner, Howard 301
Gardner, Martin 18
general practitioner 288
general practitioners (GPs) 42
Genome-Wide Association Study (GWAS) 245
Georgieva, Kristalina 15
Gigerenzer, Gerd 112
Gi-Jitsu 159
Ginza 297
Global trends 157
Goleman, Daniel 172
Good abstraction 178
Green Hub 52, 53
Grohl, Dave 166
Grove, Andy 8
Guha, Ramachandra 220

## H

HADOOP 123
Harnessing insights
  barriers for impact 26
Hastings, Reed 13
head of insights 279
Head of Insights 274
healers 187
Hidden pattern 186
Hirschman, Albert O. 30, 52
Hirschman's intellectual style 30
Hirschman's petit idee 40
Hobbies
  developing skills through 196
  pragmatic polymathy 292
Holmes, Sherlock 165
hormone replacement therapy (HRT) 42
Huang, Jensen 211, 221
Hyper-specialised people
  focused on one class of methodologies 123, 124

methodology-based silos 124, 125
hypothesis tree 103

# I

Ideas 66
Illumination 70
Imagination vs. reality 61, 62
Imaging
   artists, associated with 181
   thinking mode, mental visualisation 181, 182, 183, 184, 185
   tool in quantitative analysis 183
Immersive approaches 35
Implicit Association Testing (IAT) 159
Improvisation
   business strategy, crucial role in 190
   qualitative research, crucial in 189
Improvising
   thinking mode, by doing 187, 188, 189, 190, 191
Incubation 70
Indian Market Research Bureau (IMRB) 1
Inflation 26
innovators 187
Insight
   and mindfulness 271
   archetypes, business leaders of 256, 257
   barriers to 254
   barriers to harnessing for impact 24, 25, 26, 27, 28, 29
   Christensen's 92
   desire for control 25
   development 281
   factors limiting ability to generate transformational 27, 28
   high-quality facts for development 26
   intangible/inconspicuous/unpredictable nature 24, 25
   layers of organisations, not transmit 29
   mastering basics of methodologies 149, 150
   mistakes due to lacking 150
   mastering basics of methodologies
   mistakes due to lacking 151
   more relevant now 15
   observation, first step in developing 165
   relationship between truth and 110
   relation with truth 110
   serendipitous examples 13, 14
   striking 170
   systemic challenges faces 27, 28
Insight Dojo 2, 128, 139, 222, 276, 282, 285, 291, 306
Insight generation 32
Insights
   aspects, applicable in business practice 40
   choose where to look 40
   ground-reality check 41
   implement actions,

inspiring stakeholders
to 43
subjective interpretation
41, 42
willing to move away from
traditional research
designs 42
as visions 182
defining and understanding its
mechanisms 43, 44
definition 44, 82
effective real-world,
developing 32
foundation for 36
game changing 31
lived experience, abstract data
world 33, 34
mechanisms for 47, 48
analogies 50
connecting disparate
elements 48
experiencing dissonance
48, 49
overcoming obstacles 52,
53
seeing hidden variables or
patterns 51
non-linear relationship
between, information and
34, 35, 36
transformational power of 32
using to reverse plateauing
sales 37, 38, 39, 40, 41, 42
wheel to transcend one-
sidedness 56, 57
Insights

McKinsey & Company in 2
Insights archetypes

applying framework 269, 270
business leaders, of 256, 257
Insights Visionaries, value to
257
Seasoned Insights Practitioner
260, 261, 262
that inhibit insight
Insights Controllers 266,
267
politicians 268, 269
undervalue insight
Insights Delegator 265, 266
'Show Me the Value' 262,
263, 264
Insights Controllers 266
summary 267
Insights Delegator archetypes 265
summary 266
Insights fuel innovation 14
Insights leaders
sufficient intuition 158
Insights practitioner
eliciting knowledge from deep
experts
follow expert's lead 250
preparing for future 232, 233
adapting hybrid approaches
237, 238
analysing trends 234, 235,
236
being flexible 241, 242, 243
business leaders, focusing on
critical decisions of 234
creating plausible scenarios
240, 241
diverse and selective
interviewing 237
future thinking for 238,
239, 240

simplify complexity 243
  deploying interactional
    expertise 246, 247
  identifying unique
    dimensions 244, 245,
    246
  reducing ambiguity 243,
    244
insights practitioners 84
insights professional 3
Insights professionals 113
  and modelling 192
  classroom training for 198, 199
  imaging 182
  on-the-job training for 199,
    200
Insights Series 195
Insights visionaries
  value insight 257
Insights Visionaries
  value insight 258, 259
insights visionary 279
  CEO 280
Insights Visionary
  summary 259
insights visionary archetype 258
Institute of Physics (IOP) 85
Interactional expertise 246
  eliciting knowledge from deep
    experts 248
  asymmetry of knowledge,
    be comfortable with
    249
  engage experts 251, 252
  follow expert's lead 250
  mindset approach before
    interview 249
  physicist and biologist
    thinking to 250, 251

probe experts 249
guidelines
  agile, curious, and gritty
    mindset 247
  diverse sources and testing
    knowledge 248
  explicit time for learning 248
Internalising fundamental 248
Internal political issues 97
Intuition vs. analysis 62, 63
Intuit's Quicken 217
Ioannidis, John 112
issue tree 101, 102

## J

Jarrett, Keith 196
jazz 196, 299
Jazz 190
  good improvisation 191
Jobs, Steve 24, 35, 61, 179, 211,
  259
Job, Steve 13
Johnson, Stephen 49, 69
judo and karate 301
Just Do It slogan 211

## K

Kahneman, Daniel 29, 65
karate 301
kata 302
Kay, John 87
Kelvin, Lord 87
Key Performance Indicators
  (KPIs) 35
killing cash 12
Kindle 169
King, Mervyn 87
Kissinger, Henry 307

Klein, Gary 48, 49, 51
   'Pre-Mortem' technique 96
   triple path model 52
Knowledge 156, 157
KPIs (Key Performance Indicators) 73
Kuhn, Thomas 49
Kumar, Poonam 206
Kumbaya story 229, 230, 231, 232
kung fu 301

## L

Leaders
   impact of macro trends, need to assess 90
LeCun, Yann 18
left hemisphere 54
likeability score 217
LinkedIn 58
London Interdisciplinary School (LIS) 4, 246, 303
Longitudinal data 143
loonshots 210

## M

machine learning 282
Machine learning 245
machine learning models 122
making the strange familiar 83
Malthus, Thomas 51
Mandelbrot distribution 117
Marie-Thérèse 285
Marketing
   relying too heavily on correlations 121
Market research agencies 212
   stereotype for 212
Markkula, Mike 211
martial arts 302
Mastercard 11, 110
'MasterCard, the heart of commerce' slogan 11
Mastery 66, 273
   allow deep experts 275
   basics of methodologies 149, 150
      mistakes due to lacking 150, 151
   enable continuous learning and skill development 274, 275
   expertise from outside the organization 275
   time to develop insights 275
Mathematical models 145
Maugham, William Somerset 286
Mayo Clinic 195
McCartney, Paul 36
McGilchrist, Iain 37, 53, 55
   'Divided brain' 53
McKenzzie, Dana 113
McKinsey 78
McKinsey & Company
   insights, in 2
McKinsey Customer Insights 274
Mead, Margaret 204
Mental preparation 69
Metcalfe, Janet 45
Meyer, Richard 44
Michelangelo 286
micro-mastery 302
Miller, Larry 207
Mindfulness 127
   creating conducive environment 271, 272, 273
   develop awareness of its importance
   integrate in every step of project 272

integrate in every step of project 273
Mindset first, truth always 127
relation with insight 271
Mindset first, truth always 126
create ownership 127
ground rules interaction rules, set norms 127
mindfulness and 127
plan for serendipity 128
Modelling
thinking mode, by doing 191, 192, 193
Models 191
physical 192
Modern-day paradox 21, 22
Molnar Christoph 60
moment of truth 218
monk, Zen 46
Monty Hall problem 198
Moore's Law 211
Morse code 286
Morse, Samuel 286
Multi-modal thinker 57, 58
Mundie, Craig 307
Musk, Elon 141
mutually exclusive and collectively exhaustive (MECE) 102

## N

Nakamura 23
Narrative fallacy 113
National Institute for Health and Care Excellence (NICE) 42
natural believers 42
Netflix 88, 92
network of enterprise 299
neural networks 179, 180

Nhat Hanh, Thich 46
Nilekani, Nandan 14
non-linearity 32
Nooyi, Indra 14, 17
Norman, Donald A. 166
Nothing Official About It! campaign 210
"Nothing Official About it", Pepsico campaign 214, 215
Novel ads 217
novel business model 83
Novice activities 302

## O

Objectivity 59
and subjectivity 59, 60
Observation
human behaviour, valuable understanding in 166
thinking mode, direct experience 165, 166, 167, 168
Observation
developing insight, first step in 165
Olsen, Ken 87
On-the-job training
insights professionals for 199, 200
Organisation
empowering to implement 98
kind of resources 99
main players and role 98, 99
strengths and weaknesses of organisation 99, 100
Over-fitting
weak pattern recognition 118, 119

Over-fitting risk 209

## P

Patterns
  behavioural 185
  false 187
  hidden 186
  thinking mode, mental visualisation 185, 186, 187
Pearl, Judea 113, 145
PepsiCo India 2
Petites idees
  and transformation 30, 31
Physical models 192
physical prototypes testing 137
Physicians
  quantitative segmentation of 77
Physics
  as A-level subject 224
Playing
  thinking mode, by doing 187, 188, 189, 190, 191
Poincare, Henri 69
Politicians
  insight archetypes as 268, 269
  summary 269
Polymathy 298
Popova, Maria 14
Portfolio of interests
  considerations to design
    complementarity 302
    enjoyment 300
    Independence (orthogonality) of activities 301
    Novice activities 302
    purpose 300
  cross-pollinate deliberately 304
  Cross-pollinate deliberately 303
  insight with joie de vivre, creating 305, 306, 307
  micro-mastery and learning 302
Post-it Notes 166
pragmatic polymath 289
Pragmatic polymathy 276, 286, 287, 292
  broaden talent pipeline 276, 277
  defined 290
  implicitly/explicitly cross-pollinating 289
  loving learning 289
  overarching purpose 289
  tension, feeling 297
Pragmatic Polymathy 284
Probability distributions 117
Problem definition
  and structuring process, tips to improve issues 105
Problem difinition
  and structuring process, tips to improve issues 106
Programming 157
Prototypes 192
  designers 192
Puri, Anjali 206
Purpose 300
PWC 26th Annual Global Survey 90
Python 123

## Q

Qualitative approaches 114
Qualitative research 220

Quantitative approaches
 measurements are facts,
  believing in 114, 115, 116
Quantitative information
 unquestioning belief in 116, 117
Quantitative metrics 117
Quantitative modelling 118
quantitative research 137

## R

Radio Immunotherapy (RIT) 222
randomized control trials 120
Range 289
Real Beauty 217
'Real Beauty' campaign 60
Real Beauty campaign 181
Real Clear Polling 21
reality distortion field (RDF) 61
Real-world problems 41
Renoldi, Marco 6, 260, 261
right hemisphere 54
Rishi, Vibha 7, 37, 214, 215
Rishi, Vibha Paul 256, 258
Risk 117
Rittel, Horst 16
Robust
 designing methods
  causality, improving
   inferences about 140, 141
  checking construct validity 139, 140
  sampling 138, 139
Robust sampling 115, 116
Root-Bernstein, Michèle 63, 161, 181, 187
Root-Bernstein, Robert 63, 161, 181, 187
Ross, Mike 49

'rub-pat' barrier 295
Rumelt, Richard 17, 61
Russia–Ukraine war 17

## S

Samaj Pragati Sahayog (SPS) 5
Schmidt, Eric 307
Schoemaker, Paul J.H. 87
seasoned insights practitioner 279
Seasoned Insights Practitioner 260, 261
 summary 262
Seeing 165
Segmentation 79
Sejnowski, Terrence J. 179
selection theory 51
selective combination 48
Selectivity 178
Sennet, Richard 125
sensei 304
serendipity 68
Serendipity-purposeful enquiry 68, 69
 illumination 70
 incubation 70
 mental preparation 69
 validation 70
Serif, Sans 35
Sharma, Ruchir 48
 prediction about America's fiscal deficit 48
Sharpening questions 104
Show Me the Value archetype 262, 263, 264
 summary 264
Silver, Spencer 166
Skin-in-the-game 72
Sloman, Steven 113

sophisticated users 124
Specialists 287
Sportspeople 197
Sternberg, Robert 4
'Straight No Chasers' 46
Strategy
    tactics practice, link with 278
studying analogous 137
Subjectivity 59, 60
    and objectivity 59, 60
    associated with qualitative thinking 60
Substantial business
    creating advantage 93, 94
        behaviour needs to change 97, 98
        C-suite worried 95, 96, 97
        goals and obstacles 94, 95
Suits 49
Suzuki, Shunryu 65
Swiffer 90

**T**

Tagore, Rabindranath 286
Takenoshita, Takashi 6, 257, 259
Taleb, Nassim Nicholas 87, 116
Tanishq 207, 208
Tate Modern 128
Technology
    over reliance on 22, 23
Tension
    navigating between width and depth 297, 298
    seeing insight as assimilative field 298, 299
Testing novel
    benefit 218
Tetlock, Phillip 241
Tett, Gillian 172
The Apple Marketing Philosophy 211
The Art of Thought 70
*The Bull* by Picasso 176
The Kumbaya Story 5
Thelonius Monk tune 46
The Nature of Insight 4
theory of relativity 59
thick description 118
Thinking differently
    systematic ways of 161
Thinking mode
    direct experience
        observation 165, 166, 167, 168
    mental visualisation
        abstracting 174, 175, 176, 177, 178, 179
        analogising 179, 180, 181
        imaging 181, 182, 183, 184, 185
        pattern recognition 185, 186, 187
    thinking by doing
        modelling 191, 192, 193
        playing/improvising 187, 188, 189, 190, 191
    training on 194
        developing skills through hobbies 196, 197
        seeking inspiration, expanding through 194, 195
        sharpening thinking with puzzles and paradoxes 197, 198
Thinking modes 162
    categories 164
    coaching and feedback 199

raising awareness of 199
Top-of-Mind Awareness (TOM) 143
Toynbee, Arnold 26
transformational success 83
Translators
  importance and scarcity of 78
Transtheoretical Model 223
Triangulating 146
Trump campaign 141
Trump, Donald 21
Truth
  barriers to 112, 113, 114
  crafting methods to reveal 107
  elusive nature of 111, 112
  relation with insight 110
Tufte, Edward 185
Tversky, Amos 65
Twigger, Robert 158, 295, 302
Two brain hemispheres
  role of 53, 54

## U

Uncertainty 117
  ignorance of risk and 116, 117
Under-fitting
  weak pattern recognition 118, 119
Unknown
  types of
    what is hidden in relevant context 82
Unknowns
  types of 82
    entrenched attitudes and behaviours, changing deeply 85, 86
    making creative idea relevant and practical 83, 84, 85
    preparing for future 86, 87
    simplifying complexity 91
    what is hidden in relevant context 83

## V

Validation 70
visualization software 123
Vital engagement 23

## W

Wable, Neerja 5, 206
Wadhwa, Hitendra 4, 62
Wallace, Graham 70
Walmart 186
Waza 159
Webber, Melvin 16
Webster's New World Dictionary 44
Wicked problems 16
Wiebe, David 45
Willingness
  creating 224
Witnessing 72
Women's Health Initiative (WHI) 42
Working
  establishing ways of 199
World Bank 11
World Cup 52
World Uncertainty Index (WUI) 15
Worm's eye 71, 72

## X

X 145

## Y

Yadav, Yogendra 108
  election and human judgement 108
  quantitative survey methods, expertise in 109
  Senior Fellow at CSDS 108
  travelling and truth uncover 109
yin and yang of insight 57

# Acknowledgements

Cross-pollination has been at the heart of my approach to insights, and there are many people to thank from different walks of life – those directly involved in the creation of the book, people from my professional network, my teachers and friends related to my hobbies, and my near and dear ones.

I will begin by thanking all the people who agreed to be interviewed by me. Your inputs were invaluable. My deep gratitude to Ed Fidoe and Santosh Desai for taking the time to read the book and for their generous testimonials – with special thanks to Santosh for a foreword that captures the essence of the book with remarkable clarity.

I would also like to extend my thanks to Caroline Webb, Gaurav Bhatnagar, and Rohit Prasad for generously sharing advice on the intricacies of getting a book published, including how to write a proposal. Special shoutout to Rohit for being a sounding board, always willing to answer my questions throughout this journey.

The book is largely based on work done at Insight Dojo. My gratitude and regards to the team: Daniel Rayner, Genevieve Hall (especially for partnering with me on many of the case studies shared in this book), George Cox, Ryoko Ward, Simon Walne, and Zoé Duhaldeborde for their creative contributions to our work. My sincere thanks to long-term collaborators and believers in Insight Dojo: Marco Renoldi, Shunsuke Miyajima, and Takashi Takenoshita. My collaboration with Takashi began at McKinsey nearly 20 years ago, when we co-founded the behaviour change service line – I am grateful for that.

Thank you to Chiara Troncatti, Janice MacLennan, and Simona Falciai for being strong supporters through the years. And to Anna Puig, Otilia Pérez Montalbán, Sandra Grillo, and Sally Winch for being such fantastic partners.

At Dusty Foot Production, I would like to thank Imrana Khan, Rehana Khan, Reshma Manral, Rohit Gusain, Sumit Sisodia, and Vijender Sharma for being an extension of the Insight Dojo team.

Thank you to all my clients for their trust and support.

I am also grateful to the previous companies where I have worked – McKinsey felt like one of the finest schools I have attended. The lessons I learned through exposure to tough business problems, across industries and geographies, and amongst brilliant colleagues, were priceless.

Within it, I am particularly grateful to the global marketing and customer insights practice – especially my mentors, colleagues, and friends: Alexandru Degeratu, Angela Lovejoy, Anil Kaul, Biljana Cvetanovski, David Cheifitz, David Court, David Honigman, David Sackin,

Hai Ye, Hitendra Wadhwa, Gene Zelazny (late), Gioia Ghezzi, John Copeland, John Forsyth, Kevin Nuffer, Kevin Sneader, Leah Boucher, Mike Sherman, Rukku Motiwala, Sudeep Haldar, Tamara Charm, Tom French, Trond Riiber Knudsen, Yihua Jing, and Yvonne Staack.

Thank you, James Naylor and David Honigman, for helping me further develop the idea of the pragmatic polymath.

My gratitude to the Behaviour Change group in London – especially my friends Bérangère Bragard and Sundiatu Dixon-Fyles, who have remained close friends beyond McKinsey.

Thank you, Tim Kibbey, for being a great friend and teaching me about ethnography.

At Pepsi, I was taught by some of the finest marketers. Thank you especially to my mentor Vibha Rishi, and to Lloyd Mathias, both of whom have continued to inspire me in marketing.

Pepsi also taught me the importance of being in the trenches with the frontline, and the value of execution and passion. I am grateful to all the business leaders who allowed me to work closely with them – visiting factories, jumping on delivery trucks, and gaining a first-hand view of serving retailers.

I entered the world of insight through my first job at IMRB. Thank you to my bosses and mentors – Archana Gidwani, Arun Joshi, Bhupendra Mathur (late), and Neerja Wable – for mentoring me and building my confidence. Thank you to my team for the great work and banter: Amar Wadhwa, Ashutosh Tyagi, Hardeep Gupta, and

Srinivas Bhattacharya. Thank you to my IMRB friends: Aman Makkar, Anjali Puri, Ashish Bansal, Ashu Sabharwal, Biswajit Mohapatra, Goutam Mitra, Kiran Khanna, LK Gupta, Mohan Krishnan, Rickie Khosla, Ritesh Ghosal, Shruti Agarwal, Tanmay Jaiswal, and Vivek Khattar.

Music and jazz have had a huge influence on how I think about insight and creativity. I am immensely grateful to my teachers, mentors, and fellow musicians: George Whitmore (my friend and jazz coach), Jane Parker, Jeananne Albee (late), Karen Greenhouse, Sumit Nahar, and Tim Richards. Thank you to Marianne Windham and Guildford Jazz for creating opportunities to both play and experience jazz in my neighbourhood – a gift that deeply enriched the book-writing process.

Thank you to my karate teacher, Sensei Yoshinobu Ohta, for training me and helping me earn my two dans. Many insights have come from his classes – both from what he said and demonstrated. Thank you to the Oasis Shotokan Karate Club, Japan Karate England, and Worldwide, for creating a fantastic community that supported the disciplined pursuit of this great and difficult martial art.

My life changed after I learned how to meditate. I am grateful to Thich Nhat Hanh (*Thay*), the Zen monk who taught me the fundamentals of mindfulness.

I am also deeply indebted to Swami Niranjanananda Saraswati and the Bihar School of Yoga for teaching the yogic and meditative practices that have become a core part of my life. Special thanks to Mahesh Ji for helping me internalise these practices over the last two years.

Finally, I must thank the most important people in my life. Thank you to my parents, Debashis and Mridula Banerji, who nurtured my early interest in music, literature, sports, and science – and filled my life with so much love that risk-taking has always felt safe.

From jazz I have learned that any creative work needs a solid foundation.

My warmest and most sincere thanks my wife and best friend, Kathleen Puech, for creating the space for me to work freely on this book and for going through early drafts with her laser-sharp mind. I remain eternally grateful for her love, support, and companionship. Thank you to my children, Anisha and Nathan, for being insightful sounding boards and for pressure-testing my ideas.

Thank you to my sisters, Nivedita Banerji, Rita Banerji, Shubha Pande, and my brother-in-law Rangu Rao – not just for always being there for me, but for exposing me to the transformational work of the organisations they founded: Samaj Pragati Sahayog, Kumbaya, Green Hub, and Dusty Foot Productions.

Through these organisations, I have formed many lifelong friendships. Special thanks to: Mekhala Krishnamurthy, Mihir Shah, Shakir Khan, Shibani Chaudhury, and Shoma Chaudhury, for conversations that, in some way, have influenced this book.

My thanks to the team at Hachette India. I am incredibly grateful to Thomas Abraham, who looked at the first draft of my proposal and immediately said he would consider it for publishing. Even so, he was generous enough to introduce me to other publishers, in case I wanted to explore more options. He has been accessible and supportive, offering helpful advice along the way.

Thank you to Abhivyakti Singh for collaborating so closely on the book – for being a thought partner, offering feedback to help me understand the reader's perspective, taking ownership of important aspects, and always encouraging me. To Anna Thomas for enthusiastically and creatively working on many iterations of the cover design, as well as other graphic work. To Nayantara Roy for copy-editing and to Anupama Manral for her attention to detail and careful handling of the text. To Riti Jagoorie and Abhishek Roy for handling the book's outreach. And to Haider for the elegant typesetting and Shikha Nautiyal for charting the index.

Lastly, my gratitude to you, the reader, for picking up the book and making your way through it.

ALSO FROM JOHN MURRAY

**Ben Renshaw**
Author of *LOVEWORK*

# HOW TO BE A CEO

PURPOSE • PEOPLE • PERFORMANCE

'A proven approach for CEOs to help organizations thrive'
AMY C. EDMONDSON
Novartis Professor of Leadership and Management, Harvard Business School

ISBN: 9781399809795

## ALSO FROM JOHN MURRAY

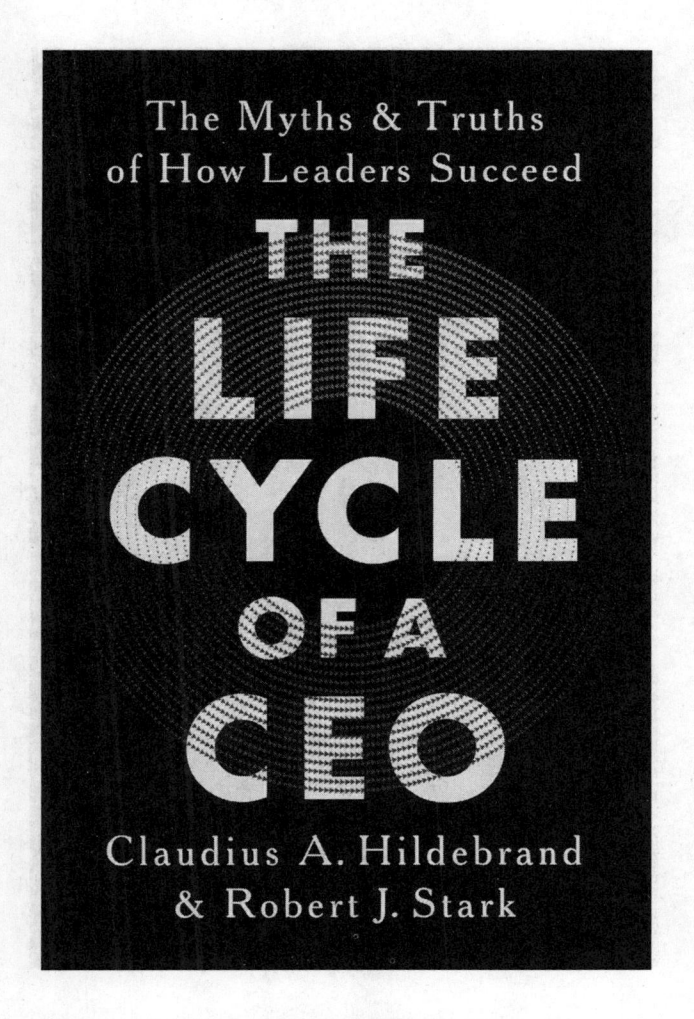

The Myths & Truths of How Leaders Succeed

**THE LIFE CYCLE OF A CEO**

Claudius A. Hildebrand & Robert J. Stark

ISBN: 9781399822244

ALSO FROM JOHN MURRAY

# REINVENTING CAPITALISM

*In the Age of*

# BIG DATA

Viktor Mayer-Schönberger
Coauthor of *Big Data*

and Thomas Ramge

ISBN: 9781473656529

## ALSO FROM JOHN MURRAY

**NEW YORK TIMES BESTSELLER**

'A personal, intuitive, powerful way to look at making an impact with your work' Seth Godin, author of *Purple Cow*

# SMALL DATA

### THE TINY CLUES THAT UNCOVER HUGE TRENDS

**MARTIN LINDSTROM**

ISBN: 9781473630130